PIT OF SHAME

THE REAL BALLAD OF READING GAOL

Pit of Shame
The Real Ballad of Reading Gaol

Published by
WATERSIDE PRESS
Sherfield Gables
Sherfield on Loddon
Hook, Hampshire RG27 0JG
United Kingdom

Online catalogue www.WatersidePress.co.uk
Email enquiries@watersidepress.co.uk
Telephone +44 (0)1256 882250

Copyright © 2007 Anthony Stokes. All rights are hereby reserved and asserted by the author in accordance with current UK and international law. No part of this book may be reproduced, stored in any retrieval system or transmitted in any form or by any means, including over the internet, without the prior permission of the publishers to whom copyright has been assigned for the purposes of this edition.

Foreword © 2007 Theodore Dalrymple subject to the same terms and conditions as above. 'Arrested Development' (*Appendix 1*) © 2002 Theodore Dalrymple.

ISBN 978-1-904380-21-4 (Paperback), ISBN 978-1-906534-45-5 (PDF ebook).

Cataloguing-In-Publication Data A catalogue record for this book can be obtained from the British Library.

Cover design Waterside Press. Front cover image of the Centre at Reading Gaol soon after 1844, from *Prison Discipline* (see also page 95). Back cover image of Oscar Wilde's cell, C.3.3 as it is today (see also the further image of this cell on page 126).

Printing Lightning Source.

North American distribution Ingram Book Company, One Ingram Blvd, La Vergne, TN 37086, USA. Tel: (+1) 615 793 5000; inquiry@ingramcontent.com

PIT OF SHAME

THE REAL BALLAD OF READING GAOL

Anthony Stokes

With a Foreword by **Theodore Dalrymple**

WATERSIDE PRESS

Acknowledgements

First I must thank all those people who have helped and supported me with the collection of data and materials for this book: from the many members of the general public who came into the prison during the open day sessions mentioned in the *Preface* and who brought with them letters and artefacts relating to the prison to the many others in libraries and public record offices up and down the country. But as with all things in life there are a few people who make that special difference.

Bryan Gibson of Waterside Press had the belief and trust necessary for me to turn the items at my disposal into a book that he thought might be of value to a range of people interested in penal reform, English literature, or both. I also owe a debt of gratitude to Jane Green, his house editor, for her untiring efforts dealing with the manuscript and her help in bringing it to its present level. Any remaining mistakes are, of course, my own.

Nick Leader, the former Governing Governor at Reading who I mention in *Chapter 13* had the belief and insight that allowed me to expand the historical display at the prison—and did not run off too many times when I began to enthuse about Reading Gaol and its history with the various dignitaries and high profile visitors who have visited the place.

I am also especially indebted to: Pauline Bryant, my present Governing Governor and her senior colleagues; Don Mead and Michael Seeney of the Oscar Wilde Society; Matthew Williams of Reading Museum; Mark Preston of the Canadian Veterans' Association; Theodore Dalrymple for agreeing to write the Foreword, and all those members of staff at Reading whom I have not mentioned by name but who have supported me in my research from time-to-time; and the many prisoners who, following their time at Reading, have reinforced my confidence that we can make a difference and help such people to change their lives for the better.

Finally and most importantly, I am beholden to my wife and soulmate, Jacquie and my beautiful children, Christopher and Sophie, for your special support and understanding, following me to the ends of Berkshire and beyond in my research, helping me to transcribe the manuscript into a readable text and making those all important cups of tea. I could never have completed this book without it. I will always be in your debt.

Anthony Stokes
April 2007

A Note from Reading's Governing Governor

As the first woman to be in overall charge at Reading I was conscious that I was opening up yet another new chapter in the long history of the prison and building on what had already been achieved over the years. Reading has an unusually interesting past, but also needs to conform to the regulations and practices of a modern, twenty-first century Prison Service. I welcome Anthony Stokes' initiative and hard work in recognising the importance of preserving facts, information and materials for future generations in this great book.

Pauline Bryant
Governor
Her Majesty's Prison and Young Offender Institution Reading
April 2007

About the author

Anthony Stokes was born and educated in Cardiff, South Wales where he joined HM Prison Service at Cardiff Prison in 1988. After training at the Prison Service Training College at Newbold Revel in Warwickshire he was posted to Reading Prison in Berkshire where he is now a Senior Prison Officer. He holds a Certificate in Education (Further Education) from Reading University, is a Member of the Institute of Carpenters and a fully qualified prison locksmith. He has been twice commended: by HM Prison Service, after he saved the life of a prisoner (1992); and by the Director General of HM Prison Service, for his part in helping to quell the riot that took place at Reading Prison on Boxing Day 1992 and which is described in *Chapter 11* (1993). In 2003, his ground-breaking work in setting up a Vocational Training Department at Reading led to his being nominated for a Butler Trust Award, one of the highest in this field. He lives in Berkshire with his wife, Jacquie and two children and spends what spare time he can taking part in water-sports and driving his speedboat off England's South Coast.

The author of the Foreword

Theodore Dalrymple was for many years a hospital and prison doctor. He wrote a regular column for *The Spectator* for 14 years, and is contributing editor to the *City Journal* of New York. His latest of a line of thought-provoking books is *Romancing Opiates: Pharmacological Lies and the Addiction Bureaucracy* (2005) (Natl Book Network).

PIT OF SHAME

CONTENTS

Acknowledgements	iv
A Note from Reading's Governing Governor	v
About the author	vi
List of illustrations	viii
Foreword	ix
Preface	xi
Timeline	xiii

CHAPTER

1	The Old Reading Gaols	17
2	The New Prison	30
3	Punishments of Former Times	44
4	Executions	52
5	Prisoner C.3.3 Oscar Wilde	77
	Illustrations	95
6	The Ballad of Reading Gaol	103
	Illustrations	119
7	The Easter Rising and Internment	127
8	Invisible Prisoners	139
9	A Pioneering Borstal Correctional Centre	144
10	Starting Again with a Clean Sheet	148
11	Life as a Local Prison	153
12	HM Remand Centre and Young Offender Institution	159
13	'Reading Gaol' Today and in the Future	165

APPENDIX

1	*'Arrested Development' by Theodore Dalrymple*	174
2	*Rules for Prisoners (c.1850)*	181
3	*Prison Dietary Scales (c.1850)*	183
4	*List of Executions*	185

Primary Sources, Internet Sites and Select Bibliography	187
Index	189

List of illustrations

Page xvi

Victorian 'Centre Box' and floor tiles before their removal in the 1960s.

Pages 95-102

Old print of the Centre at the time of the separate system.
Prisoner 973 Arabella Earles (c.1891).
The elaborate 1844 Gatehouse.
The Canadians arriving in 1945.
Prisoner Q.311 William Clarke.
Facing east down A-wing on Level 2 today.
Visiting Committee Book entry for 10 July 1896.
'There is no Chapel on the day they hang a man'.
The front of the prison around 1960.
Execution Log open at the entry for Charles Thomas Wooldridge.

Pages 119-126

Architectural gem. An old print of Reading Gaol (c.1850).
Skylights in the Centre roof.
View along A.3 landing.
E-wing showing proximity to Huntley & Palmers.
Typical view looking upwards.
The separate system. Old print (c.1860).
The top landing today – with safety net.
Top bags for top people at knock down prices.
Plans of the Execution Centre (c.1900) and Reading Gaol (c.1850).
The front gate from inside and outside.
View from Level 3 during conversion work in the late 1960s.
Plan of Reading Gaol in 1865.
Oscar Wilde's cell, C.3.3.

Foreword Theodore Dalrymple

Historians face a seemingly insoluble dilemma: they can either burrow away in the archives and produce monographs of limited overall significance, of interest mainly to specialists, or they can produce wide-ranging histories that, by excluding detail, risk sweeping and inaccurate generalisation.

Anthony Stokes' history of Reading Gaol solves this dilemma very neatly. A prison officer of many years' experience, his researches into the history of the prison in which he serves were obviously a labour of love, which has been amply requited in this book. In giving us so detailed and fascinating a picture of Reading Gaol through the ages, he causes us to reflect on penal policy, the nature of crime and man's perpetual temptation to cruelty. I don't think anyone could read his book, for example, and conclude that the harsh treatment of prisoners is either a good idea or morally justified. Here is a detailed history of a single institution that is of wide philosophical significance and that could be read with great profit and enjoyment by the intelligent and enquiring general reader.

Of course, Reading Gaol is mostly famous among the general public for having been the subject of the greatest, and most moving, poem about prison in our language, or possibly any language, Oscar Wilde's *The Ballad of Reading Gaol*. Anthony Stokes sheds fascinating new light on Wilde's imprisonment, but he recounts many other cases that are in their way (precisely because they were less famous or notorious) just as fascinating. No one will be able to resist his stories of escapees, incompetent criminals who leave their addresses at the scene of their crimes, prisoners, executioners, eccentrics and corrupt warders. His selection of detail is very telling: the bureaucratic thought that went into the regulations concerning the administration and physical properties of the lash, for example, tell us a great deal about the mentality of the age. Moreover, much of what goes on in any prison is very funny, and the author captures this aspect of prison life, often unsuspected by people who have no experience of prison, very well.

If I had to recommend a single book about the history of imprisonment in this country, this would be it. The horror, the humour, the misery, the difficulties, the successes and failures—all are here. A history such as this, written by a man who is idealistic without sentimentality, could have been written about any large prison in Britain, but it has taken Anthony Stokes to do so.

I am honoured to have been given the opportunity to write this foreword.

Preface

This book represents the end product of a passion that began soon after I arrived in Reading, Berkshire almost 20 years ago now. It is based on many years of investigation, research and detective work. Sometimes this has involved me in exploring old manuscripts kept in places where few people have trodden; at other times in scrutinising the large collection of artefacts and historical data from official and public sources that I have amassed during my years as a prison officer. It is also informed by my close, daily proximity to the fabric of Reading Gaol, its sometimes brooding and austere atmosphere, and its ghosts.

A long and proud history
The history of Reading Gaol is as vast as it is complex, stretching from the days of Henry VIII and beyond, through the penal Dark Age of the separate system of imprisonment of the Victorian era under which Oscar Wilde served his sentence, to the more enlightened times of the present day. Perhaps no other prison in England and Wales can boast such a diverse and varied pattern of uses and roles. None, I think has come to be associated with both penal reform and English literature in quite the way that Reading Gaol has.

Reading has had a gaol of one kind or another for over five hundred years. It attracted worldwide renown as the setting for Wilde's classic poem of 1896 after he was imprisoned there. *The Ballad of Reading Gaol* is featured at length in *Chapter 6*: it has become a touchstone for penal reformers at home and abroad and Wilde's imprisonment, though lawful by the standards of his day, is now a *cause célèbre* in the history of criminal justice. The ballad is a good place to start for anyone who needs to understand that prisons are not all sweetness and light; and that imprisonment must always be about far more than punishment, retribution or incarceration if, as Wilde put matters, the 'vilest deeds' are not to 'bloom well in prison air'.

But though Oscar Wilde and Reading Gaol have become inseparable in many people's minds, there is so much more to the place, as I hope readers will discover from the pages that follow. It has a black history of what would nowadays be seen as barbaric punishments (*Chapter 3*) and executions (*Chapter 4*); and the uses to which the buildings have been put range from Irish internment (*Chapter 7*) to a Canadian military prison (in which prisoners were made invisible: *Chapter 8*), a borstal correctional centre (*Chapter 9*), and a young offender institution and remand centre today (*Chapter 12*). In between times it has been a place of safety for vulnerable prisoners (including 'supergrasses'), a food store, an army surplus depot and a driving test centre!

During 2004 I arranged an open day for the general public: a chance, as I put it, to walk in the footsteps of Oscar Wilde. Over two hundred people came into the prison over a fortnight. I was astounded by their response. Despite their initial disbelief, I think they found that good work does go on inside prisons. This made me yet more resolute to bring out this aspect in the book.

A few practical remarks
So, if I can 'talk business' for a moment, I should mention that, to be sure, there are some staff who may have lost their initial spark and rationale for working with offenders. There may even be those who have become 'bitter and twisted'. They may have been fresh and raring to go at one time, but became worn down by the daily grind and constant exposure to a side of life that most people might prefer to ignore and hide behind prison walls. These may, in fact, be the same kind of people who in my early days at Reading Gaol just could not fathom out why I was at all interested in the prison itself, 'the poet', the Execution Log, where the unmarked graves were, why fine Victorian architecture and fittings had been replaced, or where important records and artefacts had gone. At times this amounted to outright opposition from those who saw the history of the place as a hindrance or millstone.

But in truth such people are in the minority—increasingly so over the years both at Reading and also elsewhere within the modern-day Prison Service. Prison officers are nowadays more likely to be dedicated to their tasks, working as part of a well-trained and highly professional team, focused on making a lasting difference to the lives of prisoners, treating them with humanity, dignity and instilling into them a sense of achievement, self-belief and self-esteem. There is considerable satisfaction to be gained from this: making that one difference to somebody's life that steers them away from a cycle of drugs, violence, dishonesty and returning to prison towards a better life. I count myself lucky that I became a prison officer and would recommend it to other people seeking such a challenge. Examples of both the 'old guard' and the new appear within the book.

'In Reading Gaol by Reading Town there is a Pit of Shame'
The title of this book, *Pit of Shame*, I have unashamedly taken from a metaphor of Oscar Wilde that appears in the opening lines of Part VI of his ballad. The book distils all the historical data I could find and verify about this onetime 'pit of shame' and explains how it has been rehabilitated (*Chapter 13*). Within the book I have drawn a number of personal conclusions for which I take full responsibility, including about Wilde's time at the prison (mainly in *Chapters 5* and *6*). These are based on close study, privileged access to documents and materials, and long reflection. So I hope that the book provides at least some fresh insights—and that my passion for Reading Gaol, its history and legacy comes through in its pages.

Anthony Stokes April 2007

Timeline

1071	Berkshire County Gaol at Wallingford receives its first state prisoner, the Abbot of Abingdon, suspected of complicity in Hereward's Rising.
1290	Berkshire County gaol is moved by Edward I from Wallingford to Windsor.
1537	A blacksmith from Wallingford is alleged to have spread a false rumour that the King was dead. He is whipped at Wallingford market-place, placed in a cart and then whipped again through the town. Next day he is taken to Reading and whipped there, then finally cast into Reading Gaol.
1571	A felon named Newman is hanged in the market-place in the centre of the town.
1574	John Nabb is the first person to be born inside Reading Gaol.
1625	Anyone caught begging is to be committed to Reading House of Correction. Prior to this, two constables are employed to administer whippings to beggars.
1634	William and Edith Wallis are accused of witchcraft. William is cleared because a suspected witch's mark, a spot on his back, bleeds when pricked—a 'test' of a witch. Edith is sent to Reading Gaol, lucky not to have been burned at the stake.
1683	Richard Marshall and Mary Elton, both prisoners in Reading Gaol, become the first people to marry there.
1755	July 17: Margaret Wright is hanged for the murder of her infant child.
1761	March 21: Ann Giles is hanged for arson.
1779	The penal reformer John Howard first visits Reading Gaol.
1785	A new gaol - often referred to as the 'first gaol' to distinguish it from that of 1844 onwards - is built on the site of the old abbey and opens fully in 1786.
1793	'Forbury House of Correction' opens.
1799	Reading is at the centre of a nationwide constitutional *cause célèbre* concerning *habeus corpus*, ending in the trial and acquittal of its governor after he refuses access to certain prisoners: *Chapter 1*.
1822	The treadmill is introduced for hard labour.
1828	In-cell sanitation is removed from the 'first' Reading Goal of 1786-1842.
1842	The first goal closes for demolition to make way for the 'new gaol'.
1844	The new gaol – a cross between Pentonville Prison and Warwick Castle - is built on the site of the old one at a cost of over £40,000. This imposing building is supposedly constructed with all 'mod cons' including in-cell sanitation. One of the first prisoners is Abraham Boswell, sentenced to six months with hard labour for the attempted rape and indecent assault of a two year old child.
1845	First public execution at the new gaol, of Thomas Jennings and a possible miscarriage of justice: *Chapter 4*.[1]
1847	Reading Gaol accepts 'Government convicts': *Chapter 2*.
1857	March 3: Thomas Gorman, a 23-year-old-blacksmith, is sentenced to transportation for 14 years for attempted murder; after attacking Principal Warder William Brewer, who is saved by the prisoner in the next cell dragging the unconscious officer into his cell.
1862	Last public execution at Reading, of John Gould, above the gatehouse: *Chapter 4*.

---

[1] A full 'timeline' for executions after 1844 appears in *Appendix 4: List of Executions.*

1864	The Prison Ministers Act 1863 allows Roman Catholic priests into the gaol.
1865	Some time after the Prison Act 1865, in-cell sanitation is removed, during the austere 'Du Cane era' of 'Hard Fare, Hard Labour and Hard Bed'—a time of harsh attitudes in society generally (except for a minority of reformers) about how people who were 'different' should be treated; and prevent communication.
1868	Last public executions in Britain, on the roof of Horsemonger Lane Goal, London, of Michael Barrett and other Fenians re the Clerkenwell Explosion. Subsequently all executions are held inside prisons pursuant to the Capital Punishment Within Prisons Act of the same year.
1870	John Owen is released from Reading Gaol on May 20 vowing revenge on Emanuel Marshall for past wrongdoings. He goes straight to Marshall's house and murders him, his wife, mother, sister and three children in what becomes known as the 'Denham Murders'. For this Owen is executed at Aylesbury Gaol on 8 August 1870.
1876	Prison clothes are supplied by local department store Heelas, now John Lewis.
1877	The Prison Act of that year nationalises the prisons. First private executions (i.e. behind prison walls) of Henry Tidbury and Francis Tidbury, brothers, for the murder of two police officers.
1879	May 2: Ada Chamberlain becomes the first person to escape from the prison. December 12: A major fire breaks out forcing the evacuation of the women's wing (E-wing). It is extinguished by the local Volunteer Fire Brigade.
1882	Roderick Maclean is arrested at Windsor Railway Station for the attempted assassination of Queen Victoria—having fired a pistol at her, but missed. He is charged with High Treason and remanded to Reading Gaol; found not guilty by reason of insanity, branded a dangerous lunatic and sent to Broadmoor Lunatic Asylum (as it was). He dies after nearly 40 years there in 1921.
1889	April 14: Henry Strong commits suicide by jumping off the top gallery (A3) and landing on the floor of the centre hall three storeys below.
1892	October 10: five members of the Salvation Army are sent to Reading Gaol, sentenced to five days' imprisonment each for non-payment of a fine imposed for obstructing the highway at Windsor in pursuit of their beliefs.
1985	Oscar Wilde arrives on November 20 (though he claims it was November 13).
1896	April 4: Amelia Dyer is arrested and charged with the murder of three infants entrusted to her care as a foster mother for a fee of £10 each. In total, seven small bodies are found in the River Thames. She remains in Reading Gaol until May 2 when she is committed for trial at The Old Bailey and thence transferred to Newgate Prison where she is executed on 10 June 1896. July 7: Execution of Trooper Charles Thomas Wooldridge (the C.T.W. of the *Ballad of Reading Gaol*). Major J B Nelson arrives as Governor at Reading.
1897	Oscar Wilde is released after being handed his notes for *De Profundis*.
1898	*Ballad of Reading Gaol* is first published by Leonard Smithers of London.
1910	June 4: on the accession to the throne of King George V there is a general amnesty: the entire prisoner population at the gaol is granted special remission and released—a total of 70 men and four women.
1913	Last execution at Reading, that of Eric James Sedgewick: *Chapter 4*.
1916	The prison becomes a Place of Internment (or POI): *Chapter 7*.

1917   Following determined efforts, four prisoners escape: *Chapter 7*.
1919   Reading Gaol closes as a prison.
1920   January 8: 100 tonnes of tinned salmon are secured inside the gaol.
1925   The prison workshop is used by the army as a surplus clothing store.
1936   The Chaplain's quarter becomes the Berkshire driving test centre.
1937   The Governor's quarter is used as a headquarters for the ARP (air raid wardens).
1938   September 7: Councillor T. Smart visits the empty gaol and requests that it be handed over to the council for use as a local government administrative centre.
1939   Offices within the gaol become the County Censor's Office responsible for the checking of all news prior to publication at the outbreak of World War II.
1940   A padded cell in E-wing is used to store the county's ration books.
1945   April 9: the prison is handed over to the Canadian Military to be used as a detention centre but this is kept secret from the general public.
May: 370 Canadian rioters from Headley Detention Barracks moved to Reading.
1946   August: the gaol re-opens as a local prison and an 'overflow' prison.
1951   Reading becomes one of the first Borstal Correctional Centres: *Chapter 9*.
1961   Re-roled as a Borstal Recall and Correctional Centre.
1964   Last executions in Britain, simultaneously at Walton Gaol, Liverpool and Strangeways Prison, Manchester at 8 a.m. on 13 August 1964, of Peter Anthony Allen and Gwynne Owen Evans, respectively.
1965   Murder (Abolition of Death Penalty) Act suspends capital punishment for murder.
1967   The Criminal Justice Act 1967 finally abolishes corporal punishment in prisons.
1968   Allegations of brutality in the national press force an inquiry into events at Reading, culminating in its closure by 14 January 1969.
1969   Reading reopens as a local prison when a major rebuilding programme starts. Capital punishment for murder abolished permanently by way of a Commencement Order signed by James Callaghan, Home Secretary.
1970   April 8: Re-opens as a 'Rule 43 Prison', i.e. for vulnerable prisoners.
1980   Reclassified as a Category B local prison holding adult and young offenders; also a new Supergrass Unit opens within the old segregation unit (E-wing).
1984   American film actor Stacey Keach serves time at Reading for drug offences.
1990   In-cell sanitation is re-installed throughout, 125 years after it was last removed.
1992   The prison is re-roled as a Remand Centre for young offenders (aged 18 to 21). December 26: a major disturbance—the 'Boxing Day riot'—takes place, in which staff are attacked and 49 prisoners run riot doing damage worth £153,000.
1993   December 21: seven of the rioters are sentenced for prison mutiny pursuant to the still novel Prison Security Act 1992.
1996   Again re-roled: as HM Remand Centre and Young Offender Institution. The Kennet Unit (*Chapter 12*) is opened by ex-England footballer, Trevor Brooking.
2000   Wilde Walk, Reading commemorates the centenary of Oscar Wilde's death.
2001   UK ratifies Protocol Six to the European Convention On Human Rights (ECHR) signed by Jack Straw, Home Secretary in 1999, so as to completely outlaw capital punishment in peacetime.
2003   A new Vocational Training Centre (VTC) opens at Reading.
2004   UK implements Protocol 13 to the ECHR ending capital punishment in war time. Pauline Bryant becomes the first woman governing-governor at Reading Gaol.

The Centre at Reading Gaol, Level 1, showing the Victorian 'Centre Box' before its removal and disappearance in the 1960s. The black and red floor tiles from 1844 were lifted up around the same time.

CHAPTER 1

The Old Reading Gaols

No doubt there were private gaols in the keeps and dungeons of the more powerful people of Reading and its surrounding area that go back into the mists of time. This book starts at the point when prisons of various kinds, whether for locking up people to await trial (or in some cases to await execution) or as a form of punishment for their crimes were beginning to move out of private ownership and to take on a more public aspect right across the country: more or less at the point where local authorities and modern forms of local justice first started.

SIXTEENTH AND SEVENTEENTH CENTURIES

The very first establishment to acquire the name 'Reading Gaol' was situated in a quite different location to that of Oscar Wilde's day and thereafter; earliest references indicate that as long ago as 1537 there was a county gaol in Castle Street, which still runs through the old part of the town today, on the site of the present-day St Mary's Church.

Reading Bridewell
Reading, in common with many other English towns, had more than one gaol, or 'bridewell'. The County Bridewell was a small building in Castle Street measuring just 100ft by 90ft (almost 30 metres square), that was used as a remand prison for people who were awaiting trial. It also housed more serious offenders, known as 'felons', from all over the county of Berkshire and served as the Town Bridewell for petty criminals from the town itself as well as being a prison for common debtors. In addition there was the very small Reading Town Gaol consisting of just three rooms in a local tavern, the Reading Arms, which only seems to have held two or three prisoners at any one time.

These gaols were administered and funded locally, with only a modest workforce to oversee a wide range of different types of offender, from women and children accused of petty crimes, through common debtors to hardened murderers.

Details from the sixteenth and seventeenth centuries are few, but it is known, e.g. that in 1537 a blacksmith from Wallingford (nowadays a township on the River Thames to the north of Reading) was cast into this version of Reading Gaol by order of King Henry VIII. The first recorded execution in the town took place in 1571—that of an offender named Newman, who was hanged in the marketplace—and the first recorded birth in the gaol was that of John Nabb, whilst his mother was incarcerated there in 1574.

In 1683 the first recorded marriage at the gaol took place between a couple called Richard Marshall and Mary Elton.

EIGHTEENTH AND EARLY NINETEENTH CENTURIES

Women as well as men were publicly executed for their crimes: in 1755 Margaret Wright was hanged in Reading for murdering her infant child and in 1761 Ann Giles was hanged for arson.

Conditions in prisons across the land in those days were brutal and dehumanising. Generally speaking, most prisoners were people who were poor and who had committed crimes to obtain money or goods of which they felt themselves to be—or were—deprived. Many goods which are mass-produced cheaply today were at that time hand-made and expensive to buy. These included handkerchiefs, clothing, pots and pans, wooden or iron goods—all of which were frequently stolen and easily sold on. The most serious criminal offences—felonies—included highway robbery and, as now, rape and various forms of homicide but also many crimes that are now considered to be less serious such as bigamy, assault and many property crimes. The sentences were severe, and the gallows awaited almost everyone convicted of felony, including many types of theft such as pick-pocketing, shoplifting, burglary, embezzlement and receiving stolen goods. The best that an offender could hope for under the 'Bloody Code' was a sympathetic jury who, often reluctant to sentence men and women to death for minor offences, would sometimes reduce the charge. For example, in larceny cases where the value of the goods stolen was less than 12 pence the sentence might be transportation, branding with a hot iron, whipping or imprisonment rather than capital punishment.

The Reverend Field and John Howard

The Reverend John Field was the chaplain who, along with the keeper, maintained the smooth running of the County and Town Bridewell in Reading for many years. He later became an authority on prison discipline and the noted author of four books on the subject. He wrote of Reading Bridewell in 1848:

> It is a spacious room, with four dark huts on one side for night-rooms. The county pays rent to the corporation. It is dirty and out of repair. Women and men are together in the day time.

Above the door leading into the street the following verse was transcribed:

> Oh ye whose hours exempt from sorrow flow,
> Behold the seat of pain, and want, and woe:
> Think, while your hands th'entreated alms extend,
> That what to us ye give, to God ye Lend.

In 1779 the Bridewell was visited by the prison reformer John Howard (in whose name the Howard League for Penal Reform was later founded in 1866) who described it thus:

> Debtors and felons have their courts separated by iron rails ... felons have a day room for men and women. The night room for men is a large dungeon down some steps; the prisoners escaped recently. A separate night room for women. The Turnkey's lodgings over the dungeon with an alarm bell so that escape will be more difficult.
> (Field: 1848)

Field has also left us a contemporary account of the procedures when new prisoners arrived at the gaol:

> When felons come into prison, they are washed and put on clothes supplied by the county. The men have a Russian drab coat with breeches, flannel waist-coat, two check shirts and two pair of yarn hose. For the women, a linsey Woolsey gown and petticoat, flannel petticoat, two dowlas shifts and two pair of yarn hose. Their own clothes are ticketed and hung up till their court appearance. The county clothes are then purified in an oven and washed. The cost of clothing in 1773 to the county for twenty men and five women is £26. 6s. 8d. (Field: 1848).

As part of the annual returns which he made, the Reverend Field noted that felons were given a prison allowance of three pence a day and petty offenders received two five-farthing loaves each, every Sunday and once during the week. Further allowances were:

> Keeper's salary, £18. From the county and £2. From the town: fees 4s. 4d. licence for beer and allowed to keep half the profit from the prisoners' work. The common side debtors pay 1s. 6d. whilst the master's-side pays 2s. 6d. a week for lodging.

Conditions in the gaol were poor even by the standards of the day, with serious overcrowding and typhus ('gaol fever') often raging, so much so that on 28 January 1786 debtors at the prison petitioned the Secretary of State 'Praying for Relief'. The petition was however ordered 'to lie on the table': no action was deemed necessary, although the option was kept open to review things later (*The Times*, 28 January 1786).

Field tells us that in 1729 the gaol committee discussed at length the demoralising custom of licensing gaolers to sell beer, which appears to have been almost universal. The committee expressed their concerns about 'the evils' resulting from keepers having a tap-house, with the effect of 'promoting riot, drunkenness and ... midnight revels' (Field: 1848). Years later, when John Howard was revisiting the gaols of Berkshire in 1789 he found that the old keeper of Windsor Castle Prison had been murdered by his prisoners in his tap-room. Soon after this the sale of beer by gaolers was prohibited and their salaries were increased to accommodate their potential loss of earnings (Field: 1848).

To the dismay of John Howard, however, the keepers were simply replaced as vendors of beer by the debtors:

> Thus at Newgate Prison I found some of the debtors had in their apartments casks of beer for sale.

Debtors could arrange for food and beer to be sent to them for a small fee, then the more street-wise among them would sell the provisions on to less fortunate people at an extravagant price.

1783: Forbury House of Correction

The number of prisoners was increasing substantially and the Castle Street site was deemed too small for expansion so that in 1783 the County of Berkshire petitioned Parliament for a new house of correction, to be built on the eastern end of an area called Forbury—the ruined site of a former abbey standing in pastures outside the town. This abbey had been founded in 1121 by Henry I the youngest son of William the Conqueror, and was demolished in Tudor times by Henry VIII during the Dissolution of the Monasteries. The Prison Act had been passed in 1781 making it compulsory for justices of the peace to provide accommodation for all felons and that kept them separate from each other, according to the latest penal reform ideas, rather than all together during the day and in single sex dormitories at night. The proposed new prison building at Reading would conform to all the new ideas of this Act:

> Justices in settling and adjusting plans of new buildings, are hereby required to provide separate apartments for all persons committed upon charges of felony, and convicted of theft or larceny and committed to the house of correction for punishment by hard labour ... in order to prevent any communication between them and other prisoners. (22 Geo. III.c.54.)

So in 1785 a new house of correction for 60 prisoners was built on the site of the old abbey, where the modern-day Reading Gaol still stands. John Howard wrote about it in 1789:

> The new prison, consisting of six close cells for refractory, eight solitary cells and six wards for prisoners permitted to being together.

According to the Reverend Field (1848), the staff allowances were as follows:

Gaoler — the Widow Wiseman [who replaced her deceased husband, J. Hill]
Salary — £20
Fees — debtors, 16s. 10d.
Felons, 14s. 4d.
Transports, £2 2s. each
Licence, beer and wine.
Prisoners'Allowance, debtors, none.
Felons, 2s. 6d

Chaplain — Rev. Mr. Webster
On duty — Sunday and Wednesday
Salary — £31 10s.

Surgeon — Mr. Tylleard
Salary — £10 for Gaol and Bridewell

Debtors had to pay for their own keep: the total income from all debtors amounted to 16s 10d. This could cause further financial hardship to people who were already in custody for debt. In a letter dated 5 November 1841, William Inwood, a debtor in Reading Gaol, complained bitterly to his sister that he had been obliged to part with everything, even his clothes, to the keeper. He also bemoaned the fact that he was starving and begged her to contact Mr Thenham (the person he owed the debt to) and to ask him to show mercy and release him from his indebtedness.

A rising prison population — and overcrowding
The ever increasing numbers of prisoners and the conditions that they were held in continued to cause concern with visiting justices and in the Michaelmas Sessions in the autumn of 1791 two options were seriously considered: the enlargement of either the old premises in Castle Street or of the new house of correction at Forbury (Southerton: 1975). Castle Street was deemed inappropriate so the latter option was chosen.

Taking in all the recommendations of the reformer John Howard, the architect chosen was Robert Fruze Brettingham of London and tenders were invited for the construction of a two-storey building to accommodate 30 felons and the same number of debtors, a chapel, store rooms, in-cell sanitation and a keeper's house. William Collier of Reading was awarded the contract for the princely sum of £3,000.

Unfortunately Collier had not taken into account the position of the new gaol: the solid flint foundations of the former abbey were to prove a mighty obstacle that somehow would need to be overcome. However, construction work progressed and the building was ready for occupation by September 1793 — when all the county felons were moved there. The Castle Street premises also remained in use as a debtors' prison until 1796 (Southerton: 1975).

The quality of the building work, however, was of a poor standard, so much so that the gaol committee withheld £138. 12s. from Brettingham's fee, a considerable sum in those days. The roof leaked and the timber used was of an inferior quality—indeed it was later to prove instrumental in a prisoner escaping from, of all places, the condemned cell (*The Times*, 8 October 1839). The repair of these defects fell to the unfortunate keeper, who had to both fix the roof and strengthen the doors and floor panels, trying to patch up the below par workmanship of the builder.

Despite the expansion, overcrowding continued to be a problem for Reading Gaol. A report in *The Times* of 7 July 1819 into the state of prisons in England and Wales showed Reading to be overcrowded: designed for 60 prisoners yet holding up to 73 prisoners at times during 1818.

Introduction of the treadmill

In 1822 Reading became one of the first prisons in England and Wales to introduce a treadmill. Invented by Sir William Cubitt and installed by Penn, millwrights of Greenwich, at a cost of £1,700, the treadmill used prison labour to grind flour. It was designed to accommodate 32 prisoners climbing a wooden cylinder with steps attached. It was said that, working continuously for ten hours, a prisoner would climb the equivalent of 13,300 feet. The building that housed the treadmill consisted of a two-storey block some 33 feet in length and divided into four compartments (Southerton: 1975). Prisoners who had been sentenced to hard labour were forced to climb the treadmill for many hours every day; it was a notorious punishment that exhausted men and women and broke their health. As the Reverend Field noted in 1848:

> A futile attempt was made to amend the morals and to reform the offender by means of bodily suffering and fatigue.

According to the local newspaper, the *Reading Mercury*, the treadmill was first brought into use on 15 November 1822 and almost immediately there was a mass refusal to work by prisoners who complained that their wooden soled shoes needed to be replaced with shoes with softer leather soles. The prisoners found the wooden shoes extremely painful after only a short time walking on the treadmill. To prevent a mutiny breaking out the authorities advertised for and appointed a second turnkey (gaoler):

> Wanted at the County Gaol and Bridewell at Reading a steady honest and sober middle aged man, who can bear confinement as Assistant Turnkey, at the said gaol .... if he is a married man he cannot be accommodated with apartments for his family .... the wages will be 18s. per week. (*Reading Mercury*, 28 January 1823)

Concern over prison conditions begins to grow

In 1824 alterations were made to the existing building to accommodate the growing number of prisoners, including women, being sent to the already overcrowded gaol and it was extended to accept female prisoners properly. By 1830 the visiting justices complained that a gaol designed to accommodate 100 prisoners was now expected to hold 142—there being three prisoners to a cell measuring in some cases just ten feet by eight feet. One Augustus Schultz, Esq. left a bequest of £1,000 to be used for the construction of a prison exclusively for juvenile offenders, but the money was actually used to build a separate ward (or what we would nowadays call a 'wing'), together with an infirmary (Field: 1848).

Whilst some parts of the gaol had been modernised the debtors, who were viewed as petty criminals and housed separately from the felons, had been more or less forgotten. A reporter from the *Reading Mercury* was so appalled by a visit in May 1829 that he wrote:

> The debtors' sitting apartment is dark and dreary ... the temperature was at least ten degrees higher than outside with no windows or ventilation ... in the debtors' yard there is a dung heap of rotting vegetables ... in one room there is a bed with six emaciated faces crouched around a small fire ... another room was ten feet by eight with three beds some one foot apart ... there is no water within the walls it can only be obtained from the gaoler by knocking at the outer door of the prison.

The following month the *Reading Mercury* reported that the conditions within the prison had led to an escape attempt by the debtors, who had managed to excavate a large hole by the outer wall, only to be stopped by the rock solid foundations of the abbey.

Prison diet and other conditions

Other aspects of the gaol, and particularly of the diet, which is detailed in *Appendix 3*, were also unsatisfactory. The local newspapers reported on a meeting on July 2 when the visiting justices had complained that the diet of 'number three class prisoners' (those sentenced to over one months' imprisonment) was wholly insufficient and that both the chapel and the solitary cells were in an appalling state. Mr Balley, the prison surgeon, had defended the prison:

> The dietary of the class referred to was not insufficient for the maintenance of prisoners.

But Mr Walter, one of the visiting justices, had stated:

> I was particularly stuck with the allowance. I deem it more as scanty and severe ... the No. 3 diet consisted of a pint of gruel [a kind of watery porridge] for breakfast

nothing for dinner and another pint for supper ... I may take this chance to mention the appalling state of the solitary cells and the small chapel.

Mr Hackett, the prison governor, had then read out a lengthy report in which he complained that in his view the treadmill was

> unjust, and injurious in every sense it often produces great exhaustion of the physical strength ... I have known prisoners wounding their legs, another chalking their tongue ... starving themselves to an emaciated state with five loafs of bread secreted within their cell [in order to absent themselves from the treadmill due to ill health] ... I therefore think that labour of the treadmill is highly unfavourable to reformation ... As to the cells and the chapel there is no ventilation which makes them extremely offensive and when you consider that there are 33 cells only and at times there will be three to a cell the size being seven feet by nine.

The chairman put the motion of Mr Walter,

> That the allowance of prisoners in class 1 and 2 [which allowed them more food: extra potatoes and bread] be extended to all prisoners on Monday, Wednesday and Friday and to everyone on Sundays.

The motion was rejected by a majority of eight to two.

Prison inspections and more calls for reform
By 1841 the Inspector of Prisons had also begun to question the deficiencies at Reading, a concern that culminated in a critical report by the Home Secretary, Sir James Graham. With the appalling state that the gaol was in, things had to change. In August 1842 a meeting of over 40 Berkshire magistrates took place in Abingdon (now in Oxfordshire). The purpose was to decide on the building of a new gaol to serve the entire county. A report had been commissioned by a new Gaol Committee that had been set up earlier, consisting of 22 members. The committee strongly recommended that a new building be commenced immediately and reported that they had considered nine tenders and had selected one of these, that of a Mr Jay.

According to a report of this meeting in *The Times* (5 July 1842), an amendment was then proposed by the Reverend N. Dodson, which would have meant that the building work would be postponed until the following February. The magistrates were unable to agree or disagree and the chair, Viscount Barrington, cast the deciding vote ensuring that work would start immediately. The architects Messrs. Scott and Moffatt's design for a gaol to hold 213 prisoners along with rooms for different classifications of prisoner was to be 'forthwith proceeded with'. Lord Barrington then asked leave to apply to the Home Secretary for the use of part of the new model prison at Pentonville, London, for the safe custody of Berkshire's prisoners during the rebuilding of the gaol.

SOME INTERESTING EARLY PRISONERS

In some of the later chapters of this book information is given about various prisoners of particular interest who have passed through the gate of Reading Goal, including those who did so on the way to the condemned cell and scaffold. But prisoners frequently arrive in notable circumstances of one kind or another, of which the following are some early examples.

A case of suspected witchcraft
In 1632 William and Edith Wallis decided to increase their income by letting out one the rooms in their farmhouse in Reading. Edward Bonavant a local man decided to take up the offer and moved into the farmhouse. Almost immediately he began to have convulsions or fits. William and Edith were accused of 'bewitching' him. Fortunately for William, when examined he was found to have no pimples on his body except for a blue spot which, happily for him, bled when pricked. Edith was not so lucky and was sent to Reading Gaol.

The fasting man
In 1841 Bernard Cavanagh arrived in Reading from Ireland where he had a massive public following, claiming to have miraculously abstained from food and drink for five years and six months. On November 18 the Lord Mayor of Reading decided that the man was no more than a rogue and a vagabond under the Vagrancy Act 1824, being someone deemed to be a vagrant from 'going about as a gatherer or collector of alms ... [to] procure charitable contributions of any kind'. He was sent to prison for three months with hard labour.

Such was the public curiosity that a reporter from *The Times* travelled from London to the prison to see this living legend. Inside the gaol a battle had begun between the surgeon, Mr Bulley, on the one hand and the chaplain and the governor, Lieutenant Hackett, on the other. As part of his punishment, Cavanagh was required to work on the prison treadmill but the surgeon, in disagreement with both of the others and concerned about the man's health, kept taking him off. After nine days the mayor decided to remove the hard labour element of the punishment as an act of mercy and kindness. Cavanagh was still fasting. All food and drink given to him was weighed both before and after meals and it was confirmed via *The Times* to a fascinated public that he had not indeed taken any substance to date (*The Times*, 27 November 1841). Cavanagh lasted to the eleventh day before he could take no more and began to eat. He died four years after his release from Reading in 1845 at the age of 32.

The one-legged sailor

In 1832 Denis Collins was arrested at Ascot Races for throwing a stone and hitting His Majesty King William IV. Collins, who had been held on remand at Reading Gaol, created a stir at his trial in March 1833 due to his physical appearance. He had a wooden leg (having lost his real one during naval service) which was painted a bright, sky blue and he wore a blue cloth cap with a red border and a white tassel attached to the top of it. He was also dressed in the two-coloured prison uniform consisting of bright yellow all down the right hand side and a shade of purplish brown down the left. Collins was found guilty of high treason and ordered to be transported for life (*The Times*, 28 March 1833).

The army 'deserter'

On 18 July 1836 soldier William Nichols was brought before Windsor magistrates claiming to be a deserter from the 43rd Regiment. Upon investigation, it transpired that he was not in fact a deserter but had been discharged from the British Army in 1834 with a pension of one shilling per day and, furthermore, that he had been imprisoned at Ipswich in 1835 on a similar charge. Nichols was sent to prison for one month for wasting the court's time.

Further investigation revealed that after his discharge he married a much younger woman with several children from a previous marriage. The marriage got into difficulties and she arranged via the overseers of their parish to have his pension paid direct to her, leaving him destitute. Enraged, Nichols concluded that the only way to stop the payments to her was to be charged as a deserter and have his pension stopped. He was sentenced to two months' imprisonment, as a rogue and vagabond, and taken to Reading Gaol.

A question of privilege and right

In 1679 Parliament passed the Habeas Corpus Act which guaranteed that someone detained by the authorities would be brought before a court of law rather than flounder in some dungeon or prison. In 1793 William Pitt, the Prime Minister, suspended the Act allowing the Secretary of State for the Home Office to send someone to prison for the offence of high treason, and without their ever having been formally charged in a court of law and proved guilty. Someone who was so accused could be incarcerated for an indefinite term, solely at the discretion of the Home Secretary. Critics claimed that this was open to abuse in that it allowed enemies of the government to be conveniently locked up including for long periods of time. There were at least two instances of this in the history of Reading Gaol.

Hodgson, Le Maitre and Galloway
A letter addressed to the keeper of Reading Gaol from Whitehall, 8 August 1799, gave explicit instructions as to how three prisoners detained for treasonable practices—Richard Hodgson, Paul Thomas Le Maitre and Alexander Galloway—were to be treated while in custody. In particular, these prisoners were not to communicate with any person without the express permission of one of His Majesty's Principal Secretaries of State. The keeper was paid 13s. 4p per week for his services with regard to this, deemed to be a reasonable rate to cover expenses.

Nearly a year and a half later, in December 1800, one of the men, Le Maitre, petitioned the Government praying for relief. He continued to be held in Reading Gaol, still with no formal charge being made against him. Le Maitre had been implicated in the so-called 'Pop-gun plot': a conspiracy hatched for the assassination of King George III in which poison was to be fired by dart from a pop-gun. The plan was foiled and those who were implicated sent to prison for treason.

Hodgson was a member of the London Corresponding Society, a group of people who supported Parliamentary reform. However, with the passing of the Corresponding Societies Act 1799 it became illegal for this society and others like it to meet so this and similar organizations came to an end. Hodgson was tried for high treason in Dublin in 1794, and later exiled to France where he met Arthur Thistlewood (the main conspirator in the famous Cato Street Conspiracy).

Knight, Hutton and Sellars
In another celebrated case that placed Reading Gaol at the centre of constitutional affairs and the powers of the executive, three prisoners named Knight, Hutton and Sellars were detained in Reading Gaol for treason. Lord Folkestone, visiting magistrate of the County Gaol, wished to visit the men but he was denied access to them by the keeper who said he had received orders from Lord Sidmouth, the Secretary of State, that on no account should anyone visit these men without his (Sidmouth's) prior permission.

A lengthy debate then ensued in the House of Commons, with opponents arguing that Sidmouth's orders were in violation of the law. However, after heated discussion, the House determined otherwise and Lord Folkestone's motion demanding access to the prisoners was defeated by a majority of 29.

Such was the outcry at this abuse of power that, according to local newspapers, after his defeat Lord Folkestone stood up and said:

> We would wish our countrymen to consider for a moment in what state the nation is placed by this decision. The Secretary of State might imprison whom he pleased and for as long as he pleased—no mortal could approach them, without his permission to hear their griefs, to hear their defence, excuses and receive and present their petitions. They were entirely put out of the pale of humanity, in a way that makes the heart tremble—it will be observed that the prisoners are not to be brought to trial in

conformity of the revered constitution of the realm; they are to be imprisoned without trial. So that, according to the decision of the House of Commons, they were being placed beyond the possibility of being heard, even in mitigation of their suffering, except by him, or with his consent, who subjected them to those sufferings.

A couple of days later Lord Folkestone again went to Reading Gaol and demanded to enter, but he was again refused access to the famous prisoners by the gaoler. Lord Folkestone was so incensed that he initiated criminal proceedings against Mr. Eastaff, the gaoler, accusing him of:

> being the keeper of the common gaol, with having, on the 6th of October, in the 57th year of reign of His Majesty, wilfully knowingly and unlawfully, refused to admit Lord Folkestone into the said gaol.

The case was heard on 3 March 1818 and after nine hours the jury found the gaoler not guilty. In a landmark summing up that foreshadowed debates over centuries to come about the treatment of political prisoners, the judge, Mr Justice Parks, concluded that, in cases of treason, it was for the Secretary of State to commit to close and safer custody, and nowhere in any statute did it authorise a justice to demand access to the prisoners of state confined in His Majesty's gaols.

ESCAPE

There were several escape attempts at Reading County Gaol in the nineteenth century, some successful, others not so. Some of the cases—as well as illustrating the inventiveness of prisoners—confirm the poor quality of the building work and materials that the Gaol Committee had complained about years earlier!

The horse-stealer
Prisoner Webb, a notorious horse-stealer, managed to escape from Reading Gaol during the Assizes held in the town in March 1818, by breaking his way out through the roof of the prison. He was waiting to be brought into the dock for trial and had he been found guilty of horse-stealing he would certainly have hanged.

The ten prisoners
Ten prisoners mounted an infamous but unsuccessful escape attempt one night in October 1826. Three men dug their way out of their cell using handles from frying pans and gridirons. They got into the courtyard and over a low wall into the day ward (where the prisoners mingled during daytime). The other seven prisoners who were waiting there started to tear up their blankets to knot the strips together as escape rope, whilst the first three set to work trying to undermine the foundations under the door. One young lad hid up the chimney

and remained there while the unsuspecting turnkey locked up and went to bed. The young man then produced an old knife which he had fashioned into a screwdriver and proceeded to try and remove the door lock. Unfortunately for him, the plan proved ineffective and a subsequent account in the local press told how he 'was found in the morning shivering in his shirt and terrified at the approaching turnkey' (*Reading Mercury*).

All ten prisoners were apprehended and put on trial for attempting to escape from lawful custody. The magistrates ordered that four of them be placed in solitary cells for one month and that the others be put into close confinement at the discretion of the keeper.

The mop-and-broom escape

At six o'clock one evening in September 1827 seven prisoners made a successful escape from the exercise yard. They had removed the benches attached to the wall and placed them on top of the privy (toilets). They were thereby able to climb up and reach the coping of the external wall. With the aid of a broom and a mop tied together with a handkerchief, they lowered themselves down on the other side and escaped into Kings Meadow, the pastureland that then stood opposite to the front of the gaol.

According to a contemporary account the escape was discovered and the alarm raised by Mr Ferry, the deputy gaoler, whose son and other turnkeys gave chase. Six prisoners were caught about a mile away on the bridge over the River Thames, but the seventh man, Charles Dormer, had already crossed the river and got away. Dormer had recently returned from transportation, having been sentenced to ten years in Botany Bay, Australia.

The four condemned men

Four prisoners under sentence of death who were being held together in the condemned cell made a determined attempt to escape the noose in October 1839. They found the lintel above the door and the door itself to be of such poor construction that they were able to remove the lintel and use it as a battering-ram to demolish the door! Farrar, Burgess, Vickers and Embling, all notorious criminals, headed for North Wales, after receiving clothes and money from friends. Farrar and Burgess went off in one direction and Vickers and Embling made their way to an ale house in Corwen, where they were quickly caught and locked up in Dolgelly Gaol.

These two then escaped again, from Dolgelly, by attacking and nearly killing the gaoler there. His wife released a debtor who managed to capture Vickers but the other three prisoners were never found.

CHAPTER 2

The New Prison

> In Reading Gaol by Reading Town
> There is a Pit of Shame
> (*The Ballad of Reading Gaol*, Oscar Wilde)

The backdrop to the major rebuilding of Reading Gaol in 1844 was a debate that was raging at that time over the issues and complexities of two quite different types of prison discipline that were in use in Great Britain and many other parts of the world. These were the 'silent system' and the 'separate system' and they each required a quite different style of prison construction.

The silent system
Based on a system practised in New York, USA, the silent method of prison discipline required prisoners to maintain total silence at all times. They worked and slept together in large open areas or dormitories where the turnkeys could easily keep a lookout for any sign of talking and punish the offender accordingly. The system was difficult to manage and control, but its main advantage was the low cost of construction with regard to this type of prison regime: large open spaces rather than the more expensive cellular configuration of the separate system.

The separate system
This system also originated in the USA and it had recently been introduced into Britain at 'the model penitentiary', Pentonville Prison, in north London, which opened in 1842. The central idea was to keep prisoners apart from one another as much as possible: as part of their punishment and also to discourage further corruption from mixing with hardened criminals. Whenever prisoners left their cells they each had to wear a baseball style cap (called a 'Scottish cap') over the head which had a large flat peak that extended down over the face creating a kind of mask. The peak was also made so that the prisoner could only see through narrow slits within it when walking around. Strict isolation was observed at all times; even the chapel was designed with individual cubicles rather than continuous pews, so that during religious services the prisoners remained completely segregated from one another and the only person they could see was the chaplain.

Within this system the chaplain played an important part, encouraging prisoners to turn away from their previous ways and to look to religion. The disadvantage of the system lay in the negative psychological effect of the total isolation and associated solitary confinement when in a cell; it was claimed that prisoners had gone mad from the intensity of the silence.

BUILDING THE NEW PRISON

The separate system won the day in the debate over the design of the new Reading Gaol and it was decided to build it on the same lines as Pentonville. Nevertheless, even in the latter stages of signing the contract, disagreements between supporters of the silent and separate systems continued. On 10 January 1843 a report of a meeting revealed a fascinating insight into problems of delay, disputes and soaring costs some of which remain familiar even today. The Reverend Dobson, who had made it clear that he was wholly against the separate system and the extra cost it would entail, complained at the Quarter Sessions held in the Bridewell Hall in Abingdon on 9 January 1843 concerning:

> the slow progress ... the number of men engaged upon the works having dwindled down from hundreds to about twenty. If this state of things continued, there would be little probability of the completion until a much later period.

The delay had been caused by the building firm having gone bankrupt. However the Gaol Committee acted quickly and appointed a new firm, Messrs Baker and Son from Lambeth, London.

It was believed that the reason the first builders had gone bankrupt was that they had failed to measure their work properly. The new contractors were to ensure that a full and comprehensive measurement of the site was carried out. All remnants of the previous gaol had been removed, leaving just a small section of four cells accommodating a few male debtors and the chapel. There had also been a delay in procuring materials, but this was soon remedied and building work started apace (*The Times*, 10 January 1843).

A year later, in January 1844, a report submitted to the Epiphany Sessions by the Gaol Committee caused uproar at the meeting. The committee reported that the original estimate as to the cost of the new gaol was set at £24,000 in 1842. This money had been secured with arrangements made with the Crown Assurance Company at a cost of four per cent: which only came to light from the seventh report of the Inspector of Prisons. There appeared to have been a massive accounting error as stated in the *Berkshire Chronicle*: 'By some strange and unaccountable forgetfulness no estimate had been framed of the expense which must be incurred in warming and ventilating the prison.' This additional work would increase the cost to £32,000. Ten days later, the magistrates were informed that the cost had increased by a further £6,000 to complete all the building work, taking the total cost of the new gaol to £40,000.

Those dissenters amongst the magistrates who had all along complained at every opportunity seized upon this and called for a halt until this type of prison had been 'more fully tried on other places and in the event of it not succeeding they might be called upon greater expense [with regard to] to further alterations'. The Reverend G. S. Evans was amongst the most vocal and took exception to the extra expense of all the ornate and decorative work being carried out.

Work continued, nonetheless, and by 1 July 1844 at the Midsummer Sessions the Gaol Committee declared the gaol to be fit and ready for occupation. The first person reported to have been sentenced to a term of imprisonment at the new Reading Gaol was Abraham Boswell, indicted for the offence of attempted rape of a minor (a two-year-old child) and sentenced to six months' imprisonment with hard labour (Southerton, 1975). Fifty years later Reading's most famous prisoner, Oscar Wilde, would be admitted through the same gates.

THE PRISON LAYOUT

> On the rising ground, at the entrance to Reading, and close to the venerable abbey, this new prison is from every side the most conspicuous building, and architecturally, by far the greatest ornament in the town.
>
> (*Illustrated London News*, 17 February 1844)

When the prison was finished it instantly became the new focal point of the town of Reading, a stone's throw from the town's main railway station and visible to travellers. It was the largest building situated on the rising ground at the eastern entrance to the town, commanding unsurpassed views and with the River Thames in the distance. A visitor's first view of Reading Gaol would have included an imposing and commanding building with four turrets and a castellated Gothic style outer wall.

The new prison had 250 cells (including those for debtors) allowing total isolation for all prisoners. Each prisoner had his or her own cell which in that sense was a vast improvement over the situation in the previous gaol, which consisted of dormitory-style accommodation. Further improvements enabled women prisoners to be housed in their own ward (E-ward). The chaplain's house to the right and the governor's house were either side of the gatehouse. Both were beautifully designed, each having four bedrooms and being built with many luxuries denoting the high status of their occupants within the community. On each of the four corners was a turret, designed with both ornamental appearance and functional use in mind, as noted by the *Illustrated London News* in a long and approving article which took the reader on an imaginary tour:

Through their grated windows they may command the flank walls both externally and internally ... facilitate the detection of any attempt to escape from within or to afford aid to such an attempt from without.

The turret to the left of the main gate was occupied by the matron, the only access being through the gaol, so that whenever she went out she had to be back before the prison had closed for the night. The right-hand turret housed the deputy-governor and the remaining two turrets were occupied by other staff. The last person to live in one of these turrets was John Smith (a prison officer).[1] He had lived there until they were demolished in the major rebuild of 1969 (see *Chapter 10*). John was real character within the prison, who could talk at great length about the problems of living in a turret. He said there was a feeling of claustrophobia and the tiny spiral staircase presented great difficulties when moving furniture in and out. His favourite story was about the time when he had to cut a new bed in half in order to get it up the stairs—then weld it back together again before his wife saw it!

The gatehouse had a flat roof specifically designed to accommodate executions—which at that time were always held in full view of the general public—and the roof was used for that purpose for the first time a year later for the hanging of Thomas Jennings (see *Chapter 4*). Past the main gate and inside the walls was a small courtyard, with the women's prison (E-ward) to the left. Totally separate from the main prison, it contained 30 cells with two additional punishment cells. This ward (or 'wing' as they are known today) was virtually self-contained, with a small infirmary and a bathroom coupled with the main prison laundry. The only time women and girls entered the main prison was for chapel services. Women prisoners, as well as men, were held at Reading until the twentieth century.

The most notorious of these was Amelia Dyer who in 1896 was hanged following the multiple murders of children given into her care as a foster mother. Dyer was a 56-year-old woman who had made a living out of other people's misfortunes. Advertising herself as a foster mother in local newspapers, she would take in young babies for a fee of £10 each and within a day of the child being in her care she would murder it and throw the body into the local River Thames. By the time of her arrest seven bodies had been recovered from the river, all of children murdered in the same way—by strangulation. It later transpired that Amelia Dyer had earlier been plying her dubious 'trade' in other parts of England and Wales. Whenever the local police became suspicious, she would claim insanity and on two occasions had been admitted to a lunatic asylum. She would then discharge herself and simply move on to another location. Whilst at Reading Gaol, Dyer made a full written confession and asked

---

[1] A friend of the author's, who died in 2006.

the prison matron, Ellen Gibbs, to give it to the police, stating, 'I have now eased my mind'. Amelia Dyer was only ever charged with and convicted of the murder of one four-month-old baby girl. She is reputed to have been carrying out her gruesome practices for over 15 years, making her one of the most prolific child serial killers of all time.

It was not until 1915, when the prison was reclassified as a place of internment for political prisoners in the wake of Dublin's Easter Rising (*Chapter 7*), that the gaol became the single-sex institution that it is today.

Within the prison wall was the main building, constructed according to the radical new Pentonville design in the shape of a four-spoked wheel. The four main cellblocks (wards A, B, C and D), radiated out from the centre in the points of the compass. A-ward held remand and trial prisoners prior to their conviction, acquittal or sentence; C-ward convicted prisoners; B-ward convicted and later government prisoners; and D-ward reception prisoners (those newly arrived at the prison) and debtors as well as the administrative offices.

The focal point of the prison was the 'centre' or inspection hall at the hub of the wheel: a large open area that commanded a full view of all wards as they radiated out from it; enabling security and control to be maintained from a single, central point by a minimum of prison officers. According to the *Illustrated London News* (1844): 'The Governor, when seated in his office, has complete command over every cell door in the prison'. Attached to the centre were two rooms for use by the visiting justices and – when there was an execution – for the obligatory coroner's inquest held after every hanging.

The wards were all identical in design: a broad passageway down the middle with a row of cells on either side of it and a huge, high window at the end. Halfway along each ward there rose a light iron staircase, resembling the cordage of a galleon and designed so as to allow staff an unimpeded view of both storeys. Prisoners walked up these to reach their respective 'landings' and along the galleries that hugged the walls to their cells.

The cells

All cells were identical: 13 feet long by 7 feet wide by 10 feet high (approximately 3 metres x 2 metres x 2.5 metres). Even as long ago as 1844 they were designed to be kept at an optimum temperature of 54 degrees Fahrenheit, by a sophisticated warm-air heating system. Each cell was simply furnished with a small stool, a table, shelves and a drawer to contain all the prisoner's requirements for washing. A hammock made out of cocoa-nut fibre was suspended from iron fastenings in one of the side walls. In one corner was a small cistern, also a copper basin for washing and other purposes. Each cell was given an allotted six gallons (27 litres) of water every morning, which had to last the prisoner all day and cover all his or her needs, including for bodily functions. A gas light hung over the table and four compulsory notices were positioned around the walls:

- prison rules and diet;
- particulars of the prisoner;
- nature of their offence and order of the court; and
- morning and evening prayers.[2]

Lastly, every cell was furnished with a Bible, a prayer book and any other book that the chaplain deemed 'advantageous in the [prisoner's] future circumstances in life'. One of these books, entitled *Friendly Advice to a Prisoner*, was written by the Reverend John Field and purchased by the prison.

The only times when a prisoner left his or her cell were for chapel services, exercise and visits received at the prison. Meals were brought to the cells and passed in through a hatch built into the door; above which a small inspection hole covered in gauze allowed the turnkey to scrutinise the prisoner. Other contact with the turnkeys was by means of a gong operated from within each cell; when a prisoner pulled a cord a small plate inscribed with his or her cell number lifted up outside the cell concerned indicating at a glance for the turnkey which prisoner in which cell had called for assistance. Misuse was severely punished.

A-ward

A-ward held prisoners awaiting trial and was distinguished as 'the gaol' in which safe custody alone was the objective to be sought and ensured (as opposed to 'the house of correction' comprising the other wards for convicted criminals). Beneath A-ward were the County Stores, accessible only from outside via an underground passageway leading to the guardroom of the Reading Militia. This storeroom was totally separate from prison control and contained all the armoury stores for the county.

B-ward

B-ward—along with A-ward—consisted of four landings: one below the centre level and three landings above. B-ward's lower level consisted of bathing area cells (cells with bathing facilities) and the dark punishment cells for refractory prisoners (people who offended against good order and discipline). The three landings above were for convicted prisoners only and later used extensively for government convicts (see further p. 40).

C-ward

This was the only ward with just three landings and no lower level. It was used for convicted prisoners and by the very nature of this long-term type of prisoner this landing would be quieter and easier to manage for the warders. Even to this

---

[2] The full text of these rules appears in *Appendix 2*.

day the layout of the cells is identical, with the brickwork and metal framing of the landings still as per the originals of 1844. It was on C-ward that Oscar Wilde would be held in cell C.3.3.

D-ward
Through the main entranceway and up a small flight of stairs was the entrance to D-ward. On the right was the office of the clerk and to the left was the debtors' prison. This comprised two wards: these being occupied by prisoners during the day allowing both sexes to mingle along with some 20 small rooms for sleeping. Exercise took place in A-yard, known as 'the debtor's airing yard', behind a massive wall whose height made impossible any communication or contact with the rest of the prison.

Next to the clerk's office were visiting rooms: each divided into three small compartments, separated by iron rails. The prisoner being visited was placed on one side, his or her visitors on the other side, whilst the officer in attendance occupied the middle space ensuring that no inappropriate conversation took place. Prisoners awaiting trial were entitled to one 20-minute visit per day; convicted prisoners just one 20-minute visit every three months.

Next door was a room for prisoners to consult with their legal adviser. It was in this room that Oscar Wilde received his last visit from his wife, Constance, on 19 February 1896 when she informed him of the death of his mother.

From the main prison entrance after entering D-ward were stairs to the sides going up and going down and leading to the basement, which contained ten cells for the reception of new prisoners (see, also, 'New arrivals', below). Along the corridors were various store rooms, the kitchen and the warder's mess-room until B1 landing where the four refractory cells and the prison bath-house were accommodated. Below this level was the boiler house, where coal fired boilers delivered heat and ventilation throughout the gaol and steam for the kitchen. The apparatus was designed and installed by George and James Haden of Trowbridge and was in use with the original boiler right up until 1972; since then the boilers have been changed three times but the rest of the old system is still functioning today.

From B1 landing a doorway led into the pump-house, divided into ten compartments, in which the crank was worked by prisoners as a form of hard labour, pumping water into an overhead cistern on the roof of the gaol. This tank supplied water throughout the gaol.

The gardens
Outside into the gardens 'designed to be pleasing to the eye' (*Illustrated London News*, 1844) the visitor came to the exercise yards for the prisoners. Designed along the same lines as those at Pentonville Prison, they resembled a massive carriage-wheel with 20 spokes radiating from a central hub that housed the ever

watchful warder standing on a raised platform who ensured that no communication took place between prisoners. The walls of the spokes were some 40 feet in length and seven feet across at the furthest point from the hub; prisoners would walk around their segment for the required length of time. Women and girls had their own exercise area, in A-yard facing the main prison, consisting of six walled walking areas, each 40 feet by 10 feet (approximately 12 metres x 3 metres) with a matron pacing at one end to enforce strict compliance with the rules of the separate system.

The chapel

At that time one of the most important places was the chapel. Under the separate system all prisoners had to attend chapel, the construction of which was identical to that at Pentonville.

Rows of individual pews or stalls were constructed one above the other: small enough to accommodate a grown man, but not large enough to allow movement or much comfort. When a prisoner entered his or her allotted cubicle, the only human being visible was the chaplain. Prisoners had to take off the brass plates engraved with their cell numbers that they each wore and hang them on hooks. The cubicles were constructed so as to block all other prisoners from view. Women prisoners had to wear thick veils over their faces, rather than the prison masks. They and the debtors were allowed bench seating at the bottom of the pews. All prisoners had to wear either masks or veils throughout.

In 1894 the chapel underwent a wholesale reconstruction in which all the old oak cubicles were removed and replaced with a more humane arrangement of bench seating, the plan of which is on display within the prison today.

PRISON LIFE: THE DAY-TO-DAY REGIME

The daily routine for prisoners in 1844 was set down in staccato form as follows:

5:30 a.m. – Warder on night duty ring bell for officers to rise
6:00 a.m. – Unlock of cells for cleaning
8:00 a.m. – Assistant warders' and prisoners' breakfast
8:30 a.m. – Principle warder breakfast - prison locked up
9:00 a.m. – Warders muster in central hall
9:10 a.m. – Bell rung for chapel
10:00 a.m. – Prisoners to labour
12:00 noon – Prisoners dine
12:30 p.m. – Knives and tins collected from cells
2:00 – 6:00 p.m. – Core routine, labour and exercise
6:00 p.m. – Prisoners' supper
7:30 p.m. – Warders remove tools
7:45 p.m. – Bell rung to prepare for bed
8:00 p.m. – Bed

New arrivals

The first view a new prisoner would have had of the inside of the gaol would have been when the outer doors had been slammed shut and the inner gate opened up leading into a small courtyard. He or she would then be taken down some steps on the north facing ward (D-ward) into what was known as 'reception', where the cells for receiving new prisoners were situated. Here the attending officer would inspect the documents authorising confinement. At this point responsibility for the prisoner transferred from the police (such as they were at that time) to the prison, and the constable who brought the prisoner to the prison was no longer responsible for him or her. Handcuffs and leg irons were removed; the prisoner was searched and all possessions were taken away which were deemed useless or injurious. These were sealed and returned to the individual if he or she was later acquitted at his or her trial and thus released. If, however, the prisoner was convicted of a felony all of his or her money and any articles of value were forfeited to the Crown.

The prisoner was then locked up in one of ten reception cells to await the surgeon, who visited daily. After a medical examination the prisoner was then led to the baths on the lower ground floor of B-ward. On the way, the prisoner was shown the refractory cells, or 'dark cells', for unmanageable or unruly prisoners: double-doored cells designed to allow in no light. Ventilation and heating were controlled by the warder and the prisoner could be made to feel extremely uncomfortable as part of his or her punishment. The new prisoner would be placed in there for just a minute to instil a sense of fear and as a stern warning that any breach of prison rules would result in being in there for much longer.

The prisoner was then allowed a bath and all his or her clothes were taken away and fumigated (except for remand or trial prisoners, who could continue to wear their own clothes until they were sentenced). Convicted prisoners had to wear the prison uniform; on the right side bright yellow and on the left a shade of purplish brown. The prisoner would also be required to wear the prison mask and a brass badge engraved with his or her cell number (Oscar Wilde's badge read 'C.3.3': C3 landing, cell number 3). This number was the only way in which the prisoner would be identified until his or her release.

Finally the prisoner was taken up to his or her appointed cell.

Diet from the 1840s

In a letter to the local newspapers on 17 May 1843 a local magistrate, Mr J. Walter, complained at length, and not for the first time, about the diet and conditions of the prisoners at Reading Gaol:

> On September 1st 1842, in consequence of pulling down the old prison ... prisoners who had been committed from the borough of Windsor to the county prison at

Reading were sent back to Windsor. There were six ... the building which had been used as the workhouse was converted into the borough gaol, all the magistrates came to see the building and inmates ... All were labouring from severe diarrhoea, and they declared that such complaint prevailed amongst most of the prisoners at Reading.

Some of the prisoners, and their sentences, were:

James Hawkins (40): two years hard labour for passing base coin 10th January 1842
William Thomas (39): two years hard labour for passing base coin 10th January 1842
Catherine Jefferies (18): one years hard labour for passing base coin 7th April 1842
Jane Davis (40): six months for self-harming 2nd July 1842
Lawrence McCenns (25): six months with hard labour 2nd July 1842

The magistrate observed Lawrence McCenns particularly; he was a soldier of the 15th regiment and when this young man had originally been brought before him for sentence he had had the appearance of 'robust health'. The final straw came when William Thomas, who was seriously ill with 'diarrhoea and debility', subsequently died from cholera. The diet was immediately changed from the one followed at Reading which, according to the surgeon at Windsor Borough Gaol, consisted of:

A pint of rice milk night and morning
A pound and a half of bread daily
Every other day half a pound of meat with potatoes
Soup made in which that meat had been boiled on the other days.

A scale of the diet at the new gaol was posted upon all cell walls, showing what prisoners were entitled to at each level.[3]

Prison discipline

As described at the start of this chapter, the Scottish cap became synonymous with the separate system. Criminals around the country became fearful of the new discipline enforced at Reading, where the period of total isolation was for a minimum of 18 months, so that those sentenced to a lesser period would spend their whole sentence completely in isolation throughout. After 18 months the prisoner could be employed within the prison.

In 1846 a prisoner named Samuel Jones was sent to Reading to await trial at the next Assizes. On arriving at the front gate he attempted to escape from the constable escorting him; he ran around the prison then jumped over a small wall by the canal and head first into the deep water at the back of the gaol, with his

---

[3] See *Appendix 3*.

handcuffs still attached to him. Field (1848) goes into great detail about this incident stating:

> On my enquiring as to why he had thus hazarded his life, he answered, 'I had heard so much against this prison that I determined to run the risk rather than come ... I have been told that prisoners were blindfolded.

Such was the reaction to the system among the criminal community around Berkshire that Reading's prisoner numbers began to reduce dramatically. In 1840 the total number committed to Reading Gaol had been 985, rising to 1154 in 1844. The first year of operation of the new gaol saw a massive decrease in numbers to just 772 and by 1850 this number had further reduced to 637.

GOVERNMENT CONVICTS

With such low numbers, there was now a problem of under capacity rather than overcrowding. Arrangements had to be made to increase the prisoner population so that in 1847 the Secretary of State and the magistrates of Berkshire came to an agreement that Reading would take 40 prisoners from Millbank Prison in London. These prisoners were styled 'government convicts': those who had been sentenced to a period of transportation, but who were held in prisons in this country before being sent away, for a term of nine to 18 months' cellular confinement.

The first such convicts arrived at Reading from other prisons on 5 August 1847. It was decided that they should serve the first four to six weeks with no manual occupation other than 'a term of reflection to the criminal, interrupted only by necessary exercise and Divine instruction'. These prisoners were a shock to the chaplain who found: 'The state of mind of these prisoners was most unfavourable ... Hardened by repeated transgressions' (Field: 1848). Later, however, he was to inform the visiting justices that 'one of them has in two months committed to memory the four Gospels.'

For the accommodation of these prisoners a yearly rental was paid by the Government to the town of Reading of £6 for each cell used. Also paid for were two trade instructors—for tailoring and shoemaking— and an assistant schoolmaster. The instructors' report of 6 March 1848 states:

> The men have been very attentive and made good progress ... those employed in tailoring can make a suit of clothes and those in shoemaking can do the same with little instruction. (Field: 1848)

One of these convicts gave the prison staff a particularly hard time. Thomas Hirons from Henley-in-Arden had been discharged from the 26th Regiment of

Foot and in his short time at Reading he twice came close to escaping, using various implements fashioned from tools given to him with his work. He even managed to fashion a thimble into a saw but he was caught when a large piece of the cell door through which he was sawing fell to the ground and broke the silence of the gaol.

At the Quarter Sessions in April 1856 it was decided to report him to the Secretary of State, who transferred him to Portsmouth Prison. Within a week of being there he had obtained a soldier's uniform, walked straight past the sentries on the gate and escaped, with a price of £5 on his head (*The Times*, 17 April 1856).

In 1853 the Penal Servitude Act came into force and ended transportation; the supply of government convicts began to diminish and by 26 May 1856 they had all left.

HARD LABOUR: A PUNITIVE TWIST

The only form of hard labour at Reading was the mill house (the treadmill from the first gaol having been sold for scrap in 1842). This could only accommodate just ten prisoners at a time all pumping water into the prison. Complaints started to be made about the lack of 'hard labour' as a form of punishment. Speaking in the House of Lords on 6 July 1849 Lord Brougham bemoaned matters in the following terms:

> Take the case of Reading Gaol … it appeared that hard labour were excluded. But the magistrates appeared to glory in their shame. They took credit for their benevolent interventions … splendid treatment of criminals, totally forgetting that this was a place of punishment … allowed 10 hours sleep … the only labour being a hand crank pumping water for 10 convicts … the gaol might rather be called Reading University, for the only labour expected from prisoners was learning to read.

The Inspector of Prisons in his report for 1850 commended the quality of the prison and 'its highest state of order' but was critical of the lack of hard labour:

> I deeply regret again to report that the provisions of the law which require that labour or employment shall be provided for prisoners in separate confinement, have not been complied with.

Voices in high places began to complain about Reading Gaol and the Quarter Sessions in 1854 decided that some form of hard labour had to be provided. By the following year six small hand mills had been delivered, providing the prison with 'coarse but wholesome' bread from flour produced by the prisoners working these. But still the criticism continued and in 1863 stone-breaking was introduced, with the aim of having both a financial outcome (selling the broken stone to local builders) and a punitive effect upon the prisoners. 'Shot-drill' was also introduced:

this involved the prisoner lifting a 25 pound cannon ball up to chest height, moving three places to the left or right, then putting it down. This was repeated at the turnkey's discretion. All these tasks were performed near the debtors' airing yard.

In 1865 the climate became yet more punitive, with the Prison Act ('Hard Labour, Hard Fare and Hard Bed') coming into force under the stewardship of Sir Edmond Du Cane. The hammocks that the prisoners slept in were removed and replaced by wooden planks that served as beds. The sentence of hard labour was divided into two classes:

- **Class 1** – treadwheel, shot-drill, crank and stone-breaking; and
- **Class 2** – any other approved form of labour, oakum picking.

Class 1 prisoners had to be over the age of 16 and to have served at least the first three months of their sentence, after which they could apply to join Class 2. Diets had to be framed by the local justices and approved by the Secretary of State. The Act also tried to professionalise the prison system. At Reading in January 1868 a complaint had been made by the governor to the visiting justices that: 'Prison Clerk Mr Brownjohn had been drunk at his post and had lost a set of prison keys.' The keys were found in one of the reception cells and no-one had escaped but the justices stated in their report: 'Drunkenness and loss of keys by a trusted officer endangers the safety of the gaol and we have felt it our duty to dismiss Mr. Brownjohn.'

NATIONALISATION OF PRISONS

In 1877 a further Prison Act was passed which put ownership and overall control of prisons into the hands of the Government. It also provided for the creation of the Prison Commissioners: a group of five men, one of whom would be chairman. This commission had overall authority over the new prison estate and was answerable only to the Home Secretary. The justices of Berkshire still had a role with the creation of a Visiting Committee. This committee also consisted of five men, who had the responsibility of inspecting the prison regularly. The Berkshire Visiting Committee of 1896 was:

Capt. Alex W. Cobham
Charles Hay
H. Hunter
A. Harry Thursby
George W. Palmer (of the famous Reading-based Huntley & Palmers biscuit company).

Their role, reporting directly to the Prison Commissioners, was to investigate any wrongdoing, listen to prisoners' complaints, hear any charges of offences against discipline and award appropriate punishments.

One of the first tasks of the Visiting Committee at Reading was to investigate the first ever escape of a prisoner from the new gaol. Ada Chamberlain was found to have escaped from her cell on the morning of 2 May 1879—breaking a 35-year record of no escapes. A report in the Visiting Committee book indicates that the cell lock appeared to be suspect and a report was sent to the Prison Commissioners to that effect. But according to other evidence it later transpired that Ada had escaped from the matron's sitting room, through a loose bar in the matron's window. Questions were asked of the matron and following Ada's capture in a nearby town eight days later it became apparent that Ada had assumed the disguise of a young man, being just 21 years of age. Having first escaped her cell, Ada then had to go through two other locked doors before entering the matron's quarter. The matron could not explain how the prisoner came to be in her sitting room.

The next milestone in the history of Reading Gaol was when perhaps the most famous prisoner in British legal history entered through its gates. Oscar Wilde arrived there in November 1895 to serve out a two-year sentence. The story of his life behind bars is set out in *Chapter 5*.

CHAPTER 3

Punishments of Former Times

> For they starve the little frightened child
> Till it weeps both night and day;
> And they scourge the weak, and flog the fool,
> And gibe the old and grey,
> And they scourge the weak, and flog the fool,
> And some grow mad, and all grow bad,
> And none a word may say.
> (*The Ballad of Reading Gaol*, Oscar Wilde)

Punishments were used at Reading Gaol across the centuries with a view to reformation and as a deterrent and way of enforcing conformity to the Prison Rules, known as 'discipline'. Lesser punishments consisted of: the removal of visiting rights (i.e. the right to receive visitors periodically); denial of letters (in or out of the prison); reduction of dietary status and class; the use of physical restraints such as handcuffs and straight jackets; and—most commonly—sensory deprivation and degradation, i.e. being placed into a dark cell for days on end with only bread and water until the term of this punishment expired or the prisoner undertook to conform to the rules. Another form of punishment and humiliation used in the gaol from 1786 was the gag:

> This instrument when applied was fastened around the neck, the mouth was kept open by means of a rough piece of iron which pressed upon the tongue, and the head-dress attached is decorated with a red feather; the whole evidently intended to excite ridicule, as well as to produce pain. (Field: 1848)

Flogging with the birch (a wooden cane used as a whip) or the 'cat-o-nine tails' (a 20 inch handled whip with nine cords each 33 inches in length) was seen as a last resort. The ultimate act of physical punishment was loss of life: the 'death penalty'. This was the final sanction by the state and is dealt with in *Chapter 4*.

HARD LABOUR AND 'LIGHT LABOUR'

From the time that the treadmill was built at the Reading House of Correction in 1822 all prisoners would be sentenced to hard labour while they were in custody. The origins and nature of the treadmill have already been outlined in *Chapter 1*. According to the governor, Mr Hackett, speaking at the Berkshire Midsummer Sessions in 1841:

The labour of the treadwheel punishes the bodily system, but as a punishment, I think it unjust, unequal and injurious to every sense ... I think it is highly unfavourable to reformation; it hardens the offender, rendering him more cunning and skilful in the art of deception.

From 1844 with the building of the new gaol, it was decided that the main form of hard labour would be the hand crank. As noted in *Chapter 2*, this was a large wheel turned manually by up to ten prisoners at any one time which was located in the pump-house to pump water up into the prison. This was also unpopular and the cause of numerous offences against prison discipline:

18th February 1882, Charles Gilbert was reported to the Visiting Committee for idleness at the pump and sentenced to 7 days in the dark cell.

Other forms of hard labour were stonebreaking and shot-drill as also noted in *Chapter 2*. 'Light labour' or second class hard labour was oakum picking and sewing mail bags. Oakum picking consisted of unravelling old tarred ropes to produce fibres which were then used in the caulking of wooden planked ships. Oscar Wilde complained bitterly about this in *The Ballad of Reading Gaol*:

We tore the tarry rope to shreds
With blunt and bleeding nails.

Wilde also deeply resented the governor at the time, Colonel Isaacson, claiming he was 'harsh and stupid and lacking in imagination'.

PRISON RULES

A major problem with all types of punishment has always been the potential for abuse and corruption. For example, in 1626 the local council at Reading enacted a law that people caught begging would be committed to the House of Correction. This rule had to be introduced purely because, prior to that time, the local council had punished beggars by flogging and employed two constables who were paid 13 shillings and four pence to administer the whippings to anyone who was caught. However, in 1625 these constables submitted a substantially higher claim for 41 shillings and four pence due to their allegedly increased workload. The council thought it preferable to regulate the situation by bringing in the new law.

Under the stewardship of Sir Edmond Du Cane, the Prison Act 1865 provided for the creation of Visiting Committees which allowed independent tribunals to allot punishment rather than the prison staff themselves. This was seen as a major step forward at that time, but due to different gaols and regions of the country interpreting the rules in different ways it was not until the nationalisation of prisons under the Prison Act 1877 that true uniformity across the discipline system came about.

The sending of someone to prison is a punishment in itself, but under the separate system described in *Chapter 2* involved both being sent to prison and also having to conform to an austere regime. Strict silence had to be observed in the prison at all times, and any infringement was harshly punished. Displayed on a wall in every cell were the 'County Gaol Rules', which listed prohibited behaviour for which prisoners could also be quite severely punished:

- Talking, shouting, cursing, swearing, singing, whistling, attempting to communicate by signs, by writing or in any other way.
- Unnecessarily looking around or about at any time.
- Having in possession or attempting to receive money, tobacco, knives.
- Looking out, or attempting to look out, at window or door of a cell.
- Not folding a bed in the proper manner ... in bed after 6 a.m. or before 8 in the evening.
- Stealing any property of the prison or of a prisoner ... trying to take anything left from other prisoners' meals.
- Spitting on, or disfiguring the prison walls and floors.
- Irreverent behaviour in chapel either before, during, or after service.
- Striking, or in any way assaulting or threatening, another prisoner or officer.
- Attempting to escape, or assist others to do so.
- Not folding up clothing in a proper manner.
- Not washing feet twice a week, prior to using the water to clean the cell.
- Not ready to leave cell when unlocked by officer for exercise, chapel.[1]

In relation to talking, prisoners soon acquired the art of communicating without moving their lips. Oscar Wilde first learned about the prisoner Charles Thomas Wooldridge, who was under sentence of death and became the subject of Wilde's *Ballad of Reading Gaol,* from other prisoners:

> I walked, with other souls in pain,
> Within another ring,
> And was wondering if the man had done
> A great or little thing,
> When a voice behind me whispered low,
> 'That fellow's got to swing'.

Prisoners had to place the peaks of their caps over their faces upon leaving their cells; this was to isolate them and prevent them from associating with criminals they might recognise upon release. Even female prisoners had to abide

---

[1] The text of these rules appears in *Appendix 2*.

by these rules; except that they had to wear very thick black veils over their heads instead.

Prisoners were also kept in their cells for 24 hours a day except for chapel, exercise or visits from friends and family. When they were moving from one place to another there had to be exactly five paces in between those in the line. A warder was placed along the route to identify immediately any infringement and the culprit would be brought before the governor and punished by three days in the dark cell with only bread and water to live on. This punishment was administered to all prisoners, even women and children.

Physical, (sometimes called 'mechanical') restraints, either for the prisoner's safety or that of the staff were sometimes used, such as handcuffs and the straight jacket. Some further information appears under the next heading. For lesser offences, prisoners were often punished by several days' solitary confinement on bread and water, as the old prison records show:

> **21st February 1885** Harriet Wiggins was reported for breaking several panes of glass, pulling down the gas pipe, destroying her bonnet. She was sentenced to 3 days in the dark cell.

> **15th March 1884** Samuel Clark using threatening language towards Warder Harrison — sentenced to 2 days in the dark cell.

For more serious offences the governor would inform the Visiting Committee and there would be an inquiry at which a minimum of two committee members and the governor heard from all relevant parties. This 'inquiry board' would consider all the facts of the case and apportion punishment where necessary.

RESTRAINT

Restraints of one sort or another have been in use within British prisons for centuries; at Reading the use of restraint was not common and was usually to prevent personal injury to a prisoner. If the prisoner was deemed to be of unsound mind he or she could be restrained using either handcuffs or a straight jacket until the medical officer deemed him or her to be stable. On the 2 March 1859 an open letter appeared in *The Times* written by a Salisbury doctor, W. C. Finch, about a young woman called Mary Newell, aged 21, who had been brought to the local asylum from Reading Gaol restrained in a straight jacket escorted by three members of the staff of the prison. The doctor in his letter pleaded her case not to be sent back to Reading; although an order had been signed by the Secretary of State allowing her to be transferred to the asylum for a period of assessment only and requiring her return to Reading.

The earliest instance of the use of the straight jacket identified by the author was in 1817, when a young lad named George Holloway (aged 18) was sentenced to death for sheep stealing. Whist awaiting his trial in Reading House of Correction, Holloway was acting as though he were mad. On May 18, Royal Mercy was extended to him and his death sentence commuted to two years' imprisonment. On May 26 he was asked by the turnkey if he was any better, and to the latter's astonishment he said, 'No'. It turned out that he had conspired with another prisoner to pretend to be mad so that he would not hang for his crime. As a punishment he was placed in a 'straight waistcoat' for a whole month.

An entry in the prison records of 9 April 1881 refers to one Thomas George being straight jacketed because he was a suicide risk. He had been brought before the governor charged with attempted suicide by tying a handkerchief around his neck and securing one end of it to the gas light within his cell. Fortunately a warder found the prisoner and was able to restrain him by placing him in handcuffs for five hours. A straight jacket was not available and the governor was informed that one had been applied for. The prisoner was a discharged soldier aged just 18 years of age.

The next prisoner to be placed in a straight jacket was Ada Chamberlain, mentioned in *Chapter 2*, who escaped in 1879. Ada was brought before the governor for threatening the matron and flooding her cell by damaging the water pipe. (It was reported that she had already been placed on a punishment diet of bread and water.) Questions were asked as to why this prisoner had two black eyes and a bruised nose; neither the matron nor Ada was able to give any clarification about the incident that caused the injuries. An enquiry by the Visiting Committee into the facts established that the injuries had been caused by the surgeon who stated:

> He had struck the prisoner in the face with a towel; he claimed this was his usual treatment in cases of hysteria. Although he admitted that he may have been a little over zealous with the force used.

Another entry in the prison records show that Ada Chamberlain had stated to the Visiting Committee that: 'What she was doing was not for herself but she wanted to get others to Heaven'. She was discharged from the prison on 28 September 1881 to a lunatic asylum in nearby Oxford, never to return.

CORPORAL PUNISHMENT

Below are extracts from various prison documents about corporal punishments administered at Reading:

7th June 1862 James Crew (16) for repeated offences against discipline received 12 lashes of the birch

20th September 1890 Prisoner Hoffman received 12 strokes of the birch for using threatening language to the Chief Warder.

25th October 1890 Prisoner Hoffman was reported to the board by the governor for repeated malingering and sentenced to 12 strokes of the 'cat.' The committee has doubts about the mental state of mind of this prisoner, punishment was adjourned.

10th January 1899 John Bowler awarded 25 strokes of the cat for irreverent behaviour in chapel.

The brutality of prison discipline appalled Oscar Wilde. He wrote an open letter to the *Daily Chronicle* on 28 May 1897 about the treatment of a prisoner named Prince (known within the prison only by his cell number: A.2.11):

On Saturday week last I was in my cell at about 1 o'clock occupied cleaning ... suddenly I was startled by the prison silence being broken by the most horrible and revolting shrieks, or rather howls, for at first I thought an animal like a bull or a cow was being unskilfully slaughtered outside the prison walls. I soon realised however, the howls proceeded from the basement of the prison, and I knew that some wretched man was being flogged ... the next day I saw the poor fellow at exercise, his weak, ugly, wretched face bloated by tears and hysteria almost beyond recognition.

All acts of corporal punishment were carried out on B1 landing next to the dark cells, in the presence of the governor and chief medical officer. The prisoner was strapped to a wooden frame, his or her hands were secured and with the prisoner facing the medical officer, the punishment would be carried out. The medical officer had the authority to stop the punishment from continuing if he felt that the victim was suffering too badly.

Guidelines were set in place in the Prison Act 1898 which reduced the use of corporal punishment to two types of serious offences only:

- gross personal violence to an officer of the prison; and
- acts of mutiny.

Such cases had to be referred to a new body called the 'Board of Visitors'. This had similar powers to the outgoing Visiting Committee but had to refer the serious offences mentioned above to the Secretary of State. According to Sir Evelyn Ruggles-Brise, the new chairman of the Prison Commission, 'the Prison Act of 1898 took away the secret tribunals that administer unauthorised floggings'.

All prisons had to use a standard type of instrument to inflict the punishments, as laid down in the regulations:

For males over 10 and up to 16 use scale B
For males over 16 use scale C

	B	C
Weight not exceeding	9 oz	12 oz
Length from end of handle to tip of spray	40 inches	48 inches
Length of handle	15 inches	22 inches
Circumference of spray at centre	6 inches	7 inches
Circumference of handle at top of binding	3½ inches	5 inches
Circumference of handle 6 inches from end	3¼ inches	3 inches

A 'cat-o-nine-tails' and birch rod must be destroyed after use and only use a cat that bears the seal of the Prison Commissioners.

In 1906 the governor of Manchester Prison, Colonel Isaacson, who was also the governor at Reading during Oscar Wilde's time there, wrote in a letter about corporal punishment:

In every large prison there is always a small fraction of the population imbued with brutality, to whom dietary punishment is absolutely useless. For these, when they resort to personal violence on an officer, I can see no alternative but the birch rod or the cat.

THE PUNISHMENT OF CHILDREN

Oscar Wilde's letter to the *Daily Chronicle* also complained about children being sentenced to imprisonment. Children had always been sent to Reading Gaol. The youngest on record was Frank Stockwell, aged seven, who was tried for an offence of arson on 15 July 1884. The chaplain, writing in his journal, complained about the case and wrote that he had asked whether it would not be better to send the young boy to reformatory school rather than gaol.

A new reformatory school had been built in 1855 at Shinfield near Reading and the courts were able to order that when a young child finished their prison sentence they should also serve a further term at such a school:

1st February 1891 - Bertie Lane (11) 14 days imprisonment then 5 years at a Reformatory School.

The idea of a reformatory school was for the children to receive education, religious instruction and some form of training. The aim was to keep them away from past associates and to try and turn them away from crime.

In 1845 there were seven children under the age of ten sentenced to imprisonment in Reading Gaol: one girl and six boys. They were each sentenced to a term of hard labour, some with a recommendation of whipping upon their release:

9th February 1892 - A. Davis (11) for poaching sentenced to 21 days hard labour and to receive 12 strokes of the birch upon his release.

Corporal punishment in prison of both adults and children continued right up until 1967, when it was abolished by section 65 of the Criminal Justice Act of that year.

A personal comment

From my personal point of view as a serving prison officer, the main problem with all forms of corporal punishment is that although they can be argued as a form of deterrent they are open to abuse and corruption, allowing certain 'unprofessional' people to exact revenge upon a prisoner whom they may have taken a dislike to. Also there are overriding issues such as the prisoner's state of mind: when the evidence of Oscar Wilde concerning prisoner A.2.11 is read, it seems that the man, who appears to have been of unsound mind, was repeatedly punished for his inappropriate behaviour. I have seen over the years a great many prisoners with severe mental health issues sent to prison pending medical examinations.

On the other hand, I can recall a more recent instance of a young paedophile prisoner charged with multiple rapes of young children, who for the 18 months prior to his sentence conducted an elaborate ruse to feign insanity. None of the medical opinions put forward by the prosecution or defence were able to agree as to his state of mind. This prisoner pretended to be unable to walk; by his actions it appeared to everyone that he was paralysed down one side and was unable to comprehend any instructions given to him. However when, on the day of his sentence, the judge at Reading Crown Court ordered life imprisonment, this prisoner stood up directly, thanked the judge and walked down the stairs into the court cells, from which he had earlier been brought in a wheelchair.

CHAPTER 4

Executions

> I have come to the conclusion that executions solve nothing, and are only an antiquated relic of a primitive desire for revenge which takes the easy way and hands over the responsibility for revenge to other people. The trouble with the death penalty has always been that nobody wanted it for everybody, everybody differed about who should get off.
>
> (Albert Pierrepoint, Executioner, 1952)

INTRODUCTION

Execution was always the ultimate punishment applied by the law and increasingly over time one of last resort. In its modern guise it dates from the Black Act 1723 when there were over 150 capital offences for which an offender could be executed, up to 222 by 1810. These ranged from such grave crimes as treason and murder to the minor, bizarre and sometimes ridiculous, such as:

- stealing a handkerchief;
- writing on London's Tower Bridge;
- damaging an orchard (the last time someone was executed for such an offence was when William Potter was hanged for cutting down an old apple tree in 1814); and
- blackening one's face or using a disguise to commit a crime.

In 1969 capital punishment was permanently abolished in England and Wales for the offence of murder (having been suspended since 1965), leaving just three offences for which someone could still, theoretically, be executed:

- treason;
- piracy with violence; and
- arson in the Royal Dockyards.

The only place where a working gallows was retained in full order after this time was Wandsworth Prison, south London; but this gallows was removed altogether in 1993. Technically, capital punishment remained a sentence in law until Jack Straw, Home Secretary, signed the Sixth Protocol of the European Convention On Human Rights on the 27 January 1999 thus ending capital punishment in peacetime. In 2002, Protocol 13 (implemented 2004) extended this to *any* time - so that barring complete separation from Europe and a wholesale reversal of penal policy that move finally dispensed with this form of punishment in the United Kingdom.

At Reading Gaol, according to the records, 35 people were executed between 1800-1913 when the final hanging, that of Eric Sedgwick (see later in the chapter), took place (see, also, *Appendix 4*). In some respects, considering the large number of relatively minor offences to which the death penalty applied, it is surprising that there were not more executions at Reading. It is perhaps likely that juries, knowing what a guilty verdict would mean for the prisoner, tended towards a charitable interpretation of the facts of the case whenever possible, sometimes even acquitting a felon rather than see him or her hang.

As time went by the public in general found executions increasingly offensive as they did the fact that people were being hung for trivial offences akin to shoplifting. They were also disturbed by cases where there was clear doubt as to whether the prisoner was in fact guilty, or indeed sane. Petitions to the King or Queen and later to the Home Secretary for leniency grew in number and there was unrest in Parliament. From 1832-1837, Sir Robert Peel's government introduced various Bills to reduce the number of capital offences

As an 'additional form of punishment' the Anatomy Act 1832 meant that all executed felons' bodies had to be buried in unconsecrated ground within the grounds of the prison where the execution took place. This was to stop the public spectacle of arguments or fighting over the body, for example between family members of the deceased (who wanted to give the prisoner a decent burial) and people employed by the local hospitals. Hospitals sometimes paid a sum of money to the executed felon prior to his or her death for the right to use his or her body for medical research or as a cadaver for junior doctors to practice their skills on.

In the archives of Reading Gaol is the prison's Executions Log, a gruesome record of those who met their untimely end within its walls, together with meticulously kept details such as the exact cause of death as certified by the prison surgeon immediately after the execution, the weight of the prisoner and even the exact distance by which his or her neck was stretched by the hangman's noose. Selected cases from the log appear later in this chapter and the full list in *Appendix 4*.

EXECUTIONERS AT READING

William Calcraft (period in office 1829-1874)
William Calcraft was reputed to be the longest serving executioner and was probably the most controversial. He was noted for his use of the 'short drop' which caused most of his victims to strangle slowly to death rather than have their vertebra snap quickly and mercifully causing instantaneous death. It is not known exactly how many executions Calcraft carried out but the estimate is about 450, including 35 women, which makes him amongst the most prolific executioners of all time. In the early days, all executions were carried out at mid-day on a Saturday

in front of large crowds of spectators, often mainly women, and Calcraft was noted as something of an entertainer.

Calcraft's controversial short drop meant that his victims were nearly always alive for a couple of minutes suspended on the rope, allowing him to act the fool in front of substantial crowds, sometimes in excess of 30,000. He became renowned for his poor taste; at times hanging onto the felon's legs and swinging from one side of the gallows to the other and at other times climbing onto their shoulders, forcing their neck to break to hasten their deaths.

Calcraft carried out the first three executions at the new Reading Gaol (from 1844). These are all described in the following pages: those of Thomas Jennings, who took over three minutes to die in front of over 10,000 people; William Spicer, for whom there is no record of how long it took for him to die, before 6,000 spectators; and John Gould, in what was Reading's last public execution, again in front of a large crowd, of nearly 4,000 people. The cases of Jennings and Gould are further dealt with later in this chapter.

William Marwood (period in office 1874-1883)

William Marwood was the first truly professional executioner; he had had a fascination with hangings for most of his life and became an executioner when he was 54. He was the inventor of the 'long drop': this meant a drop of between six and ten feet from the trapdoor to the point at which the rope tightened around the neck. Using such a large drop brought its own problems: for example, the condemned person could have his or her head severed.[1] It also meant that the condemned prisoner could die through comatose asphyxiation rather than instant death by the breaking of the neck. Marwood is also generally credited with having devised the first scale or 'Table of Drops' which was amended in 1913 following contributions by a range of executioners and latterly issued by the Home Office. The 1913 version is reproduced later in this chapter. Marwood carried out only one execution at Reading—which has the distinction of being both the first private execution there and a double hanging, of the Tidbury brothers (again, see later in the chapter).

James Billington (period in office 1884-1901)

James Billington was the head of a family 'dynasty' of executioners: all his three sons followed him into the profession. Like several other executioners he had shown a strange fascination with hanging from an early age. His first execution was at Armley Gaol in Leeds, Yorkshire in 1884. At Reading, he conducted three

---

[1] This happened once with an executioner named Berry, when hanging a condemned prisoner called Goodale, on 30 November 1885: due to the man's poor physical shape and 15 stone body weight he was unintentionally decapitated by an excessively long drop. There were two other instances where Berry nearly decapitated condemned prisoners and he was removed from office in 1892. In a modern-day context, the same thing happened in Iraq in 2006.

executions: those of John Carter for the murder of his third wife; Charles Thomas Wooldridge who was to become the most famous person ever to be executed at Reading due to his being immortalised as the central subject matter of Oscar Wilde's *Ballad of Reading Gaol* (see *Chapter 6*) and Charles Scott who murdered his partner Eliza O'Shea. According to the execution certificate, Scott had a muscular neck and so a longer drop was used but this proved to be insufficient: the medical examination found that his neck had stretched an extra three inches, the cause of death being asphyxiation.

Billington also executed the notorious Amelia Dyer (see *Chapter 2*), the baby farmer who murdered a number of newborn babies and threw their bodies into the River Thames at Reading after their mothers had paid her to foster them. Dyer was at first held in Reading Gaol for a number of days until the severity of the case was realised as the families of more and more victims came forward; she was then transferred to Newgate Prison in London, which was attached to The Old Bailey where her case was tried. Billington died in 1901 from bronchitis and his oldest son, Thomas, died ten days later. His two remaining sons carried on the family profession until 1905 when both brothers resigned.

Henry Albert Pierrepoint (period in office 1901-1910)
The Pierrepoint 'dynasty' of hangmen spanned over 55 years' service to the Crown, executing over 900 prisoners collectively. Henry was the father of probably the most famous executioner, Albert, who resigned in 1952 and who was responsible for the words at the start of this chapter. At Reading Gaol two of the famous family, Henry assisted by his older brother Thomas, executed William George Austin in 1907 for the murder and rape of Unity Alice Butler (13). Austin had been having an affair with Unity's mother; together they had been playing sexual games involving Unity and her mother at the same time. Henry was sacked in 1910 for arriving at an execution drunk and for fighting with John Ellis, then his assistant.

John Ellis (period in office 1901-1923)
John Ellis was a quiet, mild mannered man who had his own business as a barber in Rochdale, Lancashire. As a sideline he became executioner to the Crown, hanging a total of 203 people.

One strange thing that made Ellis stand out more than any other executioner was his morbid curiosity about the person he was about to hang. He would try and attend every possible trial of people he was likely to hang. He would sit at the back of the court listening intently to all the evidence and making his own judgement as to the person's guilt. As chief executioner he had the luxury of being able to pick and choose his executions. Always preferring the high profile candidate, he executed, among others, Dr Hawley Harvey Crippen for the murder of his wife. Ellis was disliked by nearly all the other executioners. They complained about his idiosyncrasies, such as dressing as a prison officer the night before an execution to watch the condemned felon, observing minutely the individual characteristics of their neck to ensure that the appropriate length of drop was used.

Ellis hated executing women. In his final year in the job he executed Edith Jessie Thompson (aged 28) on 9 January 1923 in Holloway Prison, London. She had to be carried to the gallows in a state of lifelessness and was totally unresponsive to any instructions given to her. It was said that her underwear was covered in blood afterwards and from that time forwards all women to be executed had to wear canvas underwear.

Not long after this Ellis tendered his resignation. He tried twice to commit suicide: the first time using a gun but the bullet passed through the side of his mouth; but in 1932 he cut his throat with a razor in front of his family just after completing his memoirs, *Diary of a Hangman*. These gave a unique insight into two executions held at Reading (Sedgwick, 1913; and Broome, 1910).

THE EXECUTION PROCESS AT READING

Once someone had been sentenced to death, the date for their execution would be set for the third Sunday after the sentence was imposed by the judge. No executions could actually take place on a Sunday or a Monday, so they were carried out on a Tuesday morning at eight o'clock. This provision came into effect under the Capital Punishment Act 1868; as already indicated prior to this Act all executions took place at mid-day on a Saturday, in public, in front of large crowds. Such was the public interest in these executions that a funfair and various amusements were erected close to some gaols during executions. People travelled far and wide to see these spectacles; some paying money to dealers selling seats on carts or platforms offering a better view. At one gaol, where over 34,000 people attended and due to the combination of the size of the crowd and ale being sold, a major disturbance followed the execution. Soon after this, the 1868 Act abolished all public executions.[2]

From 1844-1868 all executions at Reading were held in public on a scaffold erected above the gatehouse. Then from 1868 up until 1900 the place of execution, 'within the prison walls', was the 'Photographic House' (sometimes called the Photographic Room) situated in the courtyard between C-wing and D-wing. From 1900 a new Home Office approved 'Execution Centre' was built in D-wing. This comprised four purpose-built cells, each equipped with a bath and toilet facilities and twice the size of a normal cell. Two staff would accompany the convicted felon, 24 hours a day, eating and sleeping with him (all the people executed after this time were men). A group of six staff would do this on a rota

---

[2] The last public execution in Britain was that of Michael Barrett and other Fenians involved in the Clerkenwell Explosion that took place above the gate of Horsemonger Lane Gaol, London in 1868.

basis until 20 minutes before the time for the execution, when two totally new and impartial staff would take over. This was to prevent the phenomenon known as 'conditioning' whereby an officer might through physical proximity to the condemned person begin to empathise with him or her; and thus maybe seek to intervene to prevent the law taking its course. Two of the four special cells were attached to a corridor leading to the gallows which by this time were located in a shed fixed to the outer wall of D-wing. At the time of the execution, a cupboard in front of the doorway leading to gallows was removed and the prisoner would walk through this previously hidden door and onto the gallows.

The day before the execution the hangman would arrive at the prison and stay in the executioner's room above the centre, next to what is now an office used by the cleaning officer,[3] on the walkway between A2 landing and C2 landing. He was required to arrive no later than four in the afternoon of that day and was not permitted to leave the prison until after the execution. His time would be spent observing the condemned prisoner, looking for any unusual characteristics of his or her neck and working out the final length of rope, using the 'Table of Drops'.

The entire gallows apparatus would be meticulously tested prior to the execution and a bag of sand (of the exact weight of the condemned prisoner) would be placed onto the execution rope and left to hang all night before the execution. This was to stretch the rope and to try and remove any elasticity.

At about 6 a.m. the executioner would remove the bag of sand and recheck that everything was working, any final adjustments would be made, then the door would be locked and no-one allowed into the room without the executioner being present. When the allotted time came, the executioner would pinion the prisoner (placing leather straps around his or her arms and wrists). The governor, under sheriff, chaplain, executioner, medical officer and accompanying prison staff would walk with the prisoner into the execution shed.

There the executioner would place a white hood over the condemned person's head, then the rope would be placed around his or her neck and be adjusted to the left side of the jaw so as to force the head to twist and turn backwards, causing the neck to break. The legs of the condemned felon would then be pinioned by either the assistant executioner or the executioner himself (if working alone). This done, the executioner would operate the lever allowing the trapdoors to open and the condemned felon to fall through.

---

[3] The cleaning officer is in charge of more than 20 prisoners within the gaol responsible for the general cleaning.

EXECUTIONS-----Table of Drop (October 1913)

The length of the drop may usually be calculated by dividing 1,000 foot-pounds by the weight of the culprit and his clothing in pounds, which will give the length of the drop in feet, but no drop should exceed 8 feet 6 inches. Thus a person weighing 150 pounds in his clothing will ordinarily require a drop of 1,000 divided by 150 = 6⅔feet, i.e. 6 feet 8 inches. The following table is calculated on this basis up to the weight of 200 pounds:-

Table of Drops

Weight of the Prisoner in his clothes	Length of the Drop		Weight of Prisoner in his clothes	Length of the Drop		Weight of the Prisoner in his clothes	Length of the Drop	
Lbs.	Ft.	ins.	Lbs.	Ft.	ins.	Lbs.	Ft.	ins.
118 and under	8	6	138 and under	7	3	167 and under	6	0
119 "	8	5	140 "	7	2	169 "	5	11
120 "	8	4	141 "	7	1	171 "	5	10
121 "	8	3	143 "	7	0	174 "	5	9
122 "	8	2	145 "	6	11	176 "	5	8
124 "	8	1	146 "	6	10	179 "	5	7
125 "	8	0	148 "	6	9	182 "	5	6
126 "	7	11	150 "	6	8	185 "	5	5
128 "	7	10	152 "	6	7	188 "	5	4
129 "	7	9	154 "	6	6	190 "	5	3
130 "	7	8	156 "	6	5	194 "	5	2
132 "	7	7	158 "	6	4	197 "	5	1
133 "	7	6	160 "	6	3	200 "	5	0
135 "	7	5	162 "	6	2			
136 "	7	4	164 "	6	1			

When for any special reason, such as a diseased condition of the neck of the culprit, the Governor and Medical Officer think that there should be a departure from this table, they may inform the executioner, and advise him as to the length of the drop which should be given in that particular case.

26591-18-3-58

The entire process would go like clockwork: normally it took a convicted felon exactly 25 seconds to walk from the condemned cell at Reading to the scaffold and be hung.[4] The prison staff would listen for the bells of the local church to start the cycle of bells that led up to the eighth bell being rung to indicate eight o'clock. It is said that the saying 'for whom the bell tolls' refers to the condemned prisoner, for whom the eighth bell would sound as the trap door was sprung.

Today, Reading's execution centre has a new function; all reminders of its grizzly past have been removed. Offices have replaced the condemned cells. Inside one office which was the walkway from which condemned men and women stepped onto the gallows, it is still possible to see the two entrance doorways, now bricked up. Outside this office the author has placed a plaque on the wall inscribed: *'Place of no return'* and next to this a copy of the original plans of the execution centre allowing visitors to the prison an insight into the original function of these rooms. They are reputed to be amongst the most haunted areas of the prison: staff hear footsteps and at times see electric lights going on and off for no apparent reason. Some people refuse to walk down this wing at night, preferring to use an alternative route.

After an execution

Once an execution was over there would be a formal inquest in order to confirm that the death was lawful and that the correct prisoner had been executed. The body would then be placed into a coffin, one unique to gaols, in that its sides and ends were perforated with large holes to hasten decay. The burial plot would be against the prison wall in unconsecrated ground in an unmarked plot. There would be a burial service and the whole process was usually completed before noon on the day of execution.

EXECUTIONS AT THE NEW READING GAOL

The first person to be executed at the new Reading Gaol, i.e. at the present building that dates from 1844, was Thomas Jennings in 1845. There follows an account of those events and of other significant executions in the prison's history, compiled from contemporaneous records at the prison and reports in the local and national press.

Thomas Jennings (1808-1845)

Standing on the scaffold above the new gaol in front of more than 10,000 people who were screaming and shouting abuse at him, Thomas Jennings shook with

---

[4] Albert Pierrepoint claimed to have completed the process (at other prisons) in seven seconds flat.

fear, his head covered with the white hangman's hood, facing the large crowd and oblivious to the hangman's instructions.

Jennings stood over the trapdoor, seconds away from death and final damnation, adamantly professing to all who would listen, 'I did not do the murder!' The hangman adjusted the rope around Jennings' neck as still Jennings shouted, 'Lord save me! Make speed, oh Lord, to deliver me! Oh Lord, have mercy upon my soul!'—pleading his innocence to the end. As the chaplain, the Reverend John Field (not to be confused with the surgeon of the same name, also mentioned in the text), uttered the immortal words, 'In the midst of life we are in death' and Jennings shouted out as loudly as he could, 'I'm innocent!', the bolt was drawn and he fell through the trapdoor to his death.

But he would face one last and dreadful indignity. The hangman, William Calcraft, used too short a drop that caused Jennings a slow and painful death. In front of the large crowd, it took him three long, agonising minutes to die. His body convulsed and wriggled violently, to the horror of the onlookers, of whom the majority were female.

How had such a young man come to this fate? Thomas Jennings was a native of Thatcham, near Reading, born on 10 March 1808 and was thus just 37 years old when he died. He was the second son of a family of eight, known to the local police as a family of recidivists and not well liked within the small community. He had lived a life of vice rather than virtue, his father having already served time in Reading Gaol. He progressed from youth to manhood utterly devoid of education and was described as someone who was ignorant and totally illiterate. For most of his short life he resided within the boundaries of Thatcham, being first employed as a pig farmer, working for Chamber House Mills. This employment did not last long and soon he was on his travels, next working for Colthrop Paper Mills. But again he appears to have had itchy feet, for he then returned to his previous employer. Things did not go well for young Thomas and it was not long before he was on the move again, but this time he went to Reading, first to work for a Mr Alexander, bedstead maker, then within the service of Mr Wargent, a broker.

Before long Jenning's propensity for travelling got the better of him again and he was off to Wallingford, to be employed by a timber merchant, a Mr Sheppard. There are no details of how long he remained there, but again he returned to Thatcham and obtained employment as a gamekeeper and waterman on the Crookham estate, where he was in the habit of keeping arsenic for the destruction of vermin. This was his last job, where he worked for over six years before his arrest.

Thomas married Amy Fitter of Cold Ash Common, the daughter of a labourer, on 8 March 1835. She appears to have been a devoted wife, bearing him four children and, unbeknown to him, she was pregnant with his fifth child when he was hanged.

According to the evidence from the trial, on 21 December 1844 Amy was away for the day. At about seven o'clock in the evening the family sat down for a dinner of bacon and potatoes. Present were his four children, including Eleazar aged three-and-a-half. Also staying at the house was their niece, Maria Carter (13), who had come to stay with the family and give Amy some much needed help. In court Maria stated that during the meal Thomas got up from the table and went to the pantry, came back to his seat and placed something upon the plate of Eleazar, who sat next him, from between his thumb and forefinger. This substance resembled salt; Eleazar dipped his food into it and ate heartily. This surprised the young Maria as there was already a salt-cellar in the middle of the table. Everyone had used this except young Eleazar.

Within half-an-hour of eating his dinner Eleazar started to feel ill and over the next day or two he grew steadily worse, being violently sick. This continued up until Christmas Day when he died. This type of death was not an uncommon occurrence in Victorian times when a mortality rate of around 50 per cent was expected with young children. An inquest was held on the body and 'natural death' was the finding of the jury. During his evidence, Jennings told the jury that he had not had arsenic in his house for two years. Then, on 6 January 1845, only eleven days after Eleazar had passed away, Henry George Jennings, the third son died in mysterious circumstances.

Mr Arthur Lamb, a surgeon at Newbury had been called to the house. He claimed in court: 'On 5 January I saw the prisoner's child [Henry]; it died the next day. I had a conversation about arsenic being in his house'. The following day the surgeon had returned to the house, to carry out a post mortem on young Henry. During this examination of the body he again asked Jennings about arsenic being present in his house; Jennings replied:

> I do not mean to deny that I have arsenic, but it is not in this house, it is in a house in the wood, and I have not had any in this house for two years; nor have I taken any from the house in the wood since March last, which is the month I use it for destroying Magpies and Crows.

Jennings was present during the opening up of the child's body at his own request. In such a small community people began to talk!

Jennings began to drink heavily and talk to anyone who would listen, claiming, 'That evil child, Maria, was the murderer!' He also made one fatal mistake when he vehemently denied having any arsenic in the house for the last two years. On hearing this John Baker, the local lock-keeper, began to smell a rat: Jennings had given him some arsenic that Christmas morning to help control vermin in and around the lock-keeper's house.

Baker recalled seeing Jennings coming down the towpath, when Jennings produced a small packet from his pocket and told Baker it was from the watch-house within the woods. The small quantity was sufficient for Baker's purpose, but if he required any more, the rest was in Jennings' kitchen on top of the Welsh dresser and away from the children, especially Maria. Jennings stated that Maria had asked him what this was and had seen him place the arsenic onto the top shelf; he claimed to have scolded Maria and told her that under no circumstances must she touch it.

By January 19, the police had become aware of Jennings' lies about the arsenic. John Baker had informed them that Jennings had given him arsenic. On January 24, the police obtained a warrant and proceeded to exhume Eleazar's body. Police Constable Francis Harris of Thatcham executed the coroner's warrant and dug up poor Eleazar's body. Jennings was present and when the coffin was opened he smoothed over the child's hair and confirmed to the constable that this was indeed his child. In conversation with the constable, Jennings was asked, 'Was this child poisoned'. He had replied: 'There is no more poison in them young ones than there is in me.'

Mr Arthur Lamb, the surgeon, carried out the autopsy and stated:

> I attended at Thatcham church, and saw the coffin opened in the belfry, and opened the body in the church porch. I removed the stomach and intestines entire, and placed them in a glass bottle, having tied each extremity, so that the contents could not escape. I took the bottle and its contents to London the same day; the next day I took them to Guy's Hospital, and was present when Mr Taylor made an analysis of the contents.

Mr Alfred Taylor, of Guy's Hospital, who carried out the analysis stated: 'I found arsenic substantially in the stomach, under the arsenic the stomach was ulcerated; it would generally take about two days to produce such ulcerations'. On 4 March 1845 Thomas Jennings was indicted for the wilful murder of Eleazar Jennings by placing arsenic in his food. During the trial the prosecution case rested upon the evidence of Maria Carter, the little niece.

At Christmas last she had been living with the prisoner and his wife, her uncle and aunt, for about a year, minding the four children. Eleazar was the third child; he died on Christmas-day; the other three were then alive.

> The Sunday before we had suet pudding and potatoes and bacon for dinner. Eleazar had eaten part of it. The next day, Monday, my aunt went away about eight in the morning and returned about six; we dined that day at about 12. James, the eldest and my aunt were away. The suet pudding had been eaten on Sunday. We had bacon and potatoes for dinner. There was a salt-cellar on the table. Eleazar took no salt from it. Uncle sat down and when we began dinner; he got up again and went to the pantry, in the next room. He came back and sat next to Eleazar, who cuddled up to him. Uncle gave Eleazar some salt; I did not see him take it from the salt-cellar. He had it

in his thumb and forefinger. It was white in colour like salt. Eleazar dipped his potatoes into it and [ate] them.

Thirty minutes later Eleazar started to complain of pains in his stomach. Monday night he slept with his brother James. Tuesday he was ill, and was sick about ten o'clock in the morning, by night time he was very thirsty and slept with me. He was thirsty all night; I gave him some mint tea. Wednesday was Christmas-day, he was very ill in bed, uncle went for the doctor. The child died about an hour after uncle had gone.

Cross-examined by Mr Carrington for the defence, Maria said: 'I was on very good terms with my aunt; but she was always scolding me. Uncle was the same; he had beaten me several times.'

'Were you happy there?'

'Yes! Some of the time, the children were good with me. Eleazar and James were not troublesome to me.'

'Why did you run away?'

'Because I was not happy and my mother sent me back, to their house!'

'Did you see the bottle on the top shelf?'

'I saw uncle pick up the bottle and use a stick to take some of it out and place it onto a piece of paper; the stick, he then threw into the fire. The shelf was out of my reach; uncle never told me there was poison in it ... I never said I would be damned if I would not poison all the children, in the presence of my uncle or anyone else.'

Mary Laws, a barmaid who lived at Longbridge, stated that she:

Saw the prisoner, on Tuesday 28 January; came to the tap-room and asked for a pint of beer. He said, the girl had done it and knew all about it. He said, he took the poison home last December and laid it on the dresser shelf. He said again, 'My children were poisoned; the girl did it, and knew all about it'. He said, 'She says she will be damned and will poison them all.'

No one else was present at this conversation.

Thomas Jennings did not take to the witness stand in his defence but his evidence was read out by Police Constable Francis Harris:

About a fortnight before last Christmas John Baker, lock-shutter at Bulls Lock, Greenham asked me for some arsenic to kill some rats. I said I had none at home but I had some in the woodhouse in the wood and I'll bring some down for him.

About two days later I bumped into him again and he reminded me about the arsenic.

Two days later I went into the woodhouse and retrieved a bottle of arsenic which was full and put it into my lower right hand pocket of my coat which I wear every day. As I got to the lock I put some arsenic out into some paper, which was sufficient for him and put the bottle back into my coat.

When I got home I put the bottle onto the top shelf of the dresser; Maria Carter the girl who looks after my children saw me put the bottle onto the shelf. I saw she was looking at me and I warned her, 'Don't you touch that whatever you do'; she said 'I won't'.

I did not take the arsenic which I put in the other pocket, in paper, out at that time. I sat down for dinner; my wife was away for the day and only I and Maria were at home.

About two hours later I went Widmead lock on the Kennet and Avon canal and held out my hand to John Baker and gave him the arsenic. I told him to take great care of this stuff as this is not to be left about, as if anything goes wrong I'll be held responsible.

The bottle was in my house before the first child was ill but not when the second became ill. I had already removed it back into the woodhouse.

One thing I do remember is, I noticed that some arsenic appeared to have gone when I removed it to the woods. On returning home I asked Maria had she touched the bottle. She said no! I then again said, 'Have you touched it,' she replied 'no I have not uncle'.

The trial Judge, Mr Baron Platt, summed up at considerable length, reading over much of the evidence. He was dismissive of Jenning's assertion that the girl did it and emphasised the fact that Jennings had on two previous occasions lied about the arsenic.

The whole prosecution case rested on the girl and her version of events. All the local newspapers were scornful of the idea that such a young girl could be capable of such a crime. The jury went out to consider its verdict and returned in just ten minutes with a guilty verdict and a recommendation for mercy.

The judge placed the black cap on his head and in sentencing he said:

Prisoner at the bar you have been convicted of a most diabolical murder upon evidence which must have satisfied every person in court. Although the jury in consideration of the consequences to you, deliberated on their verdict in order that no chance of error should be left, I will venture to say that not a single person in court [would profess not to] concur with the justice of the verdict. A crime such as murder is denounced by both God and man. This crime you have committed on your own child, that you had no yearning over your offspring is a fact and you have aggravated an offence to charge upon your niece a crime for which you are now to suffer.

You have dared to charge an innocent girl with the guilt to advert from yourself, a punishment which I'll certainty be awarding you. You have now but a short time to consult those spiritual advisors you'll find in your prison. Seek from them your counsel, you so much need and in the short time left to you endeavour to obtain from Almighty God, mercy which you will not receive here. The sentence of the court is that you be taken to the place from whence you came and suffer the convenient day to the place of execution, that you then be hanged by the neck until you are dead and your body to be then buried within the walls of the prison and may God in his infinite mercy have compassion on your immortal soul.

Jennings looked on in total disbelief and shouted to the court: 'I'm innocent and falsely sworn!' He was then removed from the dock and taken immediately to Reading Gaol. The trial had lasted just six hours from start to finish.

In Reading Gaol Jennings was placed in a special condemned man's cell on B2 landing, cell 11 and 12.[5] This was totally different from all the other cells within the gaol, in that it was two cells together, with the dividing wall removed. Along with Jennings there would be two officers in the cell 24 hours a day: watching his every move, by his side morning, noon and night. There would be a nucleus of six staff looking after him, two with him at all times. These staff would be specially selected for their vigorous adherence to the rule book and for having the strength of character not to show any feelings towards the prisoner.

Jennings on his arrival continued to protest his innocence, he would protest to all who would listen. On Tuesday March 11, Jennings was visited by the Reverend V. Clementi, curate of Thatcham. He stayed for over an hour, urging Jennings to acknowledge his guilt, but to no avail: he continued to profess his innocence. Clementi, at the prisoner's request, engaged in prayer. Jennings appeared to be much moved by this chaplain.

Two petitions were sent from Reading townsfolk to Queen Victoria, praying Her Majesty to commute Jenning's sentence to a lesser one on the grounds of cruelty and the people being against capital punishment: one petition came from Mr Curwen's church congregation in Castle Street, Reading, the other from people generally of the town. Mr Lovejoy of London Street sent this latter petition with over 300 signatures and received this reply:

Whitehall, March 18th, 1845

Sir, Secretary, Sir James Graham, having carefully considered your application in behalf of Thomas Jennings, I am directed to express to you with regret that there is no sufficient grounds to justify him, consistently with his public duty, in advising Her Majesty to comply with the prayer thereof.

I am, Sir, your most obedient humble servant

SAMUEL PHILLIPPS

Not a single signature came from any person living in Thatcham.

In his last days Jennings became very anxious and worried. Every time he woke up he would instantly turn to his turnkeys (prison officers) who were always in attendance, and ask, 'Did I speak in my sleep?', only settling when told, 'No'.

On Monday March 17, Amy visited her husband for the last time. She came with his brother and sister and his two last remaining children (James and his younger sister). The visit took place in the visiting-room on D-wing. Thomas sat his little girl on his knee whilst James stood next to him, holding tightly to his father's side. They were allowed to stay for over two hours. At the end, Jennings

---

[5] Today this cell is on B1 landing.

looked at his wife, who had been crying most of the time, and gave strict instructions to her to take care of his children. As Amy was leaving she turned to him for one last time and requested him, if he did know anything about the poisoning of the child, to confess it, to which he replied: 'I can't confess what I've never done.' Then, seeing her crying, he said to her: 'My heart is as hard as stone; I wish it was as soft as yours!' He then turned to his brother and sister and pleaded with them to alter their ways and not to end up like him.

On Friday March 21 (which was Good Friday) Jennings, along with all the other prisoners at the gaol, attended divine service. The chaplain, Reverend Field, who had tried at every opportunity to get Jennings to admit to his crime, gave a very long sermon directed towards the convicted felon:

> And now it becomes more particular to apply part of the subject of our text to you, my dying fellow sinner, whose execution is so near at hand ... you have persisted in your denial of your guilt, and protested your innocence ... Evidence, as you acknowledge, so clear that neither the judge nor the jury could decide otherwise than the verdict declared. But to a fearful extent has your horrible and heinous sin of murder, and that of your own children, been aggravated by the very defence whereby you have sought to screen yourself from the dreadful and disgraceful death to which you are condemned. In that defence, you not only charge your own niece with the wilful murder of your children ... But, on the other hand, for your sake, my poor dying fellow-sinner, I thank God I may still declare that his promise has surely set pardon and salvation within your reach, if you will even now turn unto him by a humble confession of your guilt and by your earnest prayer for its forgiveness ... Look to me and ye shall be saved.

With this Jennings stood up and went back to his cell in a cool and deliberate manner. Inside the cell he turned to his two attending turnkeys (Thompson and Shade) and said: 'I could have laughed in his [the chaplain's] face when he said what he did about the children.'

Outside the gaol arrangements were being made to erect barriers all along Forbury Road in anticipation of a large crowd; the owners of the meadow opposite the gaol, Messrs Church and Ferry, had wisely opened the gates to accommodate the massive crowd expected to view such a grotesque spectacle. The authorities had drafted in extra police and special constables to help with the huge number of onlookers that was expected. Above the gaol work had started on erecting the scaffold over the gatehouse. The roof, being perfectly flat, had been designed specifically for this purpose and this was the first time it would be used for an execution. By the Friday morning all the work had been completed and the scaffold was ready for its prey.

The last night in Jennings' life was a sad and restless one for him; he went to bed at 12 midnight crying and pleading with God for mercy, awoke at 2.30 a.m., ate some food and tried to sleep. At six o'clock he rose and at seven had toast and a half-a-pint of coffee, which he consumed heartily. At ten o'clock he was summoned to the chaplain, who for the next two hours, prayed with him and tried his utmost to get Jennings to confess to the sin for which he was about to die.

Exactly as the clock on C2 landing struck noon the prison governor, Lieutenant Hackett, accompanied by the under-sheriff, Mr E. Vines, the deputy-governor, Mr Ferry, the chaplain, Mr Field, two members of the local press and the executioner, William Calcraft went to the room where Jennings was and announced that the time had come for the departure of the criminal. The turnkeys (Thompson and Shade) who had been praying with him were removed and replaced by fresh staff who had not come in contact with Jennings. The whole procession then made its slow and deliberate way along D-wing, past the debtors' cells to the press-room at the end of the wing. There Jennings was seated in a chair while the executioner pinioned his arms. Then without assistance and with a firm step, he walked out down the steps and into the courtyard in between the front of the gaol and the back of the gatehouse.

The courtyard was lined with Javelin men[6] and officers from the gaol. The chaplain began to read the Burial Service, his voice scarcely audible: he was obviously very moved by the whole process. Jennings recited the Lord's Prayer out loud and shouted, 'God have mercy on me!' The procession then advanced up the stairs beside the female wing and onto the gatehouse roof. Jennings was ushered immediately up the steps leading to the scaffold, and positioned on the white chalk mark that indicated he was over the trapdoor.

Lieutenant Hackett approached and said to Jennings: 'Have you anything to say?' Jennings replied: 'I am not guilty of the murder.' The rest, sadly, is history.

After the body had been left to hang for the obligatory one hour, the surgeon, Mr Field, confirmed death. The body was cut down and placed in the prison morgue (now the reception office). An inquest was then held in the magistrate's room, just off the main prison hall or centre, and the jury would then have had the opportunity to inspect the body. Finally, the body would have been buried in unconsecrated ground within the prison grounds. There is a plaque, placed by the author in 2004 in the prison burial ground at the exact spot indicated on the grave register where Thomas Jennings lies.

Maria Carter, the young niece whom Thomas Jennings had accused of the murder, ended up in Reading Gaol two weeks after his execution on a charge of theft from a farmer she had been staying with.

After reading all the relevant newspapers and prison documents, it seems to me that Thomas Jennings could have been the wrong person executed! In our enlightened times DNA and other evidence would be available. But for both the

---

[6] Javelin men were soldiers who each carried a large spear or javelin and were the armed guard within the gaol during an execution. Javelin men were only used for this execution, it seems, as I cannot find any other reference to them being used on other occasions.

press and the trial judge to dismiss out of hand that such a young child (Maria Carter) could do such a thing seems to have been wrong. Maria was sent to the Jenning's house to help Amy, the mother, with the domestic chores, including cooking even. It is not at all inconceivable that she might have added the poison herself to the child's food.

The last public execution at Reading: John Gould (1823-1862)

During the 1860s feelings of revulsion were growing among the general public against the death penalty and the public staging of executions. There was so much local and national antagonism to such spectacles that John Gould became the last man to be executed in public at Reading Gaol, some eight years before such executions were ended altogether and brought inside prison walls.

On 30 December 1861 seven-year-old Hannah Gould knelt on the floor, trying her best to steady herself with one hand, whilst her other hand was clutching her throat, in an effort to stop the massive flow of blood from the large wound inflicted upon her by her father. The child could feel her life ebbing away from her little body, as her murderer looked on in total disdain and satisfaction at the job he had done with his cut-throat razor. She could neither speak nor move. Then hope was in sight for Hannah saw a friendly face, Mrs Clarke, her best friend's mother from a house a couple of doors away.

Mrs Clarke had been summoned into the house by John Gould, who had come home and found that his daughter, Hannah, had not cleaned up the house to his satisfaction. John Gould was in a rage and very angry at this point; he pointed to his daughter on the floor and exclaimed: 'I have done it! I have done it!' Mrs Clarke looked into the room and to her horror she saw the little girl clutching her throat, pleading for help. With blood all over the floor, Mrs Clarke screamed and ran outside, shouting for help to all who would listen.

Gould could still not contain his anger; he picked Hannah up and threw her head first outside, so that her head smashed against a wall with a sickening, squelching noise, shouting: 'You little shit, I will die for you!'

Young Samuel Wilkins, who lived next door, saw his friend, Hannah, lying on the floor, barely breathing and struggling for life. He waited for Gould to go back into the house, then grabbed hold of her arm and dragged her into the street, again shouting for help. This arrived in the form of Mr Coker who picked up the child and ran as fast as he could to the local infirmary. But to no avail: Hannah died on the way (*Berkshire Chronicle*, 4 January 1862).

Gould remained in the doorway of his house, staring like a demon; eyes wide open and blood red, still holding the blood soaked razor. Mr Coker and Samuel Watkins returned with PC Radbourne who tried to arrest Gould. A violent struggle ensued and with the help of Mr Coker, Gould was eventually handcuffed. Realising that he could do no more, Gould went quietly to the police station. Radbourne stated in court that on their way to the station, Gould repeated three times to him: 'I've done it, I've done it, I've done it! I'm tired of my life; I'm happy now'.

At the police station Gould was charged with the wilful murder of his own child, and, being asked by Superintendent Eager as to why he had done it, he replied: 'I did do it, and I'm sorry for it, and it's all through drink. I had been drinking for a week or more'.

The coroner's inquest was a formality and Gould was indicted for the murder of Hannah Gould, aged six, and remanded to Reading Gaol (*Reading Mercury*, 4 January 1862). The trial was held on the 26 February 1862 at the Crown Court, Reading before Mr Baron Channell. Gould was charged with the wilful murder of his daughter, Hannah Gould, aged six years, in that on the 30 December 1861 in the parish of Clewer, New Windsor he did murder her by cutting her throat with a razor. Mr J. O. Griffiths conducted the prosecution and Mr George Russell was instructed by the sheriff to watch the case on behalf of the defendant.[7]

The evidence in the case was a formality in that Gould, whilst in the police station, had made a full and frank confession detailing all the events. But the trial still had to take its course in the interests of fair play. The outline of the case was shocking for all who heard it; John Gould was a 39-year-old bricklayer's labourer or hod-carrier who lived in a place called 'Clarence Clump' in Clewer. On the day of the murder, he had been drinking in the Prince of Wales beer shop at around one p.m. with a Reuben Turner. In court Mr Turner claimed that on the fateful day, Gould had stated to him that he would be locked up by the next day for murder. Reuben told him not to talk like that and said, 'What do you want to make a statement like that for!' Gould turned to him and replied: 'I shall not be alive on the first of April.' With this he got up and left the public house.

Mr George Russell for the defence asked this witness at great length as to the condition of the prisoner and to his state of mind. Reuben stated he was not drunk, but some years earlier Gould had tried to commit suicide by hanging himself from a tree. The next witness and probably the most harrowing was Harriet Clarke, aged just nine years old. She had been Hannah's best friend and was in the house with her little brother when John Gould came home. She explained in court in a low, trembling voice that when Mr Gould came home he shouted at Hannah: 'You naughty child, why didn't you clean up the place!' The child started to cry and this just made Gould even more angry. Hannah pleaded with her father saying: 'Oh father, I couldn't do it.'

Fearing for her friend's life, Harriet took hold of Hannah's hand and tried to lead her away from danger and out of the house. But John Gould was having none of it. He stopped his daughter from leaving the house saying: 'No, I want to

---

[7] This was before the days of legal representation as we know it.

do something with her.' As Harriet left the room with her brother she saw the father head off in the direction of the fireplace and then pick up a cut-throat razor.

The next witness was a Mr James Ellison, surgeon, who had carried out the autopsy. To a packed courtroom he explained that Hannah had a laceration about five inches long on the right-hand side of her throat, totally severing her jugular vein (*Reading Mercury*, 1 March 1862). The last piece of evidence was from the mouth of John Gould himself. His statement read: 'It would not have happened if I had not been drinking. As soon as I get any drink, I don't know what I am about in my head. I have had my head cut open in several places; this causes me not to know what I am at' (*Berkshire Chronicle*, 1 March 1862).

In his closing speech Mr Russell made a touching appeal to the jury; he urged them to find the prisoner not guilty on the grounds of insanity. He tried to show that there was sufficient reason for coming to the conclusion that at the time the prisoner did the act he was unable to distinguish right from wrong. Now calling on the jury, Mr Russell asked them, whilst administering justice, also to remember mercy (*The Times*, 1 March 1862). However when the jury returned from their deliberations their verdict was 'Guilty'.

The judge put on the black cap and said that, after a patient consideration of the case, the jury had found the prisoner guilty. It was now his duty to pronounce, not his own sentence, but the sentence of the law. Mr Baron Channell then said he would not aggravate the prisoner's feelings by any observations, and at once proceeded to pass the awful sentence of death in the usual form. Gould was then removed from the dock and taken to Reading Gaol.

The condemned cell on B2 landing would have been prepared and refreshed in anticipation of the arrival of a condemned man. The nucleus of specially trained staff would have had their orders and been briefed. The whole prison would have been buzzing by the time of the return of Gould from court. According to the *Berkshire Chronicle* (8 March 1862) Gould spent his last days receiving divine instruction from the Reverend J. B. Colvil the new chaplain of the gaol, who had replaced the eminent Reverend Field. Gould was quoted as saying to the chaplain: 'It is a just punishment'. He was illiterate and required help from the chaplain to write his last letter to his wife and step-daughter:

> My dear wife and daughter, I now sit down and take my pen in hand to write the few sorrowful lines to you, that by the help and blessing of God Almighty our Heavenly Father for without his help we can do no good thing of ourselves for in God do I put my trust and thank and praise him ... My dear wife and daughter, I was not the least surprised at my sentence for I know I am guilty of taking the life of my poor child, but I put my trust in the Lord to have forgiveness in the next world ... I can assure you, my dear wife, that since I have been confined in prison I have had time to seek peace with God, with the kind help of the chaplain.

From your unfortunate and unhappy husband John Gould, goodbye and God bless you all and I do forgive everybody in this world.

John Gould
Reading Gaol, Berkshire
Saturday March 1st 1862

On Monday 10 March 1862, John Gould received a visit from his sister, his wife and his step-daughter. On entering the visiting room his sister became traumatised and, shaken by the experience, fainted and had to be carried away to the medical centre next door. She was able to visit with his wife and step-daughter the next day for the last time; this meeting was sombre and tearful. Gould's step-daughter gave him her white pocket-handkerchief and bible (*Reading Mercury*, 15 March 1862).

Within the town much disquiet about the severity of the sentence was voiced by the gentry and local people. A petition of over 400 signatures was collected and on the day before the execution a deputation consisting of the mayor and two local dignitaries travelled to London to see Sir George Grey, the Home Secretary. It was reported in the *Berkshire Chronicle* (15 March 1862) that they had a difficult time trying to arrange a meeting with him; but when they did, they passed on the petition and medical evidence, but to no avail:

> Sir George Grey, the Home Secretary, heard all their arguments about the case and had taken advice from the learned judge who tried the case and found no reason for interfering with the due execution of the sentence, and the wretched man will accordingly pay the last penalty of the law.

The final hours of John Gould's life were spent with the chaplain, receiving divine instruction. It was here that he wrote a note to his fellow prisoners, giving instructions that this should be read out at the next chapel service after his execution:

> My last dying words to my fellow prisoners are that they will take warning from me, that they will abstain from drunkenness. Drink has been the ruin both of my body and soul. It has robbed my conscience, and therefore I had no fear of God before me, through drink. I hope they will pray earnestly to God to keep them from temptation and that they will live nearer to God than I have hitherto done until now.

Just before the allotted hour, the entourage assembled on B2 landing. The governor, Mr Ferry, accompanied by the under-sheriff, Mr Blandy, entered the cell and told Gould that the time had come. Gould was kneeling on the floor praying. He rose, took up the Bible and white handkerchief given to him by his step-daughter, and shook hands with each officer who had been in attendance. Then with a firm step he proceeded to the press-room, where William Calcraft, the executioner, was waiting. Gould sat down while he was pinioned and asked the governor if he could carry the Bible and white handkerchief with him, at which point tears began to fall freely from his face.

The procession then made its final journey up to the scaffold on the gatehouse roof. Gould hesitated when he saw the large crowd assembled in front of him, smaller than for the execution of Spicer, but the *Berkshire Chronicle* (15 March 1862) estimated that about 4,000 people were gathered, again a high proportion of them being women.

Calcraft ushered Gould onto the trapdoor where he performed the final act of pinioning by placing a leather strap around his legs. He then placed the white hood and the rope over Gould's head, and stepped back to pull the lever. Gould gestured to the chaplain, who was reciting the Burial Service, and asked that he take the Bible and handkerchief off him, requesting that they be returned to his step-daughter. With that he shook the hand of the chaplain and spoke his dying words: 'May the Lord bless you, and I hope he will give you many blessings for what you have done for me. Give my love to my people, and tell them I remember them'.

With that Calcraft withdrew the bolt. Gould remained alive for a minute or two, twitching and squirming, before his life finally and agonisingly ended. His body was left in the full and grotesque view of the large crowd for the obligatory hour, after which it was taken down, removed into the prison and buried in plot number three.

Such was the outcry from the local community and nationally from the newspapers that this was to be the last public execution at Reading.

The first private executions: Henry and Francis Tidbury (12 March 1877)

By 'private execution' is meant one that takes place within the walls of a prison and away from public view; and, indeed, the away from the eyes of anyone who is not part of a small, official 'execution party' (see the description later in this chapter). In response to the outcry over public hanging, government policy was changed under the Capital Punishment Act 1868 which required all executions to take place within the precincts of a gaol and out of public view. Hence, the next executions at Reading, of the Tidbury brothers in 1877, took place behind closed doors.

On the night of Monday 11 December 1876 Police Constable Golby had just started his shift and was walking down Gipsy Lane in the small village of Hungerford, Berkshire.[8] The time was around 10.30 p.m. and it was raining heavily;

---

[8] Now a small town and the site of one of Britain's most notorious crimes, the so-called Hungerford Massacre of 1987 in which 12 victims were shot and killed at random by Michael Ryan in the space of a few hours before he turned the gun on himself and committed suicide.

Golby had failed to meet his colleague, Inspector Drewitt, at a pre-determined conference point so he began his patrol alone. As he walked down the lane he noticed a body lying in the road. Thinking it was just a local drunk he shouted to try and wake him. Getting no reply, he moved towards the body and as he touched its head, his fingers went deep into the skull to a depth of three inches. Alarmed, he lit his bulls-eye police lantern so that he could see in the poor light and at that very moment the town clock chimed three-quarters of an hour past ten. The lantern light revealed that the body on the floor was in fact Golby's colleague, PC Thomas Shorter. The policeman was lying face down with a large proportion of his skull and brains strewn across the road. Later Inspector Drewitt's body was also found, 150 yards from the other dead policeman. In court Golby described the scene: 'His head was battered to pieces, and his brains was scattered all over the grass' (*The Times*, 19 February 1877).

By mid-day four local poachers had been arrested and charged with the murders. They were three Tidbury brothers: Henry (aged 26), William (aged 24) and Francis (aged 17) and William's father-in-law, Bill Day (38). Their cottages were searched and close by were found parts of two shotguns. On one the stock was broken and as to the other just a barrel remained. Such was the ferocity and violence used on the policemen that the shotguns had been smashed to pieces.

On February 19 the trial began before Mr Justice Lindley at the Berkshire Spring Assizes sitting at Reading. The case attracted a large crowd and space within the court was by ticket only. The trial lasted for a couple of days and the jury took just two hours to find Henry and Francis guilty, William guilty as an accessory to murder and Day not guilty. Next day, the judge ordered all the barristers to appear before him and spoke at length about William Tidbury. Although he was found guilty of being an accessory to murder, he had never actually been charged with this offence! He had only been charged with murder! So both William and Day walked free from court. There was such a public outcry against these acquittals that the foreman of the jury wrote an open letter to the local newspapers explaining the reason for their verdicts.

The executions were set for March 12. Both brothers had given full and frank confessions to the chaplain at Reading Gaol, Reverend Maurice Friend. A small building known as the Photographic House within the yard between C-wing and D-wing was converted for the purpose. In the centre of the floor was a brick lined pit that had been excavated. It was covered by a pair of trap doors, with a hand operated lever to one side. There was a large black stained oak beam across the middle of the pit supported by an upright at either side to which the two hangman's ropes were attached. Under the new arrangements and this being the first such execution at Reading, one member of the local press was allowed to witness and record the process:

The sentence was carried out in the Photographic Room, a small glass structure at the rear of the gaol in the stone-breaking yard ... the pit was 8 foot deep and 9ft by 6ft wide with steps leading to the bottom ... the executioner being William Marwood, of Horncastle, being paid £10 for one brother and a further £5 for the other and £2 for travelling expenses ... .the drop allowed was 6ft 6inches ... the prisoners were taken to the waiting-room where Marwood pinioned them. At 07:57 they proceeded to the gallows ... in the following order:

>   The Chaplain (reading the Burial Service)
>   Warder   Henry Tidbury   Warder
>   Warder   Francis Tidbury   Warder
>   The Executioner
>   Mr Boyce (Deputy Governor)
>   Mr Maurice (Surgeon)
>   The Governor
>   The Under-Sheriff (Mr Blandy)

At exactly eight o'clock they reached the place of execution, the warders and their prisoners entered the photographic room ... Francis screamed when he saw the two ropes hanging down from the black beam ... Marwood pinioned the prisoners' legs then placed the white hood over their heads and the rope ... as soon as the Rev. Friend finished the Lord's Prayer the executioner withdrew the bolt and at the same time the black flag was hoisted outside the gaol to indicate the execution had been carried out. The prisoners fell with a heavy jolt and a thud ... the reporters were allowed into the pit to view the bodies. (*Reading Mercury*, 17 March 1877)

The chaplain, who was opposed to capital punishment, refused to enter the photographic house, so the prison maintenance team were asked to remove a panel from the outside door to allow those inside to hear the Burial Service being read. After an hour the bodies were examined by the surgeon and placed in elm coffins. Pursuant to the 1868 Act the inquest was held within 24 hours, in the magistrates' room just off the main prison hall or centre of the gaol. The jury were taken to the Photographic Room to observe the bodies, which were placed in their elm coffins wearing the same clothes that they had worn when they killed the two policemen. The coffins were then filled with lime and the lids screwed down, and by midday the two dead brothers had been buried by warders, without ceremony, side by side in the prison graveyard next to John Gould.

The most famous execution: Charles Thomas Wooldridge (7 July 1896)
Thomas Wooldridge was to become the most famous person ever to be executed at Reading, immortalised as 'C.T.W.' in the Oscar Wilde's, *The Ballad of Reading Gaol*. The murder was one of jealousy and revenge. Wooldridge was a soldier stationed at Windsor serving in the Royal Horse Guards. He killed his wife, Laura, using a cut-throat razor then gave himself up to Police Constable Foster, who did not believe him at first.

Wooldridge was a jealous natured individual, whilst Laura was friendly and sometimes flirtatious. His temper was his undoing; he and Laura would argue for hours with both refusing to back down. Laura would talk at length to anyone and soon rumours circulated around the barracks that she was seeing another trooper. Wooldridge and Laura decided to have a break from all the arguments and lived separately for a while, but still Wooldridge could not comprehend the rumours about his beloved wife. He returned to their house on March 16 and in a fit of rage attacked Laura, blackening both her eyes and injuring her nose.[9]

Laura refused to see Wooldridge again and would go to great lengths to avoid contact with him. But on 29 March 1896 at nine in the morning Wooldridge turned up at the house to see his wife. Alice Cox, who was living with Laura at the time allowed Wooldridge in at Laura's request to avoid a scene outside—and thus began a sequence of events that were to beguile penal reformers and others to this day.

Alice went upstairs and immediately heard the arguments start; Wooldridge and Laura were shouting at each other, when Laura screamed. Wooldridge slashed Laura's throat with a cut-throat razor that he had brought with him. But it is not entirely clear where, in fact, the murder occurred, something that has seemingly been blurred by retelling of the tale and poetic licence on Wilde's part as noted in the introduction to the annotated version of *The Ballad of Reading Gaol* in *Chapter 6*. Whatever, by 20 minutes past nine Wooldridge had arrived to tell police constable Foster that he had killed his beloved Laura. Foster looked at him dismissively and carried on with what he was doing. Wooldridge repeated that he had killed Laura, was arrested and taken to the cells at Windsor Police Station.

Oscar Wilde implies that Wooldridge was resigned to his fate on the gallows. Indeed in his last weeks Wooldridge actually petitioned the Home Secretary, Sir Matthew White Ridley, not for a reprieve but to allow him to be executed. He asked if he could wear his regimental uniform at his execution. He did so because various petitions had been raised by the people of Berkshire to stop his execution; even the jury had submitted a plea for clemency when it returned its verdict of guilty. Wooldridge also told the prison chaplain that he wanted to die and thereby pay for the crime he had committed. The Home Secretary allowed Wooldridge to carry his regimental colours to the gallows and, also at his request, stopped all petitions for a reprieve. The executioner was James Billington; death by dislocation of the vertebrae. He was given a longer drop than normal, and his neck was stretched by an almost incredible eleven inches. Hence Wilde appears to have been well informed when he wrote that:

> They mocked the swollen purple throat,
> And the stark and staring eyes.

The story of Charles Thomas Wooldridge continues in *Chapter 6*.

---

[9] According to *I'll Be Hanged* (1991) by Roger Long about murder in old Berkshire.

Last execution in the Photographic House: Charles Scott (29 November 1899)

Charles Scott lived with his partner, Eliza O'Shea, in a suburb of Windsor known as South Place: an area well known for its violence and general lower class of resident. Times were hard for the two and soon trouble began at 39 South Place where they lived. Arguments and violence became the norm for Charles and Eliza, both being strong willed and opinionated. In the early hours of 3 September 1899 Charles walked into Windsor Police Station, covered in blood, stating that he had killed Eliza. Her body was found at the bottom of the stairs in their home with a large stab wound in the chest and her throat severed. Her body was a mass of bruises.

At his trial on 5 November 1899 Scott entered pleas of self-defence and provocation, but these were dismissed by the judge and the jury took just 15 minutes to find him guilty of murder. Charles Scott thus became the last person to be executed in the Photographic House in the yard between D-wing and C-wing, all subsequent executions being carried out in the new execution centre on D-wing. According to the execution certificate, Scott's neck was stretched just three inches; but he died a slow painful death, through asphyxiation.

The last ever execution at Reading: Eric James Sedgwick (4 February 1913)

Eric Sedgwick was the last person to be executed at Reading Gaol, in 1913. He was a house porter at the top English public school, Eton College, who murdered his sweetheart, Anne Davis, who worked as a maid there. Sedgwick had become possessive of Anne and had tried to control her every move. In court it was revealed that she had finished their relationship a short time before her murder, but Sedgwick would not take no for an answer. He pleaded with her to take him back; when she rebuffed him for the last time he struck out in anger and plunged a knife he was carrying into her heart.

Whilst Sedgwick was housed in the execution centre at Reading he was held in Cell 1. Across the landing in Cell 3 was Philip Truman, who had been convicted of murdering his girlfriend, Dora Hussey. On February 1 Truman received a reprieve from the Home Secretary, indicating that in his case there was no premeditation and he was sentenced to penal servitude for life. In contrast, Sedgwick had carried the knife with him to visit Anne Davis, so that there was evidence of premeditation, which in those days went against the granting of a reprieve. Instead he was condemned to die on the gallows and became a footnote in history as the last person ever to be executed at Reading Gaol.

CHAPTER 5

Prisoner C.3.3 Oscar Wilde

> I know not whether Laws be right,
> Or whether Laws be wrong;
> All that we know who lie in gaol
> Is that the wall is strong;
> And that each day is like a year,
> A year whose days are long.
> *(The Ballad of Reading Gaol)*

Oscar Fingal O'Flahertie Wilde (1854-1900) was born in Dublin, Ireland. His parents were Dr William Wilde and Jane Francesca Wilde (née Elgee); the former a leading ear and eye surgeon who would later be knighted and the latter a modestly successful poet and journalist who wrote under the name of 'Speranza'.

Wilde studied classics at Trinity College, Dublin where he was described as an outstanding student and won the prestigious Berkley Gold Medal, the highest award available to classics students. In 1874-1878 he won a scholarship to Magdalen College, Oxford, again being recognised as an exceptional student and in 1878 was awarded the Newdigate Prize for his poem *Ravenna*. He graduated with a double first-class degree, the highest available at Oxford University.

On 29 May 1884 Wilde married Constance Lloyd, the daughter of a prominent barrister. They had two sons: Cyril, born in 1885 who was killed during the First World War in France, and Vyvyan, born in 1886. When Wilde was imprisoned amid much public scandal, Constance took the surname Holland for herself and the boys. She died following spinal surgery in 1898, and was buried in Staglieno Cemetery in Genoa, Italy.

In the early years of their marriage, although Constance received a generous allowance of £250 a year Oscar Wilde began working on a woman's magazine called *Woman's World* (1887-1889) and the next six years became his most inspirational and creative period. During that time he wrote two children's books: *The Happy Prince and Other Tales* and *A House of Pomegranates*. He also wrote *The Picture of Dorian Gray*, his only novel (1891). The next year he had his first play produced, *Lady Windermere's Fan*, followed swiftly by *A Woman of No Importance* (1893), then *An Ideal Husband* and *The Importance of Being Ernest* (both 1895). These plays, which are still popular and widely produced today, firmly established Oscar Wilde's reputation as a playwright and he became a leading socialite and doyen of London society.

In the summer of 1891 Wilde met and fell in love with Lord Alfred Douglas, nicknamed 'Bosie', who was the third son of the 9th Marquis of Queensberry (after whom the Queensberry Rules in boxing are named). For the next four years the two young men were inseparable, much to the anger of Queensberry, who confronted them numerous times about the nature of their friendship. Things came to a head when Bosie's oldest brother, Viscount Drumlanrig, was killed in a shooting accident on 19 October 1894. It was rumoured that Drumlanrig had been having an affair with Lord Roseberry, who became Prime Minister (1894-1895). It was said that Drumlanrig had killed himself rather than face his father who had a reputation as a thug and a bully. Some commentators say that Wilde was a fall guy for a wider Establishment cover up.

With the death of his eldest son, Queensberry became even more incensed by Oscar Wilde and on 18th February 1895, he left a calling card at the Albemarle Club in London bearing the words: 'For Oscar Wilde, posing Somdomite'. The Marquis had actually misspelled the word 'sodomite'. He was thus accusing Wilde of indulging in sexual acts which many people then believed to be wrong and unnatural and which, perhaps more importantly, were at that time relatively serious crimes: in practice for those who got caught which, in turn, meant those who were less discreet about such matters—as Wilde was being, increasingly.

ARREST AND TRIAL

Wilde did not see the card until February 28 when he next attended the club. Incensed, angry and insulted, the following day, and as it was to turn out, disastrously, he took out proceedings against the Marquis for defamation or, as it was then known, criminal libel. The trial of the Marquis opened on April 3 at The Old Bailey. By April 5, the Marquis had been vindicated and Oscar Wilde himself was arrested by the police at 7.30 p.m. the same evening in the Cadogan Hotel, Bayswater where he was living at the time and conducting a somewhat individualistic and Bohemian lifestyle. He was charged with gross indecency under the Criminal Law Amendment Act 1885, in effect as a fall guy for a good deal of political intrigue concerning homosexuality that was around at that time. His arrest was a direct result of evidence given in the defamation proceedings.[1] Tipped off by friends, he declined to flee the country when advised to do so, thus risking the full might of the criminal law. The events were to become the subject of a poem by Poet Laureate, John Betjeman, *The Arrest of Oscar Wilde at the Cadagon Hotel*:

---

[1] These events are often cited by people (including some lawyers) who argue that the best approach to taking out legal proceedings is to avoid them at all costs!

> A thump and a murmur of voices —
> ('Oh why must they make such a din?')
> As the door of the bedroom swung open
> And TWO PLAIN CLOTHES POLICEMEN came in:
>
> 'Mr. Woilde, we 'ave come for tew take yew
> Where felons and criminals dwell:
> We must ask yew tew leave with us quoietly
> For this *is* the Cadagon Hotel.'

After two high-profile trials that scandalised London society, on 25 May 1895 Wilde was found guilty and sentenced to two years' imprisonment with hard labour. As this was a Saturday he was obliged to spend the weekend in Newgate Prison which was attached to The Old Bailey, before being transferred by cab to Pentonville Prison in north London.

WILDE IN PENTONVILLE PRISON

The reception process at Pentonville Prison was to give Wilde nightmares for years. It involved him being strip searched to ensure that no items were hidden upon his body. All relevant information would have been entered into the prison records, he would have been given a bath and a medical examination, and would then have received the prison uniform with its black arrows indicating that it was government property — and his Scottish cap, synonymous with the separate system described in *Chapter 2*.

On recounting this experience Wilde told Frank Harris, a family friend:

> The first evening they made me undress before them and get into some filthy water they called a bath and dry myself with a damp brown rag ... the cell was appalling; I could hardly breathe and the food turned my stomach; the smell and sight of it were enough. I did not eat anything for days and days ... as soon as I ate anything it produced violent diarrhoea and I was ill all day and night. (Montgomery Hyde: 1975)

One of the Prison Commissioners, R. B. Haldane, took it upon himself to visit Wilde on 12 June 1895. Haldane was one of the most powerful people within the prison system at that time. Haldane recalled this visit by saying that when he entered his cell, Wilde at first refused to talk, then:

> I put my hand on his prison-dress-clad shoulder and said that I used to know him and that I had come to say something about himself ... I would try to get for him books and pen and ink. (Ellmann, 1988)

At this, Wilde burst into tears. The idea of prisoners having books was totally against prison rules at that time and thoroughly against the whole idea of the separate system. Pentonville's governor objected to this flagrant breach of the rules and to the seemingly preferential treatment of a celebrity. Nonetheless, 15 books in all were received at Pentonville for Wilde, but his health was deteriorating. Haldane then looked to Wandsworth Prison where the chaplain, Reverend W. D. Morrison, was an outspoken critic of the separate system and might offer some support to him (Montgomery Hyde, 1975).

WILDE IN WANDSWORTH PRISON

On 4 July 1895 Wilde was moved from Pentonville to Wandsworth and on August 17 his 15 books followed him and were placed in the prison library. Wilde was allowed only one book at a time in his cell.

Despite Haldane's good intentions, Wilde's time at Wandsworth took a massive toll on his health and he approached complete physical breakdown. One morning at chapel he fell down and woke up in the prison infirmary. He was later to recall this in his penultimate work, *De Profundis*, written whilst at Reading: 'While I was in Wandsworth Prison I longed to die. It was my one desire.'

A medical team from Broadmoor, the Criminal Lunatic Asylum, sent a Dr Nicholson and others to inspect Wilde. Unknown to him he was observed talking and apparently in good spirits in the infirmary. The doctor's report stated that he appeared to show no evidence of any mental disease (Montgomery Hyde: 1975). On 11 September 1895 the deputy chaplain wrote in the newspapers that he had smelled semen on Wilde and that he had degenerated into masturbating (Ellmann, 1988). Haldane had this chaplain removed to another post and looked again for somewhere else to place his friend in safety. On the 20 or 21 November 1895 Wilde was transferred from Wandsworth Prison on the express orders of Haldane, one of the two most powerful men within the prison system (Ellmann, 1988). Hide (1975) ascribes the transfer to the influence of Sir Evelyn Ruggles-Brise, who was then Chairman of the Prison Commission, but even if this were the case it is clear that Wilde had at least one highly placed friend who may well have been looking out for him as I shall explain. It is not inconceivable that the unlikely choice of Reading was in some way influenced by this connection. Whatever, Wilde's transfer to Reading Gaol was one of the most humiliating experiences of his life. In *De Profundis* he writes:

> From two o'clock till half past two on that day I had to stand on the centre platform at Clapham Junction in convict dress and handcuffed, for the world to look at. I had been taken out of the hospital ward without a moment's notice being given to me.[2] Of all possible objects I was the most grotesque. When people saw me they laughed.

---

[2] Still in many instances the practice: known to prisoners as 'being ghosted', especially if overnight.

Each train as it came in swelled the audience. Nothing could exceed their amusement. That was, of course, before they knew who I was. As soon as they had been informed they laughed still more. For half an hour I stood there in the grey November rain surrounded by a jeering mob.

WILDE IN READING GAOL

Having worked so closely at Reading for many years and with a unique degree access to the place, records, facts and archives, I found that many questions remained unanswered. The one that has intrigued me more than any other is: why on earth did Oscar Wilde end up at Reading Gaol, then a comparatively obscure prison? What is it that was so special about Reading? At the time Reading Gaol was over 50 years old; there were far newer, more famous, notorious, progressive or high profile prisons that he could have been moved to.

As already noted, one of the Prison Commissioners was R. B. Haldane who seems to have been prepared to 'look after' Oscar Wilde; never was this more evident than at Pentonville Prison, where he gave the governor instructions to allow certain books, totally against the prison rules. Furthermore, according to Ellmann (1988), Haldane was then responsible for having Wilde moved from Pentonville to Wandsworth in 1895 and thence to Reading in November of the same year. But again the question remains: did Reading have something that other prisons could not offer?

As noted in *Chapter 2*, the Prison Act 1877 provided for the creation of a local Visiting Committee described as:

> A body selected from the local Magistracy, as the Judicial authority of a Local Prison ... a tribunal to which the Secretary of State could always refer with confidence.
> (Ruggles-Brise, 1921)

The Visiting Committee were a group of people who could come into a prison at any time, inspect and investigate any issues, and award punishments on prisoners over and above the authority of the governor. The Visiting Committee was the forerunner of Boards of Visitors—now known as Independent Monitoring Boards (or IMBs) to emphasise their independence from HM Prison Service. Visiting Committees answered only to the Prison Commission and the Government. At Reading Gaol in 1895, the year when Wilde was sent there, the local Visiting Committee comprised:

Captain Alex W. Cobham (Chairman)
Charles Hay
H. Hunter
A. Harry Thursby
George W. Palmer M.P.

The last of these, George W. Palmer was the eldest son of George Palmer, one of the founding partners of Huntley & Palmers, the famous Reading biscuit makers. Their factory was next to the gaol. By 1895 it employed over 5,000 staff and was reputed by some people to have become the largest biscuit manufacturers on the planet. George W. Palmer was, as his father had been, a member of the Visiting Committee at Reading Gaol; he became a member of Reading Council in 1882 and was Mayor in 1889-90. He served as Liberal Member of Parliament for Reading from 1892 to 1895 and again from 1898 to 1904. He was thus a man of some influence.

To continue the connection, George W. Palmer's younger brother, Walter, was married to Jean, a renowned society hostess who hosted literary parties at their home, Westfield. Oscar Wilde and his wife Constance were regular guests there; and according to documents in the Reading Museum Oscar Wilde even had a good-humoured nickname for Jean: 'Moonbeam'. Furthermore, Oscar Wilde visited the family's Reading biscuit factory in 1892, together with George Meredith, a noted wit, and Louise Jopling, the actress; as he signed the visitor's book, little did he realise that the gaol next door would in a couple of years time be his main residence.

R. B. Haldane knew that with George W. Palmer as a member of the Visiting Committee, Oscar Wilde would receive some sort of protection at Reading Gaol; evidence for this would come in the minutes of the Visiting Committee book. The governor of the gaol at this time was one Colonel Isaacson, who had been in charge there for over six years. He was blissfully unaware that Oscar Wilde would prove to be his nemesis. Isaacson addressed the staff one morning:

> A certain prisoner is about to be transferred here, and you should be proud to think that the Prison Commissioners have chosen Reading Gaol as the one most suitable for this man. (Ellmann, 1988)

But if Palmer did have a hand in matters, this must be judged in the context of an era when much was done 'on the nod' and through London clubs and social networks. Wilde certainly enjoyed favours at Reading, beyond any privileges afforded by a highly sceptical governor.

According to prison records, Wilde arrived at Reading Gaol on 20 November 1895.[3] There he spent the remainder of his two year sentence. Upon his arrival he would have been given the obligatory tour around the punishment landing and a bath as already described in *Chapter 2*. Then to add to his woes his hair would have been cut short, which we know did happen. According to a letter sent to Leonard Smithers, his publisher, he pleaded: 'Must it be cut? ... you don't know what it means to me.' At Wandsworth, his hair had been allowed to grow out a

---

[3] Although in *De Profundis* he claimed the date to be the 13th.

little, but in his new governor he would soon find a man who lived by the rules and without deviation (Ellmann, 1988).

Wilde was placed in cell number 3 on C3 landing in C block; he was also provided with the Scottish cap, the grey prison uniform with black arrows and a brass badge inscribed 'C.3.3'. From henceforth he was known simply by this number. Cleverly perhaps, he was able to turn this to account by using it as the pseudonym under which he published *The Ballad of Reading Gaol*. His cell was furnished according to the basic requirements of the Prison Act 1865: 'Hard labour, hard fare and hard bed'. The earlier in-cell sanitation had been removed for a more austere regime: by a chamber pot which could only be emptied three times a day. After his release Wilde wrote to *The Daily Chronicle* (28 May 1897): 'One of the most horrible things in prison is the badness of the sanitary arrangements.' He was also later to recall seeing on three separate occasions warders becoming violently sick when opening up cells in the morning (Ellmann, 1988).

The routine was one of repetition and, for Wilde, hardship: 'All the rigours of the system were applied to him relentlessly. He had to pick his quantity of oakum ... turn the monotonous crank' (Sherard, 1928). For Wilde, the picking of oakum from tarred rope was exceptionally hard, he complained of his fingers bleeding, being torn to shreds. At eight o'clock every evening all of the day's completed tasks would be collected by the warder; and if Wilde did not submit his quota he would be punished.

Wilde complained bitterly about the prison governor, Isaacson, claiming that he was 'Harsh and stupid and lacking in imagination'. Colonel Isaacson was indeed renowned for his harshness. When Frank Harris visited, the governor told him that he would: 'Knock the nonsense out of Wilde' (Hyde, 1975). To another visitor Wilde called him: 'A mulberry-coloured dictator.' Indeed, Oscar Wilde was no model prisoner; he would be punished for the smallest of offences, was unable to clean his cell satisfactorily and, according to Ellmann (1988), as long as Isaacson was in charge, Wilde was caught up in a never-ending cycle of punishments. Talking to André Gide after his release, Wilde stated: 'After I had been at Reading for six weeks, I heard someone murmur, "Oscar Wilde, I pity you because you must be suffering more than we."' Wilde replied: 'No, my friend, we are all suffering equally.' A day or two later a warder called out, 'C.3.3 and C.4.8, step out of line!' The two prisoners were brought before the governor and accused of breaking prison discipline by talking. Both prisoners stated that they had started the conversation, whereupon Isaacson became mad with rage and awarded punishment of 14 days[4] in the punishment cell and added a diet of bread and water (Ellmann, 1988).

---

[4] At that time the governor only had authority to award a maximum of three days in the punishment cell. Any further time would have required the approval of the Visiting Committee, and with Wilde's friend as a member this would never have been given.

One morning Wilde was looking out through his window when the chaplain, Reverend M. T. Friend entered his cell. Wilde complained about not being able to see clearly through the window so when the chaplain turned to him and said: 'Oh my friend, let me entreat you to desist from such thoughts and not let your mind dwell on the clouds, but on Him who is above the clouds', it is said Wilde shouted at him and pushed him out of the cell (Ellmann, 1988). For such an attack on the chaplain it is almost certain that any other prisoner would have been flogged with the cat o'nine tails, bearing in mind that on 10 January 1899 a prisoner named John Bowler received 25 strokes of the cat for similarly irreverent behaviour albeit in chapel. After he had been at Reading for three months Wilde's mother died, but he was not informed of this until two weeks later when his wife, Constance, visited him with special permission from the Home Office. The visit took place in the room allotted for special visits, and this was to be the very last time he saw Constance (Sherard, 1928).

He became depressed and very low; on 13 June Frank Harris visited him privately, without any warder being present, after receiving permission from the Prison Commissioners. Wilde complained bitterly about his treatment:

> I am perpetually being punished for nothing; this governor loves to punish, and he punishes by taking my books away from me ... if you resist they drive you crazy.

He also complained about a bad ear but Harris was asked not to repeat his complaints as Wilde feared the repercussions (Ellmann, 1988).

The Prison Commissioners decided to call for a medical investigation from Dr. Nicholson who had examined him after a fall at Wandsworth. Wilde, in the meantime, decided to petition the Home Secretary on 2 July 1896. The Prison Commissioners wasted no time and ordered an inquiry to be held at the gaol by the Visiting Committee. The entry in the Visitors Book reads as follows:

> 10th July 1896 Enquiry, held at the Prison, by direction of the Prison Commissioners, on Prisoner Oscar Wylde in regard to a Petition made by him to the Home Secretary dated 2nd July 1896.
>
> 1. The Committee do not consider from the enquiry that there is danger of the Prisoner becoming insane, but as this Prisoner's petition is based upon the fear of insanity, always a difficult subject, the committee think an expert Medical Enquiry may well be held upon his case, to which an examination of his hearing and eyesight [could be added].
> 2. The Committee consider that the Prisoner has been well treated. He himself states that his treatment has been good & the dietary sufficient – He has been relieved of oakum picking, has been allowed more books, & more exercise than the other prisoners. He has increased eight pounds in weight since he entered the prison. Prison life must of course be more internal severe to a prisoner of his educational achievement than it would be to an ordinary one.

Alex W. Cobham
Charles Hay
H. Hunter
Harry Thursby
George W. Palmer

Hence Wilde was 'no ordinary' prisoner.

Events at Reading then moved at a fast pace; the next entry in the Visiting Committee book reads:

> 18th July 1896 The Committee having heard with regard that Colonel Isaacson is shortly to be summoned from this prison decided to word their appreciation ... the satisfactory condition of the prison is as much due to the kindness ... wish him every success and happiness in the enlarged sphere at Lewes to which he has been promoted.
>
> Alex W. Chobham
> George W. Palmer

This entry indicates that Colonel Isaacson was being 'promoted' to a much larger prison, making way for a more liberal and, some would say, humane governor: Major J. B. Nelson. The following week Nelson, on his arrival, immediately went to Wilde and according to Ellmann (1988) said to him: 'The Prison Commission has allowed you some books. Perhaps you would like to read this one; I have just read it myself.' Wilde must have cried and was later to praise Nelson highly in *De Profundis*: 'What a beginning! What a wonderful beginning ... I shall owe much to this personality that has altered every man in this place.'

A list of books was submitted to the Prison Commissioners by July 28. They decided that he could have some of the books up to a net value of £10. This was equal to the total budget of the gaol for a whole year's supply of books. From then on Wilde was excused most forms of hard labour and appointed 'Schoolmaster's Orderly' with the task of taking care of prison library books. Nelson knew full well that under the Prison Rules all books sent to Wilde would become the property of the Crown and end up in that library.

For Wilde, things began to change for the better. In Major Nelson he found a more humane individual than Isaacson and to add to his new found joy he was allowed to write the now famous letter to Lord Alfred Douglas, *De Profundis*. Prison Rules still applied in that he was only given small amounts of paper each day, to be returned to the warder at eight o'clock every evening, as recalled later by Warder Thomas Martin:

> Later he was allowed a more important privilege—the privilege of writing—and to this concession the world owes *De Profundis*. He wrote mostly in the evenings, when he knew he would be undisturbed. (Sherard, 1928)

During this time he received a visit from his wife's solicitor, Hargrove, in February 1897. It was to finalise the awarding of custody of his children to Constance and Adrian Hope, her cousin. Wilde was deeply affected by the loss of his children, writing in *De Profundis*:

> That the Law should decide ... I am one unfit to be with my children is something quite horrible to me. The disgrace of prison is nothing compared with it. I envy other men who tread the yard along with me. I am sure that their children wait for them.

Outside the room, unbeknown to Wilde, was his wife who had come to the prison with her solicitor. She turned to the warder in charge and asked: 'Let me have one last glimpse of my husband'. The warder moved aside and Constance saw Wilde for the last time. The warder later recounted this event in the *Evening News* (2 March 1905): 'Mrs Wilde cast one long lingering glance inside and saw the convict-poet, who, in deep mental distress ... witnessed his degradation.' Much distressed, Constance then left the prison with her solicitor, never to see her husband again (Montgomery Hyde, 1975).

It took Wilde from January through to March to finish *De Profundis*; he asked on 3 April 1897 for permission to send out this letter but was refused and the full manuscript was given to him only upon his release by Major Nelson.

Seven weeks before this a new warder appeared on C-wing: Warder Thomas Martin, a fellow Irishman, who was to become a very close friend of Wilde's and called him affectionately 'the Poet' during his last weeks in Reading.

Warder Martin broke virtually all the Prison Rules for Wilde; he supplied him with ginger biscuits—again from Huntley & Palmers—and on a daily basis brought him the *Daily Chronicle*. These actions were all banned under the rules at that time: basically he was 'trafficking', one of the most serious offences a prison officer can commit. Wilde would write him notes:

> My dear friend, what have I to write about except that if you had been an officer in Reading Prison a year ago my life would have been much happier. Everyone tells me I am looking better – and happier. That is because I have a good friend who gives me the *Chronicle* and promises me ginger biscuits.

Warder Martin had written on the bottom of the note: 'Your ungrateful I done more than promised' (Ellmann, 1988).

In Sherard's book, *Life of Oscar Wilde* (1928) there is a chapter contributed by Martin with the express instructions that it must be published as it was written without alteration. The chapter goes into detail about Wilde's last weeks at Reading. It tells of his distress at being unable to polish his shoes or comb his hair which had been allowed to grow again under Major Nelson. Whenever he received a visitor he would conceal his unshaven appearance with a red handkerchief, complaining: 'If I could but feel clean, I should not feel so utterly miserable. These awful bristles ... are horrid.'

Towards the end of Wilde's sentence the Prison Commissioners decided to introduce a new class of prisoner: star class[5] for people who were in prison for their first offence. As Martin states: 'During the later part of the Poet's imprisonment the order was issued for "first offenders" to be kept apart from the other prisoners.' These prisoners were made easily recognisable by a red star on their jacket and on their cap. The idea was to isolate first time offenders and take them away from associating with recidivists. However, this only applied to new prisoners and not to Oscar Wilde. When a star-class prisoner was passing down a landing, all other types of prisoners, including Wilde had to turn and face the wall until the person had passed. According to Martin: 'I have seen the Poet having to stand with his face to the wall whilst a villainous looking ruffian passed by.'

In March 1897 Martin entered Wilde's cell and found him still in bed, breaking the Prison Rules. On enquiring Wilde complained of pains in his side and a headache; but refused to allow the warder to report him sick and eventually got up. The warder asked again if he should get the doctor. Again this was declined except for to say that he would like something warm to drink. The warder then went off and made him a hot beef-tea, poured it into a bottle and, hiding it inside his jacket, returned to Wilde's cell. As he was going up the central staircase from C2 landing to C3 Martin was stopped by the chief warder and summoned back to the central hall below. The beef-tea had started to seep and to burn Martin's chest; unable to move he had to listen to the chief warder and try to answer his questions quickly. As Martin later described:

> I was in frightful agony. The hot bottle burned against my breast like molten lead ... I could have cried out in my agony, but dare not ... it lay there against my breast like a hot poultice ... the chief eyed me curiously. I believe he thought I had been drinking.

Martin then ran up the stairs as fast as he could and into C.3.3, Wilde's cell. On hearing what had just happened Wilde burst into laughter. This angered the warder who stormed out of the cell, saying that it was a poor reward for all he had undergone to be laughed at, slamming the cell door shut as he left. Later Martin had to return to the cell to deliver breakfast; Wilde refused to touch his food like a small child until the warder had forgiven him. The next morning Wilde handed him a note with the heading 'An Apology'. It read:

> I never thought to resume ... but yesterday morning I laughed, which showed my perversity, for I felt sorry for you. I did not mean to laugh; I had vowed never to laugh again. Then I thought it fitting when I had broken one vow to break another. I

---

[5] Even today in some prisons first timers may be nicknamed 'stars'.

never intend to laugh, nor do I intend ever again to write anything calculated to produce laughter in others. I am no longer the Sirius of Comedy ... if I write any more books, it will be to form a library of lamentations ... they will be for those who have suffered or are suffering. I understand them, and they will understand me. I shall be an enigma to the world of Pleasure, but a mouth piece for the world of pain'.

(Sherard, 1928)

On Saturday, May 15, Wilde was in his cell when he heard a prisoner being flogged on the punishment landing of B1. He was very distressed by the man's suffering and later wrote to the *Daily Chronicle* complaining about the harsh treatment given to this prisoner (see *Chapter 3*). Another incident that appalled him was seeing three young children who had been convicted of poaching and sent to Reading Gaol because they were unable to pay their fines. Wilde asked Martin if he could find out the name of the prisoner in A.2.11 (the man being flogged) and the amount of the fines for the boys, 'so I might be able to get them out'. Warder Martin was dismissed a few days later for giving one of the boys a biscuit. The young lad unknowingly had told the chief warder of his kindness and for this Martin was dismissed.

RELEASE

Oscar Wilde was eventually released from Reading Gaol late in the evening of 18 May 1897 and before leaving he received from Major Nelson the letter he had written entitled *De Profundis*. Unlike other prisoners, he was allowed to wear his own clothes and not be handcuffed; instead of being released at the prison gate he was taken by cab to Twyford Station a few miles away, then by train to London and transferred to Pentonville Prison from where he was finally set free the following morning.

Later, after a reunion with close friends, he left for France, never to set foot in England again. Wilde settled in a small hotel at Berneval-sur-Mer under the name of Sebastian Melmoth. It was here that he wrote his *Ballad of Reading Gaol*, the story of the last days of Charles T. Wooldridge, a former trooper with the Royal Horse Guards, who was held and executed at Reading for murdering his wife (see *Chapters 4* and *6*) which happened whilst Wilde was there. Hence such telling lines as:

> I walked, with other souls in pain,
> Within another ring,
> And was wondering if the man had done
> A great or little thing,
> When a voice behind me whispered low,
> 'That fellow's got to swing.'

The execution of Wooldridge, which took place in 1896, had a profound effect on Wilde, coming when he was physically and emotionally at his lowest ebb, and living simultaneously through the last weeks of this young soldier's life. He dedicated the poem to the memory of the trooper. Interestingly and indicative of the times, perhaps, the execution attracted little news coverage, much of which concerned Wooldridge's passivity and acceptance of his fate. His trial and conviction were covered only superficially by the national press and *The Times* devoted the smallest space necessary in noting that an execution had taken place at Reading Gaol on 7 July 1896. There were longer accounts in the *Hants & Berks Gazette* and in the *Reading Mercury*, but even these were largely factual—and certainly there was nothing to suggest any further public interest. As the last mentioned newspaper put matters, Wooldridge died 'bravely without a struggle or a cry ... as if he were on parade'. It also noted that the black flag flew over the prison gate for several days, which was the normal routine on such occasions.

An interesting entry in the Visiting Committee journal dated 20 June 1896 states: 'Allowed prisoner Wooldridge under sentence of death some tobacco'. Remembering that tobacco and newspapers were amongst the totally prohibited articles within prisons:

> And twice a day he smoked his pipe,
> And drank his quart of beer:
> His soul was resolute, and held
> No hiding place for fear;
> He often said that he was glad
> The Hangman's hands were near.

Could this have been at Wilde's request, an example of preferential treatment by proxy or was it maybe that the authorities were equally intrigued by Wooldridge's attitude towards his fate and were beguiled into treating him well?

THE DEATH OF OSCAR WILDE

Oscar Wilde died in France three-and-a-half years after his release in 1900 at the age of 46, and his passing was announced in England in *The Times* of December 1: 'Oscar Wilde died on November 30 of meningitis.' Some people have said that he died of a middle-ear illness first contracted in prison.

Warder Martin was dismissed for gross insubordination and an inquiry was held by the Prison Commission into Wilde's *Daily Chronicle* newspaper articles. Some of the inquiry papers were officially stamped with the words 'Closed for 99 years'. Below is an extract:

> As to Martin's dismissal this is a matter which obviously cannot be discussed in print. He was an unsatisfactory officer and it is not easy to attribute the conduct which led

to his dismissal to an excusable motive. Supposing he was a specially tender-hearted man and honestly believed the boy was suffering from hunger, he should have reported this to the governor.

To permit warders – even from humane motives – to distinguish one prisoner from another by kindly acts would obviously lead to very serious scandals, and Martin had previously been suspected of trafficking with prisoners.

Prison Commission, 15 June 1897

R. B. Haldane and Sir Evelyn Ruggles-Brise were both members of the Prison Commission and the Gladstone Committee which in 1895 looked into various aspects of imprisonment. This culminated in the Prison Act 1898 which abolished hard labour, diluted the separate system—allowing prisoners to speak for the first time—and allowed for the introduction of remission for good behaviour. It was all too late, however, for Oscar Wilde.

THOUGHTS FROM SOMEONE CLOSE AT HAND

After almost 20 years' experience of working inside Her Majesty's prisons, much of it at Reading Gaol and with unrivalled opportunities for research and contemplation, I constantly look for answers to a number of questions, in particular:

- why was not the dismissal of Martin discussed in print at the time: did the powers that be have something to hide? Could it have been that Martin was an embarrassment to someone higher up in the chain of influence? Was he a plant, sent to Reading and placed there to look after Wilde during his last weeks of imprisonment? Why else the sudden change of events?
- why was a new and junior member of staff placed on a long term 'convicted landing' (for prisoners found guilty and serving their time) and not, as is customary, on the remand wing (a remand landing will teach new members of staff all that is required for the job; they deal with a frequently changing prisoner population as prisoners go back and forth to court and new ones arrive for short periods. Remand prisoners by their very nature are more volatile and demanding: the majority believing that they are innocent and should not be there. On the 'convicted' landings, prison officers deal with a relatively static population, prisoners are resolved to doing their sentence and pre-occupied with the date at which they are to be released. They tend to be more relaxed and less stressed. New or junior staff would learn very little from this landing and in the pecking order within the prison

system, older staff would normally work this type of landing, going for the 'plum job' that means an easier, less stressful time.

It seems to have been the general view hitherto that Oscar Wilde was lucky to come across the occasional kind-hearted individual during his time in Reading. However, as a serving prison officer with an intimate knowledge of Reading Gaol past and present, I have found myself during the research for this book coming to somewhat different conclusions. Rather than by sheer good fortune, it appears to me that Wilde's path into, through and out of Reading Gaol was made smoother for him than it was for the other prisoners by assistance from the highest to the lowest levels within the prison hierarchy, Prison Commission and local Visiting Committee. The original official documents of the gaol itself are not yet in the public domain but I have had the opportunity to read all of these before forming this conclusion.

Haldane and the Prison Commissioners
R. B. Haldane clearly looked out for Oscar Wilde by using his influence to move him into the most sympathetic environment possible and by seeing to the moving around both of senior and more junior personnel with the same aim. A reconsideration of the sequence of events makes this evident. For example, in June 1895 after Wilde had been in Pentonville less than a month he is visited personally by Haldane and offered books, a pen and ink—all against the then highly restrictive Prison Rules. He receives a huge number of books by comparison with other prisoners in those days. The governor objects and three weeks later Haldane arranges for Wilde to be moved to a different prison, Wandsworth, where there is a chaplain who has criticised the regime at Pentonville. All his books, which are supposed to be the property of Pentonville Prison, follow him within a few weeks. In September the deputy chaplain makes an unfavourable written note about Wilde and is subsequently removed to another prison. A couple of months on, Wilde openly unhappy and complaining about Wandsworth, is moved to Reading, where the governor announces that the Prison Commissioners (either Haldane or his colleague Sir Evelyn Ruggles-Brise) have selected Reading Gaol as the most suitable place for him. At Reading there is an eminent, wealthy and locally influential member of the Visiting Committee whose relations are already on personal terms with Wilde, if not Palmer himself who may well have been in any event. In June 1896 the Prison Commissioners permit another friend to visit Wilde in complete privacy (again, something quite against normal rules) and he makes complaints about the staff, including the governor. Next month the Prison Commissioners arrange for the Visiting Committee to hold a formal inquiry into Wilde's treatment and the governor is subsequently 'promoted' to a different prison to be replaced by someone far more sympathetic to Wilde—who gives him preferential treatment. Seven weeks before Wilde's release a new warder arrives who allows him daily

privileges. He is released under conditions somewhat above the norm by first being taken to another prison, then escorted back to London. Shortly after his release the warder is dismissed, discredited and effectively temporarily silenced for showing a single favour to another prisoner.

The Palmer Connection

The George W. Palmer connection is one that has not been documented before and arose during my research for this book into local materials on Reading town. The Palmer family were wealthy and influential. George W. Palmer became Mayor of Reading 1889-90 and served as Member of Parliament for the town 1892-1904, with a break between 1895 and 1898. He was 'second generation' on the Visiting Committee at the prison, his father having also been a member. It is an immense irony that Wilde's signature is in the visiting book of the Huntley & Palmers biscuit factory next door to the gaol. Since Wilde is known to have been a friend of the Palmer family and to have been entertained by them frequently, it appears to me that this may be the reason why Reading was chosen by Haldane. Palmer was a pillar of Reading society and, as one of the richest men in the town and its MP, wielded considerable influence. The Visiting Committee of which he was a member had considerable powers and influence with regard to the governor, and Palmer's name was on the minutes of the inquiry into Wilde's complaints that ultimately led to the removal of Governor Isaacson. Palmer was also one of the directors of Huntley & Palmers and it was from this factory that warder Martin would collect or receive biscuits for Oscar Wilde.

Governor Nelson

It is unlikely to be mere coincidence that the new governor who replaced Isaacson was of a far more sympathetic inclination. However his actions in allowing Wilde such preferential treatment as books, writing paper, long hair, more exercise and cancellation of the hard labour part of his sentence should under normal circumstances have laid him open to disciplinary action. Such favouring of a prisoner was quite against the very strict Prison Rules of the time and for such flagrant breaches to have been allowed suggests that the Palmer connection was working and Nelson knew that the Visiting Committee were not likely to discipline him. Indeed they may even have been condoning his behaviour.

If a governor were to act like that today, totally against all the rules, he or she would be investigated and any findings of guilt would lead to his or her demotion or even dismissal. In all my years in the service I have never known a governor to be replaced other than for disciplinary or security reasons in such a short time as was Colonel Isaacson, with just a couple of weeks between his being told of his promotion and his replacement arriving at Reading. Who had replaced Nelson at such short notice at his previous gaol? There is a saying within the prison service: the fastest way to remove a member of staff is to promote them!

Warder Martin

The final person in the Wilde 'mafia' was Warder Thomas Martin. As the most junior of the four men mentioned above and the one in the front line who directly broke the rules to help Wilde, he was also the most vulnerable. Then, as now, for a prison officer to 'traffick' with or for a prisoner by bringing him or her any contraband is a dismissible offence. By favours such as bringing Wilde biscuits and newspapers daily (even to the extent of making him beef-tea when Wilde felt ill) and presumably facilitating letters to the press, Martin broke the rules in the most serious way possible for many weeks without ever being 'found out' or disciplined. Subsequently, Wilde was to take up as one of his campaigns the treatment and dismissal of Warder Martin, about which he wrote at great length to the *Daily Chronicle* in a letter published by that paper on 28 May 1897. As already noted, Wilde's other campaigns included the plight of child prisoners, the inappropriateness of prison regimes for those of tender years and the treatment of a man called Prince who was held at Reading and punished on the instructions of the visiting magistrates, despite his obvious mental impairment (see *Chapter 3*).

Even after such a long lapse of time, I sense irregularities in Martin's appointment and tenure at Reading which suggest that he was in fact a 'plant', placed in the prison to steer Wilde through his final weeks of imprisonment. Why was this new and junior member of staff supervising a convicted, high profile prisoner such as Wilde in C block and not, as is customary for new staff, the more challenging remand prisoners? This was quite against the normal practice at the time. How did Martin manage to get away with breaking the rules to such an astonishing degree without being caught? Why was he then dismissed (or sacrificed) after Wilde had left, for a transgression far more minor than many of those relating to Wilde, and why did he, despite having been 'discredited', condemn in print, in the strongest terms, his dismissal? Was he cynically disposed of by the Prison Commissioners because he had served his purpose and knew too much? Why did they seal the official papers for a century and admit that his dismissal 'obviously cannot be discussed in print'?

And what of the *Ballad* itself? We know that *De Profundis* was written at Reading and returned to Wilde on his release. Did Wilde really suddenly wake up one morning in France and write the *Ballad* down? This hardly makes sense: at some point the prison authorities must have realised that Wilde was about to launch a salvo that he was already thinking—if not already writing—about in his cell. It is only possible to surmise, more than 100 years later, precisely what was going on and whether the official and traditional accounts hold water.

An old print from *Prison Discipline* (1848) by Reading Gaol Chaplain the Reverend J. Field showing the Centre at Reading Gaol at the time of the separate system. The ornate 'Centre Box' was removed in the late-1960s.

Prisoner 973 Arabella Earles (c.1891). Prisoners were photographed in the Photographic House.

The elaborate 1844 Gatehouse just before it was demolished in 1969.

The Canadians arriving in 1945 with their 'invisible prisoners': *Chapter 8*.
Reproduced by kind permission of Reading Museum.

Prisoner Q.311 William Clarke. Note how two images were captured in one, full face and profile using the mirror. The prisoner's badge shows his cell A.2.22.

East down A-wing, Level 2 now. The central stairway gives an unobstructed view.

10th July 1896. Enquiry held at the Prison, by direction of the Prison Commissioners, on Prisoner Oscar Wylde in regard to a Petition made by him to the Home Secretary dated 2 July 1896.

1. The Committee do not consider from the enquiry that there is danger of the Prisoner becoming insane, but as the Prisoner's petition is based upon the fear of insanity, always a difficult subject, the Committee think that an expert Medical Enquiry may well be held upon his case, to include an examination of his hearing & eyesight.

2. The Committee consider that the Prisoner has been well treated. He himself states that his treatment has been good & the dietary sufficient. He has been relieved of oakum picking, has been allowed more books, & more exercise than the other prisoners. He has increased eight pounds in weight since he entered the prison. Prison life must of course be more irksome & severe to a prisoner of his education & attainments than it would be to an ordinary one.

Alex. W. Cobham.
Charles Hay.
H. Hunter.
A. Naring Thursby —
George W. Palmer.

Visiting Committee book entry for 10 July 1896 with Wilde mis-spelt 'Wylde' in the second line, signed among others by George W. Palmer: see *Chapter 5*. It deals with Wilde's petition to the Home Secretary as per the transcription on pages 84-85.

THE CHAPEL ON THE "SEPARATE SYSTEM," IN PENTONVILLE PRISON, DURING DIVINE SERVICE.

'There is no Chapel on the day they hang a man'. Old print showing the chapel at Pentonville Prison under the separate system, on which that at Reading was based.

The front of the prison around 1960.

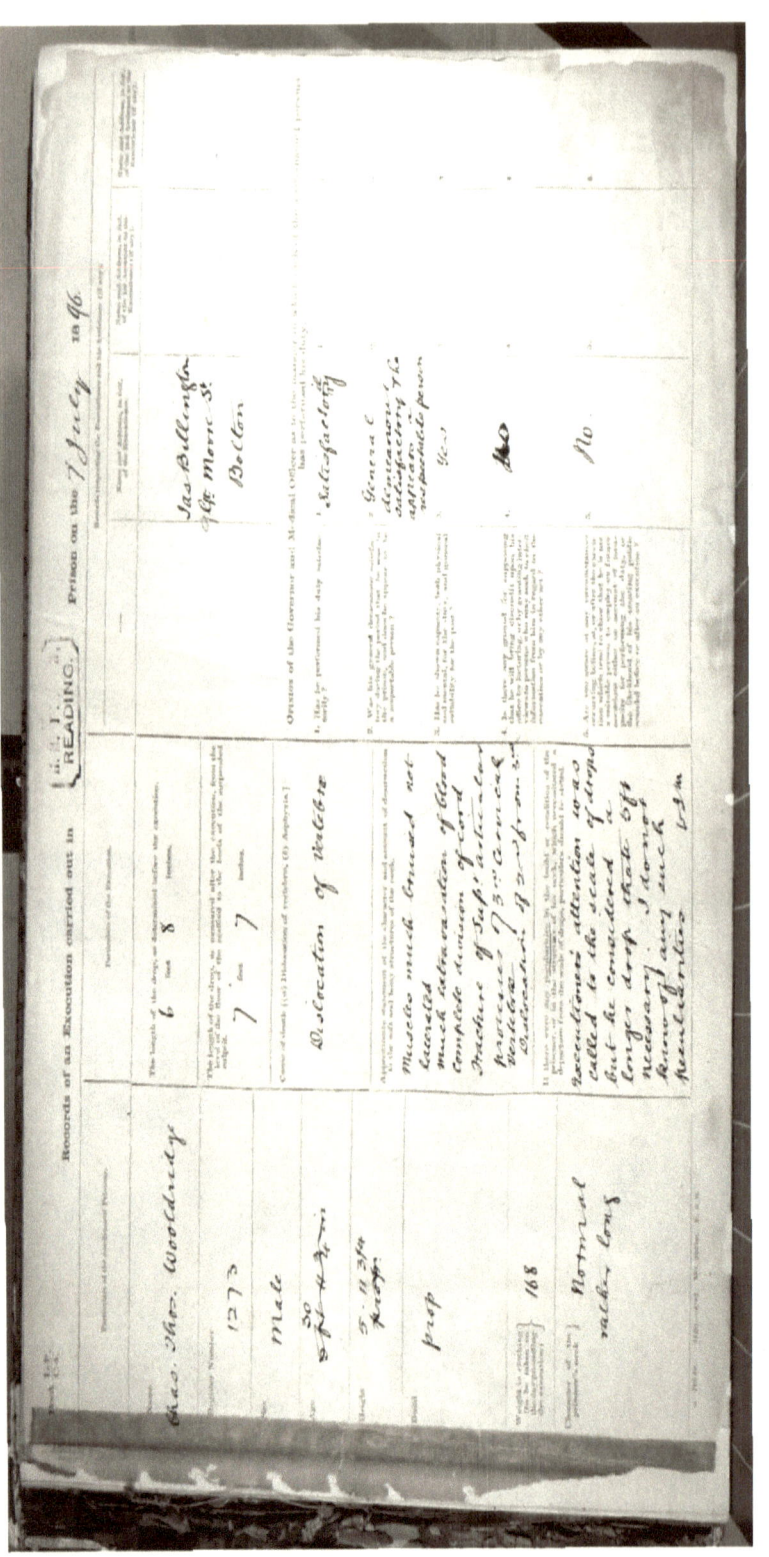

The Execution Log showing the entry for Charles Thomas Wooldridge and cause of death as 'dislocation of the vertebrae'. It also notes that executioner James Billington had his attention drawn to the Table of Drops but that he considered that a 'rather longer' drop was necessary; whereby Wooldridge's neck was stretched by a huge 11 inches (25 centimetres): *Chapter 4*. Hence 'they mocked the swollen purple throat' in *The Ballad of Reading Gaol*.

CHAPTER 6

The Ballad of Reading Gaol

The Ballad of Reading Gaol 'by C.3.3' and headed 'In Memory of C.T.W.' was written when Oscar Wilde was in France in 1897; just a couple of months after his release from Reading.[1] It is structured around the last weeks of a fellow prisoner, Trooper Charles Thomas Wooldridge (the C.T.W. of the dedication), who was executed at Reading for the murder of his wife. This part of the story has already been described in *Chapter 4* and some additional information about how Wilde came to write about Wooldridge is contained in *Chapter 5*. Perhaps most significantly, Wilde encountered Wooldridge regularly during exercise when the prisoners were walking the 'Fools' Parade': the term Wilde used to describe the prisoners walking in circles in total silence.

The ballad is at once beautiful and dark although it was not universally well received at the time of its publication: the *Daily Chronicle* having matters both ways by chiding it as 'a mixture of rubbish and excellence'. It captures the images of sheer horror and terror that must have haunted every prisoner within the gaol during Wooldridge's last days. It also portrays the deplorable conditions of prison life in the era of Sir Edmond Du Cane's 'Hard labour, hard fare and hard board' (or sometimes 'bed'): the treadmill, the frugal diet and the wooden planks that had replaced hammocks for sleeping on. This was Wilde's last artistic effort in a great literary career and it has left Reading Gaol with a huge legacy worldwide. The poem also ensures that Wooldridge's memory lives on and that he is unlikely ever to be forgotten.

On publication, Wilde's publisher, Leonard Smithers, was taken by surprise by its instant success. Only several hundred copies had been printed and there was no substantial advertising. Nonetheless, the ballad went into seven editions in the space of 18 months, each of which ran to several thousands of copies.

Aspects of the ballad explored
Wilde's final gesture with regard to his imprisonment and the prison system that he so deplored was to sign the ballad not in his own name, but using as a pseudonym the cell number by which he had been known throughout his time at Reading: C.3.3.

That cell has since acquired a form of immortality of its own and it is still in regular use today as a prison cell. It has also been at the centre of certain literary

---

[1] As intimated in *Chapter 5* it seems inconceivable that the poem was not at least in embryo during Wilde's time at Reading, if only in his head. There is no record of drafts or notes being amongst his papers—in contrast to *De Profundis* that was already complete.

debates. There are, e.g. those who say that Wilde could hardly have seen the site of Wooldridge's burial in quicklime within the prison walls from his cell. But these people have not, as the author has, carefully worked out the sightlines from the small window of Wilde's cell and, still further, had access to the original plans of the prison which show that the view was not then obstructed, as it is nowadays. As with the other such graves at Reading it now bears a small commemorative plaque placed there by the author.[2]

But there is evidence of some poetic licence: for example, Wooldridge's regiment, the Royal Horse Guards (or 'Blues'), wore bluish green coats and not the 'scarlet' of Wilde's opening line—to juxtapose this with blood and wine. Wilde himself was quite frank when challenged about this anomaly: 'I could hardly have written, "He did not wear his azure coat, for wine and blood are blue".'[3] There is similar licence in other verses, examples of which are noted in the commentary to the ballad which follows below. It is worth noting though that even within the first verse Wilde is already using 'smoke and mirrors' in order, seemingly, to move the murder from its strict location to 'her bed' and create the triple rhyme 'red', 'dead', 'bed'. Even contemporary accounts vary, but *The Times* of 1 April 1896, reporting on the inquest, states that Laura was found in the street, Wooldridge himself having left the house in a rush, slamming the door, following a heated argument. Alice Cox who lived in the same house as Laura, stated that she heard a scream then the front door slam and a further scream coming from the street outside where Laura's body was found. Most likely, I think, Laura was attacked by the front door and maybe whilst she was still inside the house but then staggered into the road before dying. However, there are various things within the ballad that connect immediately to Reading Gaol and that Wilde could only have written using his first-hand knowledge and experience of the austere post-Prison Act 1865 regime.

In what follows I have tried to draw out certain other key words and phrases, particularly in a prison or penal context and where possible with regard to Reading Gaol itself—and also from the perspective of someone whose daily life is still affected by features and images in the ballad.[4]

---

[2] Surprisingly perhaps my interest in Wilde was actively discouraged by some people in the early days: but times have changed and I believe that there is now a real pride in the prison's heritage.
[3] As noted in *The Times*, 7 July 1980 in an article by Garrett Anderson.
[4] So as to add a different, socio-medical dimension and perspective, I am grateful to Theodore Dalrymple for agreeing to my reproducing his fine article, 'Arrested Development' in *Appendix 1*.

The Ballad of Reading Gaol

In Memoriam
C. T. W.
Sometime Trooper of the Royal Horse Guards.
Obit H. M. Prison, Reading, Berkshire,
7 July 1896

I

He did not wear his scarlet coat,
For blood and wine are red,
And blood and wine were on his hands
When they found him with the dead,
The poor dead woman whom he loved,
And murdered in her bed.

He walked amongst the Trial Men
In a suit of shabby gray;
A cricket cap was on his head,
And his step seemed light and gay;
But I never saw a man who looked
So wistfully at the day.

Wilde describes Wooldridge as wearing the obligatory Scottish cap ('cricket cap') and the grey prison uniform with black arrows described in earlier chapters. Later (see below) the cap becomes 'a 'casque of scorching steel'. 'Trial men', i.e. prisoners who were on remand to prison to await their trial (and who were thus still presumed to be innocent) were in the late-1800s, as now, kept apart from convicted prisoners and were subject to a different, less harsh prison regime. Presumably therefore Wilde is at this stage referring to Wooldridge before his trial and conviction. After conviction, condemned men were normally held separately from all other prisoners (see Chapter 4*).*

I never saw a man who looked
With such a wistful eye
Upon that little tent of blue
Which prisoners call the sky,
And at every drifting cloud that went
With sails of silver by.

The 'wistfulness' that Wilde describes in this verse intrigued both Wooldridge's fellow prisoners (who watched 'with gaze of dull amaze') and the prison officers who had charge of him as noted later in the ballad and, like his acceptance of his fate, it continued with him until the very end. He had no real motivation with regard to the pleas for clemency that were made on his behalf and as the Reading Mercury, *presumably with a degree of inside knowledge, reported, Wooldridge died 'as if he were on parade'.*

I walked, with other souls in pain,
Within another ring,
And was wondering if the man had done
A great or little thing,
When a voice behind me whispered low,
'That fellow's got to swing.'

'Walking in a ring' describes the exercising prisoners, walking in total silence in a circular, clockwise direction: with time. Even to this day prisoners always walk in a clockwise direction on exercise; it is an unwritten rule to proceed in this way and not in an anti-clockwise direction, which would be 'against time'! After the line, 'That fellow's got to swing' there comes the realisation that for this unfortunate prisoner, the ultimate punishment of the law is to be applied.

Dear Christ! the very prison walls
Suddenly seemed to reel,
And the sky above my head became
Like a casque of scorching steel;
And, though I was a soul in pain,
My pain I could not feel.

The reference to the 'casque' or helmet 'of scorching steel' is another prison metaphor, recalling the hated helmet-shaped Scottish caps that prisoners all wore and which were obligatory within the separate system: see Chapter 2.

I only knew what haunted thought
Quickened his step, and why
He looked upon the garish day
With such a wistful eye;
The man had killed the thing he loved,
And so he had to die.

Yet each man kills the thing he loves,
    By each let this be heard,
Some do it with a bitter look,
    Some with a flattering word,
The coward does it with a kiss,
    The brave man with a sword!

This is one of the most telling and often quoted verses that is also repeated as the last verse of the ballad, but also the most cryptic in its juxtaposition with the violence of and to Wooldridge. Is it a reference to Lord Alfred Douglas and his betrayal of Wilde, as some commentators suggest? The lines are often interpreted as addressed to Douglas, whose article and dedication by Douglas to Wilde of a collection of poems Wilde had rejected, thereby wounding Douglas – whilst Douglas had himself 'killed' or 'destroyed' Wilde with his evidence in court.

Some kill their love when they are young,
    And some when they are old;
Some strangle with the hands of Lust,
    Some with the hands of Gold:
The kindest use a knife, because
    The dead so soon grow cold.

Some love too little, some too long,
    Some sell, and others buy;
Some do the deed with many tears,
    And some without a sigh:
For each man kills the thing he loves,
    Yet each man does not die.

He does not die a death of shame
    On a day of dark disgrace,
Nor have a noose about his neck,
    Nor a cloth upon his face,
Nor drop feet foremost through the floor
    Into an empty space.

Here Wilde dwells at length on the details of a condemned man's last hours in prison, compared to the freedom of other 'murderers' of those they love. He was horror-struck by the macabre details of the execution ritual and his empathy with the condemned prisoner's feelings is clear. The 'cloth' was a white hood placed over the prisoner's face immediately before execution.

He does not sit with silent men
    Who watch him night and day;
Who watch him when he tries to weep,
    And when he tries to pray;
Who watch him lest himself should rob
    The prison of its prey.

As also described in Chapter 4, when someone was under sentence of death, they were accompanied by two warders, day and night, to prevent suicide among other things – which would 'rob the prison of its prey'. The warders slept in the condemned cell: six staff rotated on eight hour shifts, 24 hours a day, up until 20 minutes before the execution, when two fresh staff were brought in. All were required to keep conversation to a minimum, and ensure that any incidents were logged. At all times they were expected to remain distant from the condemned felon and to show him neither empathy nor pity.

He does not wake at dawn to see
    Dread figures throng his room,
The shivering Chaplain robed in white,
    The Sheriff stern with gloom,
And the Governor all in shiny black,
    With the yellow face of Doom.

Before any execution could take place there had to be certain officials present: the chaplain, the sheriff, the governor, the medical officer – and, of course, the executioner and prisoner. A typical execution party is given in Chapter 4.

He does not rise in piteous haste
    To put on convict-clothes,
While some coarse-mouthed Doctor gloats, and notes
Each new and nerve-twitched pose,
Fingering a watch whose little ticks
    Are like horrible hammer-blows.

He does not feel that sickening thirst
    That sands one's throat, before
The hangman with his gardener's gloves
    Slips through the padded door,
And binds one with three leathern thongs,
    That the throat may thirst no more.

When looking from his cell window Wilde saw the hangman walking along B and C-yard. The executioner, James Billington (see Chapter 4*), was renowned for wearing thick 'gardener's gloves'. The leather thongs are the straps used to pinion the prisoner's hands, legs and ankles ready for the scaffold. 'Padded door' may refer to that of the condemned cell. I am most grateful to Theodore Dalrymple for his medical perspective, 'Arrested Development' that he has kindly allowed me to reproduce in* Appendix 1.

He does not bend his head to hear
The Burial Office read,
Nor, while the anguish of his soul
Tells him he is not dead,
Cross his own coffin as he moves
Into the hideous shed.

This must have been poetic licence: the coffin would have been placed in readiness at the bottom of the execution pit not along the route taken by the prisoner – when the least distraction might trigger a disturbance, making the hangman's task more difficult and risking a 'bungled execution'.

He does not stare upon the air
Through a little roof of glass:
He does not pray with lips of clay
For his agony to pass;
Nor feel upon his shuddering cheek
The kiss of Caiaphas.

The 'little roof of glass' refers to the Photographic House at Reading Gaol that served a dual purpose: as a photographic dark room for the official photographer of prisoners and also, in later times, as an execution shed for hangings. Situated in the prison yard between C-wing and D-wing, it was built in 1870 with a glass roof on the north facing side. The first time it was used as an execution shed (for the Tidbury brothers: see Chapter 4*), the chaplain refused to enter, for he was totally opposed to capital punishment. So the maintenance team constructed a glass observation panel in the door, allowing the chaplain to read the Burial Service through this to the condemned prisoner. The 'kiss of Caiaphas' refers to the Jewish High Priest, Caiaphas, to whom Jesus was taken after his arrest in the Garden of Gethsemane.*

II

Six weeks the guardsman walked the yard,
In the suit of shabby gray:
His cricket cap was on his head,
And his step was light and gay,
But I never saw a man who looked
So wistfully at the day.

I never saw a man who looked
With such a wistful eye
Upon that little tent of blue
Which prisoners call the sky,
And at every wandering cloud that trailed
Its ravelled fleeces by.

He did not wring his hands, as do
Those witless men who dare
To try to rear the changeling Hope
In the cave of black Despair:
He only looked upon the sun,
And drank the morning air.

He did not wring his hands nor weep,
Nor did he peek or pine,
But he drank the air as though it held
Some healthful anodyne;
With open mouth he drank the sun
As though it had been wine!

And I and all the souls in pain,
Who tramped the other ring
Forgot if we ourselves had done
A great or little thing,
And watched with gaze of dull amaze
The man who had to swing.

Wooldridge is now walking in isolation in a separate exercise ring, accompanied by his two escorting officers – in contrast to the situation before his trial and conviction (see earlier note). Six weeks was the standard period between sentence and execution, all barring a reprieve – which the 'wistful' Wooldridge declined to pursue. In the end he did allow representations to be made on his behalf to the Home Secretary.

For strange it was to see him pass
With a step so light and gay,
And strange it was to see him look
So wistfully at the day,
And strange it was to think that he
Had such a debt to pay.

The oak and elm have pleasant leaves
That in the spring-time shoot:
But grim to see is the gallows-tree,
With its adder-bitten root,
And, green or dry, a man must die
Before it bears its fruit!

Oak was used for the construction of the gallows and elm for the coffins. The 'gallows-tree' was an actual tree used in former times for public hangings and a regular feature of many localities, hence 'adder-bitten root'. The word 'gallows' continues in use in many place names and may signify that this is where such a tree once existed, such as Gallowstree Common, near Reading.

The loftiest place is the seat of grace
For which all worldlings try:
But who would stand in hempen band
Upon a scaffold high,
And through a murderer's collar take
His last look at the sky?

It is sweet to dance to violins
When Love and Life are fair:
To dance to flutes, to dance to lutes
Is delicate and rare:
But it is not sweet with nimble feet
To dance upon the air!

The 'hempen band' is the hangman's noose; the word hemp also carries allusions to the picking of hemp by prisoners. The vivid image of 'dancing in the air' is part licence, part reference to the former practice of hanging by slow strangulation as opposed to instant death using a trap and table of drops to break the condemned person's neck. The 'dancing man' is a gallows emblem found on many old broadsheets and Penny Dreadfuls (cheap early news sheets), often in the form of a 'stick man' dangling from a two line scaffold. The Execution Log at Reading shows that Wooldridge died from dislocation of the vertebrae (i.e. instantly); though his neck was stretched by an enormous eleven inches (see Chapter 4).

So with curious eyes and sick surmise
We watched him day by day,
And wondered if each one of us
Would end the self-same way,
For none can tell to what red Hell
His sightless soul may stray.

At last the dead man walked no more
Amongst the Trial Men
And I knew that he was standing up
In the black dock's dreadful pen,
And that never would I see his face
For weal or woe again.

This last verse refers to Wooldridge being brought up before the Assize Judge to be sentenced to death. The judge would have donned the 'black cap' before pronouncing capital punishment. The 'black dock' is a reference to the dock in the courtroom in which Wooldridge was 'penned' – though in truth passively and without resistance, accepting his inevitable fate.

Like two doomed ships that pass in storm
We had crossed each other's way:
But we made no sign, we said no word,
We had no word to say;
For we did not meet in the holy night,
But in the shameful day.

A prison wall was round us both,
Two outcast men we were:
The world had thrust us from its heart,
And God from out His care:
And the iron gin that waits for Sin
Had caught us in its snare.

The 'iron gin' is a reference to a gin trap that was used to catch wild animals, birds and, until banned, as a deterrent to poachers, burglars and other intruders. Whilst such traps were generally made of iron that word lends emphasis and may also be an allusion to the iron bars of the prison. Hence also the references to prison as an 'iron town' and to the 'iron heel', 'iron stair' and 'Life's iron chain' later in the ballad. Waiting for sin may refer to Wilde's own predicament and sexuality; but is also an allusion to the fact that the criminal process itself can sometimes be a snare.

III

In Debtors' Yard the stones are hard,
And the dripping wall is high,
So it was there he took the air
Beneath the leaden sky,
And by each side a warder walked,
For fear the man might die.

The Debtors' Airing Yard was in A-yard: so as to keep debtors separate and apart from other categories of prisoner when in the open air. This area was also used for stone breaking as hard labour. It had a 50-foot east-facing wall in almost permanent shadow that would be 'dripping' with condensation and algae. The final two lines are a reference to the perverseness or irony of the law, whereby people must be kept alive in order to die, as noted earlier. Interestingly, Wooldridge and so presumably other condemned men, walked in this separate yard away from other prisoners, whether as a privilege or for security reasons.

Or else he sat with those who watched
His anguish night and day;
Who watched him when he rose to weep,
And when he crouched to pray;
Who watched him lest himself should rob
Their scaffold of its prey.

The Governor was strong upon
The Regulations Act:
The Doctor said that Death was but
A scientific fact:
And twice a day the Chaplain called,
And left a little tract.

For a comment on 'scientific fact', see the article 'Arrested Development' by Theodore Dalrymple in Appendix 1. By 'Regulations Act' Wilde meant the provisions that laid down exactly how a prisoner under sentence of death would be looked after. However, this would appear to be a forced line in order to achieve the rhyme. Regulations are made under Acts of Parliament and are not part of them: and the notion of a Regulations Act seems somewhat fanciful. Tobacco and alcohol were strictly forbidden – but nonetheless:

And twice a day he smoked his pipe,
And drank his quart of beer:
His soul was resolute, and held
No hiding-place for fear;
He often said that he was glad
The hangman's day was near.

Here is reference to the fact that the Visiting Committee broke Prison Rules and allowed Wooldridge tobacco and beer, possibly at Wilde's instigation as noted in Chapter 5.

But why he said so strange a thing
No warder dared to ask:
For he to whom a watcher's doom
Is given as his task,
Must set a lock upon his lips,
And make his face a mask.

Or else he might be moved, and try
To comfort or console:
And what should Human Pity do
Pent up in Murderers' Hole?
What word of grace in such a place
Could help a brother's soul?

With slouch and swing around the ring
We trod the Fools' Parade!
We did not care: we knew we were
The Devils' Own Brigade:
And shaven head and feet of lead
Make a merry masquerade.

We tore the tarry rope to shreds
With blunt and bleeding nails;
We rubbed the doors, and scrubbed the floors,
And cleaned the shining rails:
And, rank by rank, we soaped the plank,
And clattered with the pails.

We sewed the sacks, we broke the stones,
We turned the dusty drill:
We banged the tins, and bawled the hymns,
And sweated on the mill:
But in the heart of every man
Terror was lying still.

In the two verses above Wilde describes the prisoners performing hard labour: oakum picking, stone breaking, mail bag sewing and turning the mill for water. Various of these tasks are noted in Chapter 3. Wilde undertook them like the other prisoners until the later part of his sentence when he enjoyed an unusual level of privileges: Chapter 5. I have already commented in that chapter as to the fact that Wilde seems to have avoided more punitive or disciplinary measures.

> So still it lay that every day
> Crawled like a weed-clogged wave:
> And we forgot the bitter lot
> That waits for fool and knave,
> Till once, as we tramped in from work,
> We passed an open grave.
>
> With yawning mouth the horrid hole
> Gaped for a living thing;
> The very mud cried out for blood
> To the thirsty asphalte ring:
> And we knew that ere one dawn grew fair
> The fellow had to swing.

Passing B and C-yards Wilde would have stepped by the open grave being dug by the outer wall.

> Right in we went, with soul intent
> On Death and Dread and Doom:
> The hangman, with his little bag,
> Went shuffling through the gloom:
> And I trembled as I groped my way
> Into my numbered tomb.

The hangman, James Billington, was required by law to attend at the prison by 4 p.m. on the day before an execution, after which time he would not be allowed to leave until the execution had taken place. Executioners used this period to observe the prisoner, sometimes disguising themselves as a warder, to assess the prisoner's build and shape of neck. From this a calculation as to the length of drop needed would be made in order to judge the distance that the prisoner needed to fall through the trapdoor so as to cause his instant death: Chapter 4.

> That night the empty corridors
> Were full of forms of Fear,
> And up and down the iron town
> Stole feet we could not hear,
> And through the bars that hide the stars
> White faces seemed to peer.
>
> He lay as one who lies and dreams
> In a pleasant meadow-land,
> The watchers watched him as he slept,
> And could not understand
> How one could sleep so sweet a sleep
> With a hangman close at hand.

As noted in Chapter 4, the executioner was required to sleep in the prison on the night before an execution; latterly within a specially constructed Execution Centre where he may have slept immediately above the condemned man.

> But there is no sleep when men must weep
> Who never yet have wept:
> So we the fool, the fraud, the knave
> That endless vigil kept,
> And through each brain on hands of pain
> Another's terror crept.
>
> Alas! it is a fearful thing
> To feel another's guilt!
> For, right within, the sword of Sin
> Pierced to its poisoned hilt,
> And as molten lead were the tears we shed
> For the blood we had not spilt.
>
> The warders with their shoes of felt
> Crept by each padlocked door,
> And peeped and saw, with eyes of awe,
> Gray figures on the floor,
> And wondered why men knelt to pray
> Who never prayed before.

The warders wore felt footwear, ensuring that the required deadly silence was always maintained within the gaol. The 'padlocks' are poetic licence, seemingly to make the line scan: by then cell doors had been fitted with standard locks.

All through the night we knelt and prayed,
    Mad mourners of a corse!
The troubled plumes of midnight shook
    Like the plumes upon a hearse:
And as bitter wine upon a sponge
    Was the savour of Remorse.

The night before an execution the whole prison would be deadly silent; the prisoners held within it praying beyond all hope that the condemned man would be reprieved and live for at least another day, week or possibly have his sentence commuted to what was then penal servitude for life.

The gray cock crew, the red cock crew,
    But never came the day:
And crooked shapes of Terror crouched,
    In the corners where we lay:
And each evil sprite that walks by night
    Before us seemed to play.

They glided past, they glided fast,
    Like travellers through a mist:
They mocked the moon in a rigadoon
    Of delicate turn and twist,
And with formal pace and loathsome grace
    The phantoms kept their tryst.

With mop and mow, we saw them go,
    Slim shadows hand in hand:
About, about, in ghostly rout
    They trod a saraband:
And the damned grotesques made arabesques,
    Like the wind upon the sand!

With the pirouettes of marionettes,
    They tripped on pointed tread:
But with flutes of Fear they filled the ear,
    As their grisly masque they led,
And loud they sang, and long they sang,
    For they sang to wake the dead.

'Oho!' they cried, 'the world is wide,
    But fettered limbs go lame!
And once, or twice, to throw the dice
    Is a gentlemanly game,
But he does not win who plays with Sin
    In the secret House of Shame.'

No things of air these antics were,
    That frolicked with such glee:
To men whose lives were held in gyves,
    And whose feet might not go free,
Ah! wounds of Christ! they were living things,
    Most terrible to see.

'Gyves' is seemingly a reference to Skeffington's gyves, named after Sir William Skeffington, Lord Deputy of Ireland, who in the sixteenth century invented (or at least imported into Europe) a portable form of torture by physical incapacitation in which the body was forced by the device into 'impossible' positions – knowledge of which may have stemmed from Wilde's Irish background.

Around, around, they waltzed and wound;
    Some wheeled in smirking pairs;
With the mincing step of a demirep
    Some sidled up the stairs:
And with subtle sneer, and fawning leer,
    Each helped us at our prayers.

The morning wind began to moan,
    But still the night went on:
Through its giant loom the web of gloom
    Crept till each thread was spun:
And, as we prayed, we grew afraid
    Of the Justice of the Sun.

The moaning wind went wandering round
    The weeping prison wall:
Till like a wheel of turning steel
    We felt the minutes crawl:
O moaning wind! what had we done
    To have such a seneschal?

Again the 'weeping prison' wall is a reference to condensation: but also here an allusion to sorrow. As I have noted, this is based on fact.

At last I saw the shadowed bars,
Like a lattice wrought in lead,
Move right across the whitewashed wall
That faced my three-plank bed,
And I knew that somewhere in the world
God's dreadful dawn was red.

Wilde's cell was south-facing, with the prison wings and landings built on a perfect compass. In cell C.3.3 he would have watched the shadow of his window bars, created by the morning sun, move across its whitewashed inner walls, knowing that with every inch the prospect of a man's death came closer.

At six o'clock we cleaned our cells,
At seven all was still,
But the sough and swing of a mighty wing
The prison seemed to fill,
For the Lord of Death with icy breath
Had entered in to kill.

He did not pass in purple pomp,
Nor ride a moon-white steed.
Three yards of cord and a sliding board
Are all the gallows' need:
So with rope of shame the Herald came
To do the secret deed.

We were as men who through a fen
Of filthy darkness grope:
We did not dare to breathe a prayer,
Or to give our anguish scope:
Something was dead in each of us,
And what was dead was Hope.

For Man's grim Justice goes its way
And will not swerve aside:
It slays the weak, it slays the strong,
It has a deadly stride:
With iron heel it slays the strong
The monstrous parricide!

We waited for the stroke of eight:
Each tongue was thick with thirst:
For the stroke of eight is the stroke of Fate
That makes a man accursed,
And Fate will use a running noose
For the best man and the worst.

At the time, executions outside London normally took place on the stroke of eight; London prisons nine. The last few verses above again emphasise the clinical nature of punishment and that it is 'a great leveller' – even if individuals react to it differently. It is ironic that Wilde himself probably received special treatment: Chapter 5.

We had no other thing to do,
Save to wait for the sign to come:
So, like things of stone in a valley lone,
Quiet we sat and dumb:
But each man's heart beat thick and quick,
Like a madman on a drum!

With sudden shock the prison-clock
Smote on the shivering air,
And from all the gaol rose up a wail
Of impotent despair,
Like the sound the frightened marshes hear
From some leper in his lair.

And as one sees most fearful things
In the crystal of a dream,
We saw the greasy hempen rope
Hooked to the blackened beam,
And heard the prayer the hangman's snare
Strangled into a scream.

As already noted, the hangman's rope was made of hemp and the gallows beam was painted black. When eight o'clock arrived all the prisoners within the gaol fell deadly silent; if Wooldridge had screamed as he fell through the trapdoor, during that last second of his life, this would have echoed through the prison and the prisoners would most likely have heard him.

And all the woe that moved him so
That he gave that bitter cry,
And the wild regrets, and the bloody sweats,
None knew so well as I:
For he who lives more lives than one
More deaths than one must die.

IV

There is no chapel on the day
On which they hang a man:
The Chaplain's heart is far too sick,
Or his face is far too wan,
Or there is that written in his eyes
Which none should look upon.

So they kept us close till nigh on noon,
And then they rang the bell,
And the warders with their jingling keys
Opened each listening cell,
And down the iron stair we tramped,
Each from his separate Hell.

On the day of an execution the whole prison would be 'locked down' until the process was complete. After the execution the prisoner would be left to hang for one hour, supposedly to allow the soul time to leave the body. Then the medical officer would pronounce death and the body would be placed in the prison morgue. An inquest would be held at Reading in the magistrates' room – to confirm the death as lawful and the body would be buried in the pre-dug grave within the prison as prescribed by law.

Out into God's sweet air we went,
But not in wonted way,
For this man's face was white with fear,
And that man's face was gray,
And I never saw sad men who looked
So wistfully at the day.

I never saw sad men who looked
With such a wistful eye
Upon that little tent of blue
We prisoners called the sky,
And at every happy cloud that passed
In such strange freedom by.

But there were those amongst us all
Who walked with downcast head,
And knew that, had each got his due,
They should have died instead:
He had but killed a thing that lived,
Whilst they had killed the dead.

For he who sins a second time
Wakes a dead soul to pain,
And draws it from its spotted shroud
And makes it bleed again,
And makes it bleed great gouts of blood,
And makes it bleed in vain!

Like ape or clown, in monstrous garb
With crooked arrows starred,
Silently we went round and round
The slippery asphalte yard;
Silently we went round and round,
And no man spoke a word.

Wilde was later to complain bitterly about the prison uniform that convicted prisoners had to wear; 'crooked arrows' is a reference to the black arrows stamped upon the uniform, indicating Crown property. There are rare real life instances of people being sentenced to death for a second time, having been reprieved following their first murder and death sentence who went on to kill again, or to 'sin a second time'.

Silently we went round and round,
And through each hollow mind
The Memory of dreadful things
Rushed like a dreadful wind,
And Horror stalked before each man,
And Terror crept behind.

The warders strutted up and down,
And watched their herd of brutes,
Their uniforms were spick and span,
And they wore their Sunday suits,
But we knew the work they had been at,
By the quicklime on their boots.

For where a grave had opened wide,
There was no grave at all:
Only a stretch of mud and sand
By the hideous prison-wall,
And a little heap of burning lime,
That the man should have his pall.

Lime (or 'a sheet of flame') was an acid in powder form that was used until the turn of that century to speed up the decaying process; it would have been shovelled into the grave around the coffin. The body would have been stripped of clothes, wrapped in a shroud and laid in a coffin made of elm and perforated with holes.

For he has a pall, this wretched man,
  Such as few men can claim:
Deep down below a prison-yard,
  Naked, for greater shame,
He lies, with fetters on each foot,
  Wrapt in a sheet of flame!

And all the while the burning lime
  Eats flesh and bone away,
It eats the brittle bones by night,
  And the soft flesh by day,
It eats the flesh and bone by turns,
  But it eats the heart alway.

For three long years they will not sow
  Or root or seedling there:
For three long years the unblessed spot
  Will sterile be and bare,
And look upon the wondering sky
  With unreproachful stare.

Once lime was used, nothing grew above the space occupied by the grave for three years. Nor would anything have been planted there.

They think a murderer's heart would taint
  Each simple seed they sow.
It is not true! God's kindly earth
  Is kindlier than men know,
And the red rose would but glow more red,
  The white rose whiter blow.

Out of his mouth a red, red rose!
  Out of his heart a white!
For who can say by what strange way,
  Christ brings His will to light,
Since the barren staff the pilgrim bore
  Bloomed in the great Pope's sight?

But neither milk-white rose nor red
  May bloom in prison air;
The shard, the pebble, and the flint,
  Are what they give us there:
For flowers have been known to heal
  A common man's despair.

So never will wine-red rose or white,
  Petal by petal, fall
On that stretch of mud and sand that lies
  By the hideous prison-wall,
To tell the men who tramp the yard
  That God's Son died for all.

Yet though the hideous prison-wall
  Still hems him round and round,
And a spirit may not walk by night
  That is with fetters bound,
And a spirit may but weep that lies
  In such unholy ground,

The prison burial site was always thought to be by the south-east corner of the prison wall. However, during the author's research when inspecting documents in storage at the local records office, the grave register and grave plan came to light in the back of the Execution Log referred to in Chapter 4. *This plan indicates that the graves were in fact placed by the east-facing 'hideous prison-wall' at the end of C-wing.*

He is at peace this wretched man
  At peace, or will be soon:
There is no thing to make him mad,
  Nor does Terror walk at noon,
For the lampless Earth in which he lies
  Has neither Sun nor Moon.

They hanged him as a beast is hanged:
  They did not even toll
A requiem that might have brought
  Rest to his startled soul,
But hurriedly they took him out,
  And hid him in a hole.

The warders stripped him of his clothes,
  And gave him to the flies:
They mocked the swollen purple throat,
  And the stark and staring eyes:
And with laughter loud they heaped the shroud
  In which the convict lies.

As the final indignity and as part of the overall execution ritual, the bodies of felons executed after 1834 became the property of the Crown. They were placed in unconsecrated ground without any funeral service as such and with no cross to mark the grave, just a mound of earth. As already noted, according to the Execution Log Wooldridge's neck was stretched eleven inches and it appears that when the warders were burying him they were heard laughing at his swollen neck and staring eyes. In the 1980s many bodies so buried were removed from within prisons across Britain and reburied in consecrated ground. At Reading, however, none have been removed: the remains of all the eleven people executed after 1844 are there to this day, including those of Thomas Wooldridge. The author has now 'marked' the graves.

The Chaplain would not kneel to pray
By his dishonoured grave:
Nor mark it with that blessed Cross
That Christ for sinners gave,
Because the man was one of those
Whom Christ came down to save.

Yet all is well; he has but passed
To Life's appointed bourne:
And alien tears will fill for him
Pity's long-broken urn,
For his mourners be outcast men,
And outcasts always mourn.

V

I know not whether Laws be right,
Or whether Laws be wrong;
All that we know who lie in gaol
Is that the wall is strong;
And that each day is like a year,
A year whose days are long.

But this I know, that every Law
That men have made for Man,
Since first Man took His brother' life,
And the sad world began,
But straws the wheat and saves the chaff
With a most evil fan.

This too I know and wise it were
If each could know the same
That every prison that men build
Is built with bricks of shame,
And bound with bars lest Christ should see
How men their brothers maim.

Again, the first of the three verses above is one of the most quoted and for some people telling. In 1987, Wilde's metaphor 'bricks of shame' was adopted as the title of a book by penal reformer and former director of the National Association for the Care and Resettlement of Offenders (Nacro), Baroness Vivienne Stern. The allusion to imprisonment as a thing that 'straws the wheat and saves the chaff' has proved to be particularly forceful as a touchstone for reformers – as have many of the verses in Part V of the ballad. It is interesting that Wooldridge's mourners 'be outcast men'. Peter Stanford chose The Outcasts' Outcast *as the title of his biography of the late Lord Longford, one of the most idiosyncratic of penal reformers and thus himself 'an outcast', often derided for his support and associations with some of the most serious offenders, including killers. Earlier in the ballad Wilde uses the phrase 'two outcast men we were' to refer to Wooldridge and himself as if to emphasise some kind of bond between offenders.*

With bars they blur the gracious moon,
And blind the goodly sun:
And they do well to hide their Hell,
For in it things are done
That Son of things nor son of Man
Ever should look upon!

The vilest deeds like poison weeds
Bloom well in prison-air:
It is only what is good in Man
That wastes and withers there:
Pale Anguish keeps the heavy gate,
And the warder is Despair.

For they starve the little frightened child
Till it weeps both night and day:
And they scourge the weak, and flog the fool,
And gibe the old and gray,
And some grow mad, and all grow bad,
And none a word may say.

Wilde may be making a reference to two children serving sentences at Reading while he was there and the flogging of prisoner A.2.1 (a man called Prince whom he later wrote about to the newspapers: see Chapter 3) who appeared mentally unstable. Wilde wrote two letters to the press complaining of the harsh treatment afforded to children and mentally impaired people.

> Each narrow cell in which we dwell
> Is a foul and dark latrine,
> And the fetid breath of living Death
> Chokes up each grated screen,
> And all, but Lust, is turned to dust
> In Humanity's machine.

Grated screens, two in each cell, supplied the prison's heating and ventilation. In one remarkable letter, Wilde was jubilant, almost like a schoolboy responding to a challenge, about having worked the word 'latrine' into the ballad, saying that it looked 'beautiful'.

> The brackish water that we drink
> Creeps with a loathsome slime,
> And the bitter bread they weigh in scales
> Is full of chalk and lime,
> And Sleep will not lie down, but walks
> Wild-eyed, and cries to Time.
>
> But though lean Hunger and green Thirst
> Like asp with adder fight,
> We have little care of prison fare,
> For what chills and kills outright
> Is that every stone one lifts by day
> Becomes one's heart by night.
>
> With midnight always in one's heart,
> And twilight in one's cell,
> We turn the crank, or tear the rope,
> Each in his separate Hell,
> And the silence is more awful far
> Than the sound of a brazen bell.

The prison regime was governed by the toll of the prison bell; staff would wait for the bell before they commenced their daily tasks. The original bell from this time is today on display in the Vocational Training Centre (VTC) within the prison. Interestingly, later in the ballad, Wilde notes that no bell was tolled for prisoners who had been executed. It is a disappointment that many other fixtures and fittings from this time have disappeared although the original centre clock remains.

> And never a human voice comes near
> To speak a gentle word:
> And the eye that watches through the door
> Is pitiless and hard:
> And by all forgot, we rot and rot,
> With soul and body marred.
>
> And thus we rust Life's iron chain
> Degraded and alone:
> And some men curse, and some men weep,
> And some men make no moan:
> But God' eternal Laws are kind
> And break the heart of stone.
>
> And every human heart that breaks,
> In prison-cell or yard,
> Is as that broken box that gave
> Its treasure to the Lord,
> And filled the unclean leper's house
> With the scent of costliest nard.
>
> Ah! happy they whose hearts can break
> And peace of pardon win!
> How else may man make straight his plan
> And cleanse his soul from Sin?
> How else but through a broken heart
> May Lord Christ enter in?
>
> And he of the swollen purple throat,
> And the stark and staring eyes,
> Waits for the holy hands that took
> The Thief to Paradise;
> And a broken and a contrite heart
> The Lord will not despise.
>
> The man in red who reads the Law
> Gave him three weeks of life,
> Three little weeks in which to heal
> His soul of his soul's strife,
> And cleanse from every blot of blood
> The hand that held the knife.

Mr Justice Hawkins, the trial judge at Berkshire Assizes who sentenced Wooldridge, wore the standard red robe of a High Court Judge or 'Red Judge': the normal rank of a judge of assize and still so today in terms of those who sit in the Crown Court to deal with the most serious cases.

And with tears of blood he cleansed the hand,
　　The hand that held the steel:
For only blood can wipe out blood,
　　And only tears can heal:
And the crimson stain that was of Cain
　　Became Christ's snow-white seal.

VI

In Reading gaol by Reading town
　　There is a pit of shame,
And in it lies a wretched man
　　Eaten by teeth of flame,
In a burning winding-sheet he lies,
　　And his grave has got no name.

Wilde would have appreciated the fact that today there is a small brass plaque on the prison wall at every grave listed in the records and at sites shown on old plans, bearing the name of the prisoner and the date of his execution.

And there, till Christ call forth the dead,
　　In silence let him lie:
No need to waste the foolish tear,
　　Or heave the windy sigh:
The man had killed the thing he loved,
　　And so he had to die.

And all men kill the thing they love,
　　By all let this be heard,
Some do it with a bitter look,
　　Some with a flattering word,
The coward does it with a kiss,
　　The brave man with a sword!

EARLY STIRRINGS IN A LONG CAMPAIGN

In many ways, the ballad leaves the reader feeling despondent—he or she shares Wooldridge's fate, 'wistfulness' and sense of doom. It is only possible to imagine, through its words, how Wilde himself felt as he observed the hapless Wooldridge, who in a fit of anger had committed the ultimate crime for which he had to pay the ultimate penalty. He had committed what the French call a *crime passionnel* or 'crime of passion',[5] a defence or excuse that has never been tolerated in English law. The nearest equivalent, diminished responsibility, might well have been available to Wooldridge in modern times to reduce the charge that he faced from murder to manslaughter. But that defence was not introduced until 1957 after the outcry that followed the execution of Ruth Ellis, the last woman to hang in Britain.

Whether Oscar Wilde anticipated that his ballad would not only keep alive the memory of 'C.T.W' but would also become a rallying point for penal reformers everywhere—and in the process place Reading Gaol firmly on the map as a symbol of the ills of capital punishment and incarceration—I sometimes wonder. Many people already found capital punishment distasteful in the nineteenth century, but it was not particularly fashionable to oppose it (as if that would have bothered Wilde); but over the years the ballad gave encouragement and sustenance to many people during the long and arduous campaign for the abolition of the death penalty and a more decent system. Capital punishment itself was last used in Britain in 1964. It was suspended in 1965 and abolished altogether for murder in 1969. Some residual and by then largely theoretical possibilities for its use or revival were only dispensed with so far as peacetime is concerned when the United Kingdom signed the Sixth Protocol to the European Convention On Human Rights in 1999. This was ratified by Parliament in 2001 and later extended to war time situations by eventual implementation of Protocol 13 of the Convention in 2004. But the practice remains rife worldwide, including in advanced nations like the United States of America, China, Saudi Arabia and also in Iraq. So there is still much work for Wilde and Wooldridge to do.

---

[5] It is interesting to ponder what effect a more hard edged murder might have had on Wilde and the course of penal history.

Architectural gem: Reading Gaol c.1844. From *Prison Discipline*.

Skylights in the Centre roof.

View along A.3 landing.

E-wing (the former women's wing) with Huntley & Palmers (top right) next door.

Typical view looking upwards from Level 1, here on A-wing.

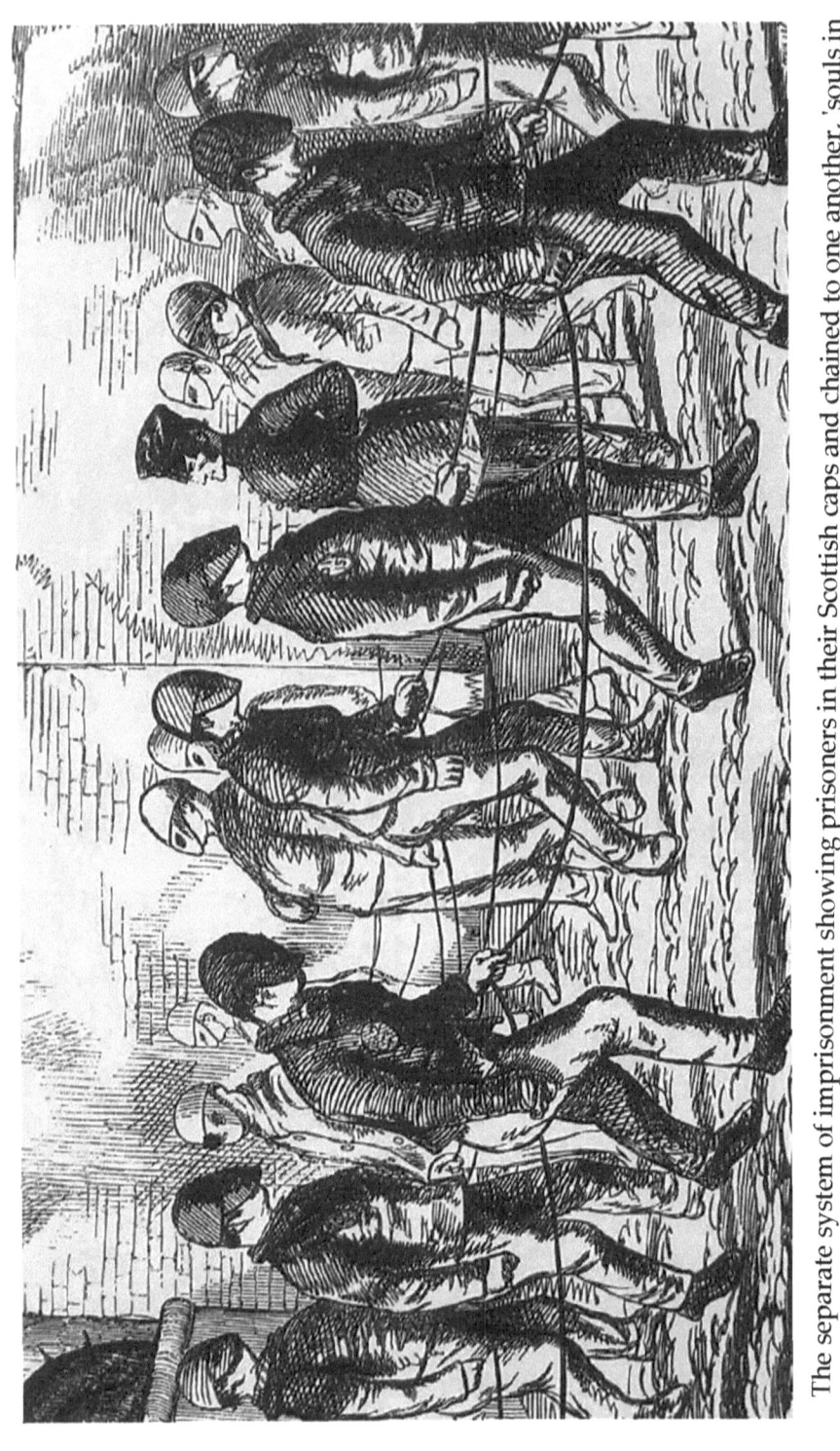

The separate system of imprisonment showing prisoners in their Scottish caps and chained to one another, 'souls in pain' within their various 'rings' - walking in complete silence. Hence the need for prisoners to learn the 'ventriloquist's art' of verbal concealment. From an old print (c.1860).

The top landing today. C-wing, showing safety net.

Top bags for top people at knock down prices!: *Chapter 11*

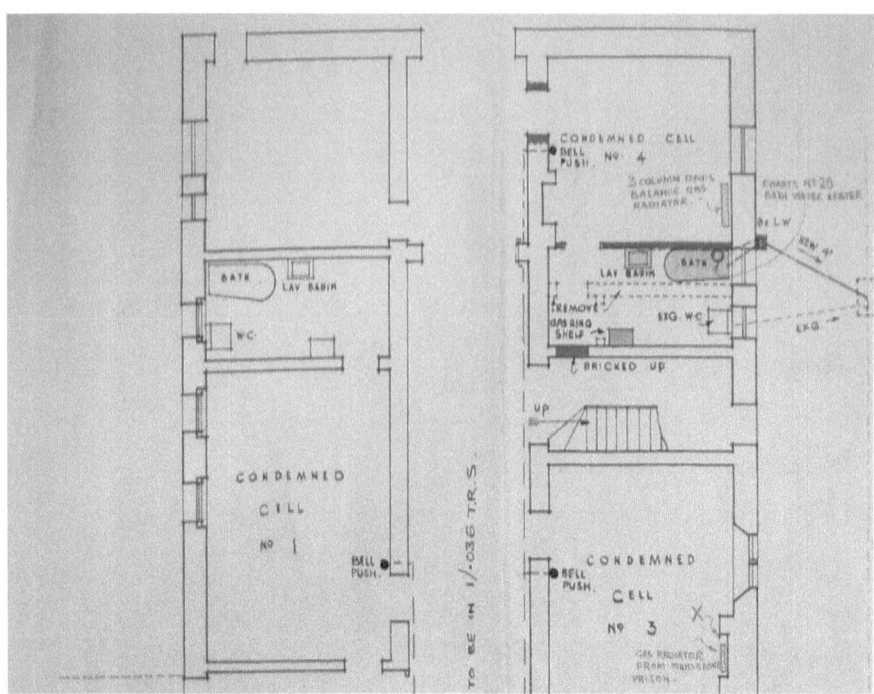

Plans of the Execution Centre (c.1900) (above) and Reading Gaol (c.1850) (below). Note the 'cartwheel' with its inner, triangular exercise segments. A guard would stand on a raised platform in the middle of the centre circle.

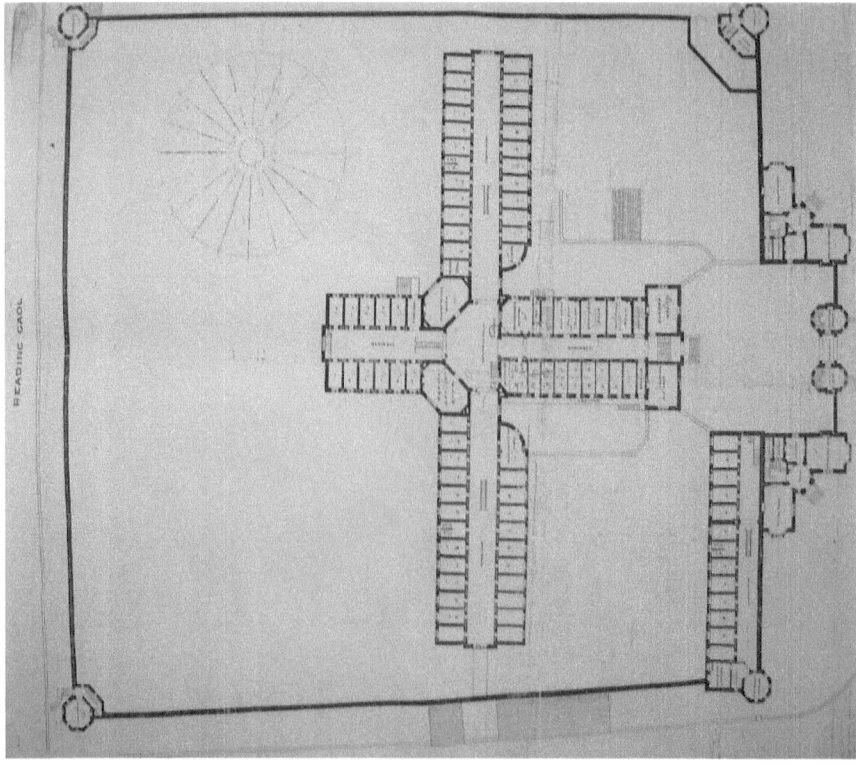

The front gate from the outside and inside, respectively.

Into the abyss. Looking down from Level 3 into the basement during conversion work. Late-1960s

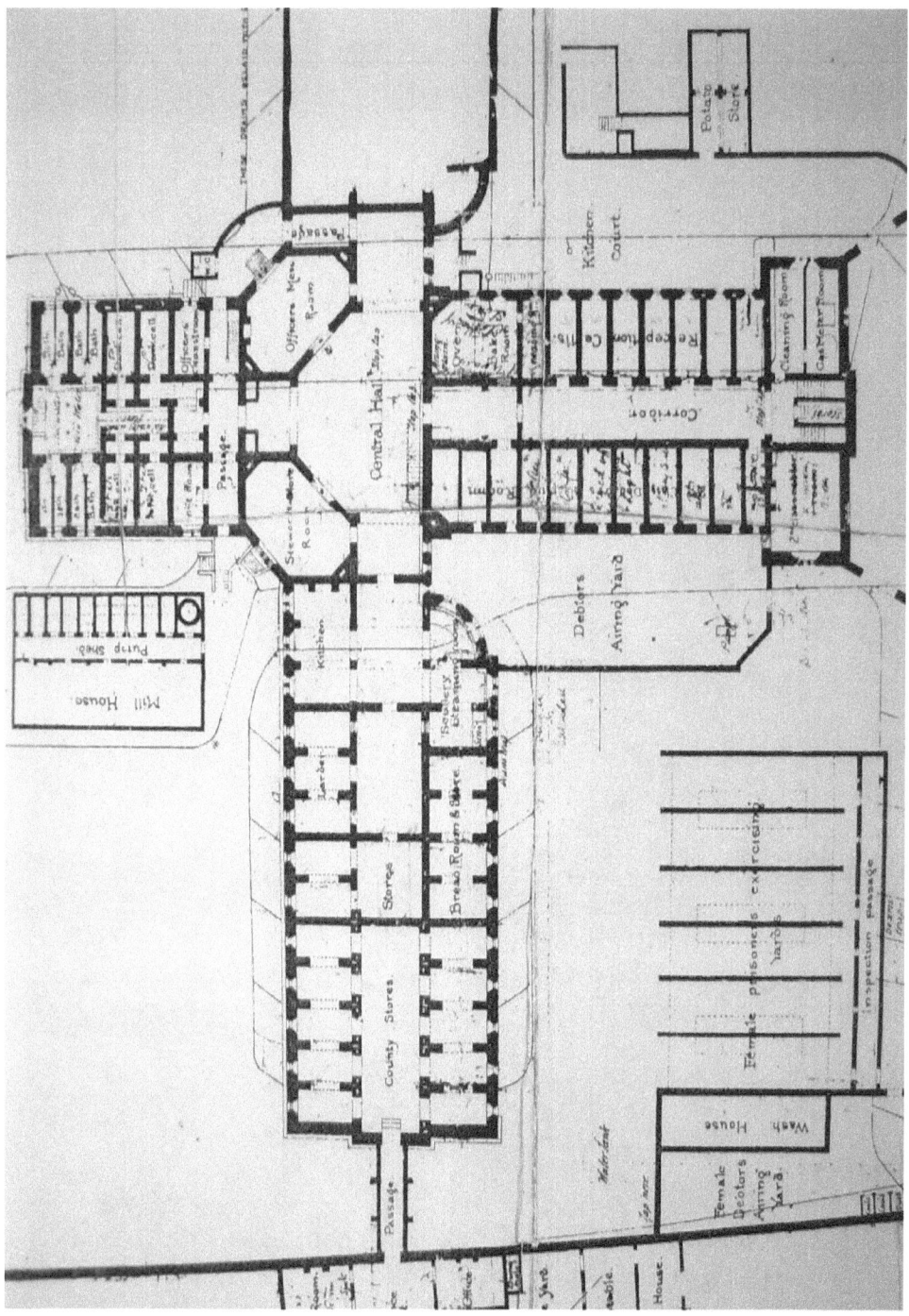

Plan of Reading Gaol in 1865 when part of the prison was used as a Militia Store with a concealed passageway to the outside. Contrast the women's exercise yard with the men's cartwheel on page 122 and note the Mill House/Pump Shed that supplied the whole prison with fresh water and was used for hard labour. The Potato Store (bottom right) became the Photographic House and Execution Shed.

C.3.3 Oscar Wilde's cell today and the earliest known photograph of a comparable cell at Reading inset ('a foul and dark latrine': see *Chapter 6*). Note the plaque on the wall placed there by the author. C.3.3 has now become C.2.3 (see page 150).

CHAPTER 7

The Easter Rising and Internment

> A prison wall was round us both,
> Two outcast men we were:
> The world had thrust us from its heart,
> And God from out His care:
> And the iron gin that waits for Sin
> Had caught us in its snare.
> (*The Ballad of Reading Gaol*, Oscar Wilde)

From 1900 up to World War I Reading Gaol underwent a massive upgrade and refurbishment. This was to try and incorporate all the recommendations of the Prison Act 1898, emanating from the Gladstone Report of 1895. This report sought to change the whole ethos of prison culture and life. There was a move from a culture of punishment and deterrence to a more liberal regime of deterrence and reformation. The main focus of the Gladstone Report was to abolish unproductive hard labour (the treadmill, crank etc.) and to increase the scope of education within prisons. Two members of the committee who contributed to the report were Sir Evelyn Ruggles-Brise and R. B. Haldane, both of whom had been instrumental in supporting Oscar Wilde as noted in *Chapter 5*. Wilde' was a lasting legacy for the prison system: his letters of complaint to the press about the harshness of the system had not gone unnoticed and, coupled with the influence of his friends in the Prison Commission, the events of that time were instrumental in bringing about change and a more humane system.

Changes at Reading Gaol

At Reading the changes involved unprecedented investment. In 1900-1901 a new and enlarged gatehouse was built to accommodate larger vehicles and carriages (or transports) carrying prisoners into and out of the prison. On C2 landing a new purpose-built classroom was constructed behind the deputy governor's office, in an effort to provide a structured educational curriculum far removed from the chaplain-dominated format that had gone before. New workshops were introduced within the prison grounds; a wire workshop was placed next to the female wing, for the use of women only and another was placed on B- and C-yard adjacent to C-wing for the men. These were designed, pursuant to the Prison Act of 1898, to allow the prisoners to associate with each other while they were working during labour and so as to let them work together on mass production lines. This was a constructive move, with the twin aims of benefitting the prison and teaching prisoners a trade that they might follow on release, so as to divert them away from crime.

This form of work, dubbed 'association labour', was classed as a privilege that could be withdrawn as a form of punishment by the governor for breaches of the Prison Rules, with the added effect that offenders would then remain locked up in their own cell for the whole day. Finally, a new purpose-built execution centre was built, with four condemned cells adjacent to it, as described in *Chapter 4*, all state of the art and conforming to the latest Prison Commission design (see *Appendix 5*).

General relaxation of the prison regime

More generally, life for the prisoners became more relaxed; they were no longer obliged to wear the Scottish cap and they were allowed to mix together and speak with one another for the first time in the history of the gaol. The days of the hated separate system were over. The Prison Commission was trying to make the experience of prison less austere and forbidding, with more emphasis on the reformation and resettlement of prisoners after their release, much in line with the principles and emphasis of the modern-day approach of HM Prison Service, of which more in *Chapter 13*.

A notable incident

But all was not sweetness and light. Around the same time, one disturbing incident involving an ex-prisoner took place which made it into the pages of the national press, including *The Times*. One of the main fears of prison staff, myself included, who work with violent and disturbed individuals is that it is impossible to know what prisoners are thinking, or what exactly they might be planning to do when they get out. At times they regard prison officers as hate figures, purely because they are people in authority, the ones with the keys and power over the minutiae of prisoners' day-to-day lives. Never have the risks that flow from this been more evident than in what took place one warm Sunday evening on 17 May 1908.

The matron of Reading Gaol, Miss Rogerson and a friend, Mrs Cushon, were leaving St. James's Roman Catholic Church next door to the prison. As the pair were entering the walkway to the prison an ex-prisoner, Mabel Truelove, who had been in Reading Gaol on numerous occasions approached the two women and threw a cup of acid over them inflicting terrible injuries. Miss Rogerson lost one eye and received severe burns down one side of her face. Her friend received minor burns to her face and arm, whilst the attacker, who had administered the assault within close range of her intended victim, herself received serious acid burns to her eyes and face:

Truelove appeared in the dock at Reading being carried by two policemen, and presented a pitiful spectacle, her face being blurred and scarred from the effects of the acid.

Truelove had asked the court that she be transferred to another gaol, and during the trial it transpired that the matron had previously had numerous altercations with this prisoner such that Truelove had vowed to get her revenge when last released from Reading. So indeed she did.

The coronation of King George V

Two years after this event, when King George V came to the throne on 4 June 1910 and by way of a 'general amnesty' all sentenced prisoners incarcerated at Reading were granted special remission allowing 70 male and four female prisoners to be released forthwith.

The last days of women prisoners at Reading

By the early years of the twentieth century the number of women prisoners being sent to Reading had dwindled until an average of just four were being held there at any one time. The Prison Commission considered that the closing of E-wing (that for women) made economic sense and so in 1915 Reading ceased to hold women prisoners at all.

The last woman held at Reading to be charged with a capital offence was a domestic servant named Winifred Amy Franks (aged 26). She had murdered her newborn son by throwing his naked body out of the window of a train whilst they were travelling from Wokingham to Reading on the night of 29 May 1913. Evidence from the prison's medical officer, Dr Freeman, was instrumental in her being found guilty but insane. Later that year she was ordered to be detained indefinitely at His Majesty's pleasure, in effect a life sentence by another name. Coincidentally, 1913 saw the very last execution at Reading: that of Eric James Sedgwick on February 4 (see *Chapter 4*).

PLACE OF INTERNMENT

During the summer of 1914, with World War I and hostilities with Germany looming for Britain and its allies, life at Reading Goal was slowly winding down and as with many aspects of life the prison was facing a bleak and uncertain future. The prison population was at an all time low and across the whole prison estate of England and Wales the population was dwindling by the day, possibly due to the fact that the reforms under the Prison Act 1898 were starting to bite or maybe it was just due to a perception of impending doom. But at Reading all of this was to alter following events across the Irish Sea.

It was a time when there was a generally increasing fear of foreigners and/or 'strangers', especially those of German or Russian origin, and the Government had deemed it necessary to bring in draconian measures to protect the nation from aliens and other potential threats under the Defence of the Realm Act 1914 (known as DORA). DORA conferred wide-ranging powers, including with regard to the requisitioning of buildings, land or property deemed necessary for the war effort. The British public were affected by many other such rules: for example, the flying of kites or lighting of bonfires was prohibited as it was feared these could be used by agents on the ground to signal to foreign Zeppelins. Similarly, there were prohibitions on the sale or purchase of binoculars, the feeding of wild animals, and discussion of any form of military or naval matters and similar measures.

At this sensitive time the authorities felt that there was a need to control all foreign nationals and anybody with possible anti-British sympathies, so that internment camps were established using existing prisons such as Reading, Brixton and various other premises up and down the country such as Alexandra Palace in London. In total over 30,000 'enemy aliens' within Britain during World War I were detained under DORA and in 1916 Reading was officially reclassified as HM Place of Internment, Reading.

Within a few weeks 68 internees had been received. Problems soon arose in the gaol as a result of having such a multi-cultural mix all housed together there; and language and cultural difficulties rapidly became apparent due to the different types of internee held. Prison documents from that time list details of internees who were classified as: enemy aliens; deportees; prisoners of war; or spies. Because they were internees rather than convicted prisoners, the regime was rather more relaxed and the inmates were allowed certain concessions, such as more time out of their cells. In correspondence with the Prison Commission the governor indicated that, within the dietary allowances for the internees, there was a quota of three puddings a week, and for Christmas 1917 the internees were permitted to purchase additional rations at their own cost: ham and sausage were omitted and wine not allowed, but beer was.

During these war years the staff had to be on their guard at all times, looking and listening for any covert or subversive actions by the prisoners. All mail was strictly censored and all visitors had to be vetted before being allowed entry into the gaol. Prison documents throw an interesting light on the problems that the governor was faced with. A letter dated 1 January 1918 from Captain Morgan (the governor) to the Prison Commissioners reveals that an internee named F. Schachere had been found in possession of a blank piece of paper, but when the warder held it up to the light he noticed 'invisible writing'. Although the paper had appeared blank it was in fact a coded letter addressed to someone outside. Scotland Yard were informed immediately and the letter sent to them.

The author cannot find any direct evidence, but it is likely that at least one of the warders would have been working for the intelligence services whilst employed at Reading—possibly even planted there to oversee the internees. This was hinted at in one letter dated 11 March 1918:

Board of Invention and Research
Victory House
Cockspur Street
SW
11 - 3 - 18

Sir

I am directed by the Board of Invention and Research to thank you for your letter of the 2nd 246/1783CF, transmitting description of Anti-Submarine proposals put forward by C. Slingeneyer in Reading P of I.

In reply, I am to state that the proposals in question have now been carefully examined and are not found to add to the information already in the possession of the Board, who would be glad if you would acquaint the inventor accordingly, at the same time, should you see no objection, conveying the thanks of the Board for bringing his proposals to notice.

I am, Sir, Your obedient servant

D Enington
Secretary

This letter has date stamps from Whitehall and the Prison Commission, indicating that it was seen by various sections within Government before arriving on the governor's desk four days later on March 15.

THE EASTER RISING

The peace and tranquillity of the goal were rudely interrupted with the arrival on 11 July 1916 of a group of 37 Irish internees, most of whom had taken part in the Easter Rising in Dublin in which a small band of republicans had seized Dublin's General Post Office and Dublin Castle. Doomed from the outset this now most famous of events in Irish history led to a wholesale rout by the British Army and the execution of the ringleaders by firing squad at Kilmainham Gaol, Dublin. Many other participants in this failed uprising and attempt to win independence from Britain were arrested and housed locally in prisons in Ireland. But there was also an overflow and maybe political reasons for bringing some prisoners to England.

At Reading, the internees were housed in the vacant female wing (E-wing) and such was the fear of unrest expected by the Prison Commissioners that the War Office supplied a contingent of soldiers to be attached to the prison. The detachment consisted of three non-commissioned officers and nine soldiers to form an armed sentry guard of the prison. The Visiting Committee had been of the opinion that in the interests of the safe custody of the aliens, an armed guard was appropriate. The guard remained until the end of 1917 when due to increasing losses on the war front the War Office put in a request to the Prison Commissioners that the guard supplied earlier in expectation of disturbances should now be discontinued. The commissioners advised the governor to try and elicit help from the local constabulary in a letter dated 22 December 1917.

The Irish prisoners were all held under section 14b of DORA; as they were classed as internees and not prisoners, they were allowed the same degree of flexibility as any other internees, but there were still restrictions on their mail and 'time out of cell'. All internees had to be in their cells by 8 p.m.

Some quite famous Irish figures were interned at Reading; and certain of them quickly made life unpleasant for the staff, as one Irish internee, Darrell Figgis, relates in his book *A Chronicle of Jails*, written in 1917, shortly after his release:

> The gaol is a handsome building, erected in red brick after the manner of an old castle, with battlements and towers ... we stood in a small cobbled yard. Behind us was the broad wall in which the double gates were set. Flanked either side by the Governor's and Steward's houses ... to the right a wall arose dividing us from the work yard ... on the left a high blind wall arose, pierced by a single door near the wall round the gaol. This was the female prison ... but for the time being our habitation ... Our first act was to elect Ceann-Phort ... to formulate our demands ... at once we took control of our affairs into our own hands ... any dealing of officials with us were with us as a whole and not as individuals.

Similar arrangements were in place at The Maze and other Northern Ireland prisons during The Troubles of the late 1970s-late 1990s with regard to both republican and loyalist internees or prisoners. The use of this type of collective made any disagreements or issues that the governor or prison officers had to raise very intimidating for the staff concerned. At once the Irish internees started to make demands, one of the first being an attempt to change the time the lights went out in the prison. Until then all internees had to be locked up by 8 p.m. with lights out by 9 p.m. The governor relented and allowed the Irish to have the lights to their cells left on until 10 p.m. (gas lights were used at this time and were controlled by staff from outside the cells). The next issue raised by the Irish was visiting arrangements: all internees at that time were allowed just one letter each month and one visit every three months. After much debate between the

Prison Commissioners and the governor it was conceded that they could have two letters each week and one visit per month.

A week after their arrival, trouble flared at another internment camp and a group of seven internees were sent from there to Reading. They initially had to be housed in the reception holding cells, as E-wing was already full. These latest internees associated and ate with everyone in E-wing going back to the holding cells during the evening. This situation was improved when a group of other internees were released on July 3, allowing all the Irish to be placed into E-wing.

According to Figgis (1917), one of the Irish internees — whose reputation must have preceded him — Patrick J. Daly, was approached by the governor and offered a deal from the Home Office that he could be liberated if he signed an undertaking to be of good behaviour. Daly replied that he was destined to be in prison a long time.

The Irish had many friends outside the gaol within the local community and beyond. All reading material was censored, but Figgis indicates what happened as soon as the identity of the censor became known:

> When a happy accident gave us the name of our censor; and it was deeply interesting to see his path among the classics of Irish literature ... In this we were assisted by our friends outside. Indeed, not the least value of our months of imprisonment was the revelation of friendship ... we had but to express a need and it was at once met by leagues and committees that had been gathered together, both at home and in England, to befriend and serve us. If our state was like that of an island, it was at least an island washed by a great sea of friendship.

This entry indicates that the censor was used as a channel for trafficking into the gaol. Whether he knew what was going on is impossible to say. But if someone knows where a book is being purchased, ordered or requested, they can get a friend to place substitute pages within the book as it makes its way to or from the bookstore. Or a book can have pages hollowed out and items secreted within it. Alternatively the censor can be terrorised into bringing items into the gaol and turning a blind eye. This is evident in another paragraph:

> The gifts cast up by the tides of that sea became embarrassing as Christmas approached ... we had altogether dispensed with the prison fare.

At 2.30 p.m. on 24 December 1916 the governor arrived in E-wing and informed the Irish that they were being repatriated. Figgis wrote: 'So at half-past four we passed out through the streets of Reading, singing our songs as we went'.

Life at the gaol must have seemed quiet after the Irish internees left but this was to be interrupted with the arrival of a new batch of internees on 25 May 1918, more militant and demanding than the first group had ever been. Many of these detainees, including W. T. Cosgrove (below), had been involved in a mutiny at Lewes Prison and had been transferred out of there.

PROMINENT IRISH INTERNEES

Five of the most prominent Irish internees are profiled below and a full list of Irish detainees held at Reading is given in the table that follows.

W T Cosgrave
William Cosgrave, affectionately known as 'W.T.', had been sentenced to death for his part in the Easter Rising. This was later commuted to penal servitude for life. He was a Sinn Fein councillor from 1909-1922 and became a Member of Parliament for Carlow-Kilkenny in 1918. In 1922 he became the first President of the Executive Council (Prime Minister of Ireland) remaining in office until 1932.

Arthur Griffith
Arthur Griffith was the founder of Sinn Fein (meaning in Irish 'We Ourselves') in 1905 and its first leader. In 1921 he was head of the treaty delegation at the Anglo-Irish Treaty talks in London led by Michael Collins. He became President of the Irish Free State in 1922 before his death of a brain haemorrhage.

Terence MacSwiney
MacSwiney was a teacher by profession. In 1913 he founded the Cork Brigade of the Irish Volunteers and became President of Sinn Fein in Cork. MacSwiney was interned at Reading on 11 July 1916 and was there at the time of a mass hunger strike instigated by the German internee, P. Meyer. MacSwiney was arrested in Cork in November 1917 and while imprisoned in the county gaol there for wearing an IRA uniform he began his first hunger strike, being released after three days. Elected as the Lord Mayor of Cork in 1919, he was again arrested in 1920 and sentenced to two years' imprisonment. He began another hunger strike and was transferred to Brixton Prison in London (as Reading had ceased to be a prison by this time) where he continued to refuse food for 74 days, before his death on 25 October 1920 — the longest hunger strike in Irish political history.

Laurence Ginnell
Also known as 'Larry', Ginnell graduated in law and became a Member of Parliament for North Westmeath and Sinn Fein's first MP in 1906. Prior to his own internment at Reading on 30 August 1918, as an MP he had visited all the Irish internees held in English gaols and was eventually banned by order of the Government, on suspicion of facilitating escape attempts.

Irish internees held at Reading Gaol (data taken from prison records)

Name	Date interned at Reading	Age	Occupation	Released
Michael Brennan	11 July 1916	31	Farmer	31 July 1916
Michael Joseph Brennan	11 July 1916	20	Farmer	24 Dec 1916
Albert W. W. Cotton	11 July 1916	25	Clerk	24 Dec 1916
Thomas Curtin	11 July 1916	32	Shopkeeper	24 Dec 1916
Patrick J. Daly	11 July 1916	45	Printer	24 Dec 1916
Cornelius Deere	11 July 1916	35	Grocer	31 July 1916
William J. Langley	11 July 1916	28	Book-Keeper	24 Dec 1916
Denis McCullough	11 July 1916	33	Musical instrument maker	2 Aug 1916
Terence MacSwiney	11 July 1916	37	Teacher	24 Dec 1916
George Nicholls	11 July 1916	30	Solicitor	24 Dec 1916
Jeremiah J O'Connell	11 July 1916	28	Instructor	24 Dec 1916
Patrick O'Malley	11 July 1916	39	Farmer	24 Dec 1916
Charles Shannon	11 July 1916	24	Clerk	
Joseph P Connolly	11 July 1916	31	House Furnisher	31 July 1916
Edward Dundon	11 July 1916	33	Doctor	2 Aug 1916
Pierce McCann	11 July 1916	34	Farmer	31 July 1916
John Milroy	11 July 1916	39	Confectioner	24 Dec 1916
Darrel Figgis	11 July 1916	54	Author	24 Dec 1916
Herbert M Pim	11 July 1916	33	Journalist	31 July 1916
Peter Sweeney	11 July 1916	45	Builder	24 Dec 1916
Arthur Griffith	11 July 1916	45	Journalist	24 Dec 1916
Walter L Cole	25 May 1918			8 March 1919
WT Cosgrave	25 May 1918	37	Insurance Clerk	6 March 1919
Richard Davis	25 May 1918	40	Clerk	8 March 1919
Frank Fahy	25 May 1918	39	Teacher	7 March 1919
Richard Hayes	25 May 1918	37	Medical Doctor	7 March 1919
John Hurley	25 May 1918	26	Printer	Transferred to Birmingham 27 Jan 1919
Dennis Daly	4 July 1918			8 March 1919
Paul Peter Galligan	6 July 1918	28	Farmer	8 March 1919
PC O'Mahony	12 July 1918	30	Organiser	9 March 1919
Thomas Walsh	12 July 1918	22	Merchant	9 March 1919
Frank McGinness	17 July 1918	51	Draper	7 March 1919
Joseph McDonagh	24 July 1918	35	Teacher	14 March 1919
Frank Thornton	25 July 1918	26	Insurance agent	9 March 1919
Laurence Ginnell	30 Aug 1918		Refused to give any information. Released 6 March 1919.	
Edward C Fleming	23 Sep 1918	25	Clerk	9 March 1919
Michael J Reynolds	28 Sept 1918	23	Clerk	9 March 1919
Patrick Cahill	2 Oct 1918	33	Cinema proprietor	7 March 1919

Whilst Ginnell was at Reading he refused to conform in any way. When he first arrived at the gaol he refused to give any details to the reception staff who were writing in the nominal register (detailing relevant information upon a person's entry into prison). Among prison documents is a letter from the governor to the Prison Commissioners dated 23 October 1918 that shows he was not popular: 'The man most offensive is L Ginnell ... he must either be taken seriously or ignored—I prefer the latter.'

Ginnell was released on 6 March 1919, immediately demanding an apology from the governor for his 'wanton imprisonment'.

Darrel Figgis

An Irish writer and independent politician, Figgis joined the Irish Volunteers in 1913. He was implicated in the Kilcoole gun-running by Irish Volunteers in 1914. He had travelled to Belgium with Robert Erskine Childers to receive guns which Roger Casement and others had purchased from the Germans. Although nothing could be proved at the time he was still implicated, interned and arrived at Reading on 11 July 1916. In his book, *A Chronicle of Jail* (1917) he goes into detail about his life inside the prison. Upon his release from Reading, Figgis was made Honorary Secretary of Sinn Fein, but was expelled from the party in 1922. His wife, Millie, committed suicide in 1924 after learning of his infidelity with a woman named Rita North. Rita died a year later and Figgis committed suicide in London during the same year.

ESCAPE

Apart from the lively activities among the Irish on E-wing, a quiet and relaxed atmosphere prevailed over the rest of the prison. However, on Saturday 3 November 1917 the calm was rudely interrupted: four prisoners escaped. This was to prove a most embarrassing incident for both the Government and the gaol. The internees involved were: two Germans, named Louis Cress (aged 22) and Burt Muller (20); an Austrian who was suspected of being a spy and when arrested had been found to be in possession of a firearm, Carl Jenlar (age unknown) and, last and most troublesome, a Spaniard named Carlos Kuhne de la Escosuras (30).

Together they had hatched a plan to escape one Saturday evening at about 7 p.m. when the night staff were starting and the day staff leaving. The prisoners had noticed that when the two groups of staff congregated there was much frivolity and banter between them, providing an opportunity for the prisoners to escape un-noticed. It seems that the four prisoners had been able to fabricate a key out of a wooden knife. In the investigation after the escape, it transpired that central to the plan was the German internee Meyer who may have been a locksmith by trade and was able to make that key.

Meyer had been arrested and interned at Reading on 12 July 1916 for being of German descent and he soon became a key player in many acts of indiscipline. According to a letter in the prison archives from the governor to the Prison Commissioners, 20 November 1917, Meyer had been the main instigator of a mass hunger strike that took place at the prison towards the end of 1916 with the prisoners demanding better facilities and more time out of their cells. Certainly, the governor was convinced that Meyer had played a leading role in the November 3 escape attempt. His letter stated:

> I am convinced in my mind from all the information I have obtained that he was the man who made the key with which the men opened the gates to the exercise yard ... His conduct is bad and today he has just completed 3 days No. 1 diet [punishment diet: bread and water] and 14 days No. 2 diet for refusing to obey orders and using filthy and grossly insubordinate language to a warder ... I would be grateful if he could be transferred to another prison or internment camp.

When the time was right, on the evening of November 3, the four prisoners used their homemade key to open the end gate of A-wing and slip out into the grounds of the prison. They made their way towards the south-west corner of the gaol wall and with ropes made from bedding they were able to secure a hold onto the top parapet of the wall and escape into the ruins of the old abbey next door. The four men passed the armed sentry guard that had been supplied by the War Office and disappeared into the night.

A massive manhunt ensued with all ports and constabularies being circulated with descriptions of the escapees. *The Times* carried the story on 5 November under the headline: 'Escape of Four War Prisoners'. Scotland Yard masterminded the manhunt but it took until the following Tuesday to track down the only prisoner to be recaptured: Carlos Kuhne de la Escosuras. He had made his way to London and entered the Spanish Embassy where he claimed Sanctuary. Carlos stayed in the embassy under virtual house arrest until 15 January 1918, when he either gave himself up or was forced out by the Embassy staff. Scotland Yard returned him to Reading on the same day and he stayed there until August 1, after which he was transferred to Brixton Prison.

The other prisoners were never caught. One of them, Louis Cress, who while he was incarcerated at Reading had shown very strong pro-German sympathies, turned up at the front gate of the prison nearly two months later, on the evening of December 23, dressed in a British Army uniform. He had enlisted into the army as a private of the 30th Battalion of the Middlesex Regiment and asked if he could return to collect some of the belongings he had left behind. The gatekeeper refused him entry and the next day the governor wrote to the Prison Commissioners informing them of the incident.

Surprisingly the escapees had committed no offence as such under existing legislation and could not be charged with any crime such as escaping from lawful custody. The next letter in the prison file is from the Secretary of State in Whitehall, dated 10 December 1917, indicating that the government had hastily passed an amendment to section 14b of DORA making it an offence to escape or to attempt to escape from a place of internment.

AN END TO HOSTILITIES AND REDUNDANCY

Once hostilities between Britain and Germany finally ceased on 11 November 1918, time at Reading Gaol must have again slowed and endless days of monotony and boredom must have set in for the remaining internees. Sharing a sense of isolation and an unknown future, they would have been anxiously wondering whether they were going to be deported, allowed to stay in Britain or, for some, exposed to the risk of being deported to a foreign land.

March 1919 saw the mass return of all internees to their homelands and with its dwindling number of occupants Reading once again faced an uncertain future for both the prison and its staff. By October there were just five internees remaining; and any new prisoners from the local courts were now being sent to Oxford Prison, 25 miles away.[1] The authorities decided that HM Place of Internment, Reading was to close and all staff were to be transferred to Chelmsford Prison. In January 1920, Reading assumed a completely new role: not as a gaol but as the county secure food store. According to *The Times* newspaper (8 January 1920), which solemnly detailed such matters, the prison now contained over 100 tonnes of tinned salmon.

---

[1] Now a hotel, shopping mall and leisure complex.

CHAPTER 8

Invisible Prisoners

> The Warders strutted up and down,
> And kept their herd of brutes
> Their uniforms were spick and span,
> And they wore their Sunday suits,
> But we knew the work they had been at,
> By the quicklime on their boots.
> *(The Ballad of Reading Gaol*, Oscar Wilde)

Over the next 20 years, the Reading Gaol buildings were used for a variety of purposes by successive governments, including for functions as diverse and seemingly inappropriate as a driving test centre (1936) and (in one of the workshops within the prison grounds) an army surplus clothing store (1925). Throughout this period (1920-1940) the main use of the prison was as a secure county food store, enabling the local council to hold large quantities of valuable produce safe and secure under lock and key!

In 1935, with World War II looming, the general tenor of life in Berkshire began to take an ominous turn and the prison was put to use by the War Department as an Army Recruiting Office. In 1937 the main governor's house, situated to the right of the gatehouse, became the headquarters for the ARP (air raid wardens)—two years before the actual outbreak of war.

By 1938 the four wings of the prison, housing all the cells, were still unused, although it had clearly lost none of its chilling atmosphere, as a visiting dignitary noted. Councillor T. S. W. Smart, on a tour of inspection of Reading Gaol in September of that year, noted his 'feeling of despondency as the big gates clanged behind us, and the echo of our footsteps reverberated through the gloomy halls and corridors'. He reported: 'It all has a ... forbidding appearance, and the gloom increased as one looked beyond the [barbed] wire to the murky base of the tower above.' Having completed his tour, which included inspection of such 'gruesome relics' as the condemned cell and the execution shed 'reminiscent of the Chamber of Horrors, the black oak beam to which the hangman would attach the execution rope, dismantled and covered with dust', he concluded that this was a building which had long outlived its purpose, even as a relic, and he recommended: 'The only practical thing seems to be to raze it to the ground, and utilise the site for a building more in keeping with our social needs'. Councillor Smart requested that the prison be handed over to the local council and used as an administrative centre for local government.

THE WAR YEARS

However, the following year more urgent priorities took over and shortly after the outbreak of World War II the prison was simply cleaned up and made ready for use as a place of internment again—although it was in the event never actually used for that purpose. Instead, in August 1940, a party of borstal boys who had survived the bombing of Portland Borstal in Dorset were transferred to Reading, the governor being Sir Almeric Rich. They remained there until October 10 when 29 of them were transferred back to Portland after the wing there had been repaired. Extracts from the governor's journals at the time capture the wartime flavour:

August 25th-	24 boys attended Church of England chapel, but those whose kit was too shabby were left in their cells. The behaviour was very good but I don't know whether going out is a good plan yet.
August 30th-	The pay not having arrived from Portland the acting steward went to borrow some money to pay the staff.
August 31st-	The relief night patrol did not arrive so Housemaster came in.
Sept 1st-	I took five leaders for a walk around the town.
Sept 4th-	A great shortage of soap for any purpose.
Sept 9th-	I dismissed staff because of an air-raid and myself and a Housemaster remained with the inmates.
Sept 10th-	Medical Officer dissatisfied with Officers' quarters, complains that they are untidy and unkept.
Sept 15th-	I took 30 lads to church at 11:00 and marched them back a much longer way round. The air-raid siren sounded whilst we were out but we came back gradually.
Sept 18th-	I had to check Officer Hilyard for cutting lads' hair too short.
Sept 21st-	Took 32 lads outside to play football on the recreation ground.
Sept 23rd-	3 lads placed on report for breaking their gas lights. Punishment of removing their mattress for 3 nights.
Sept 26th-	Clerical Officer Walker apprehended the absconder Furnace on leaving a bus in Broad Street. Gave chase and finally caught him.
Sept 29th-	In the afternoon I took 8 lads for a walk along the riverside and allowed the remainder to stay in bed.
October 10th-	29 inmates left by 2 buses and an escort of 5 officers for Sherwood. All handcuffed, Officers for transfer to Sherwood and Usk D.I. 6 lads on discharge left to clear up.

The prison closed a couple of weeks later and all remaining prisoners were released.

The Canadians: hidden prisoners

In 1943, at the request of the Royal Canadian Air Force (RCAF), it was agreed that men of that service sentenced to detention might serve their time in Canadian Army

Detention Barracks. It was explained that 'only personnel of the London headquarters of the RCAF (Royal Canadian Air force) would be involved' (memo from Wing Commander J. A. R. Mason to senior officer, CMHQ dated 23 March 1943). So part of Reading Gaol was then taken over by the military authorities and used by the RCAF as a military detention centre. Later, in another communication on 9 April 1945, the British Home Secretary informed the Canadian High Commissioner that Canada could have the whole of Reading Gaol for use as a detention barracks. Known during that period as No. 4 Canadian Military Detention Barracks, this was the only time that armed guards have ever been seen within the prison and on its landings. It was noted what a poor condition the gaol was in as it had not been used as a prison since 1919. There were no electric lights—just gas—and the sanitary arrangements consisted of 'slopping out' each morning; the Canadians, however, did their best to try and improve things for the short term.

The Canadians only used Reading for a year but in that short space of time they housed some interesting prisoners there.

The Galaher treason trial
In what the press dubbed 'the most sensational Canadian Army court case during the First and Second Great Wars', a 34-year-old Canadian private became the first Canadian serviceman ever to be charged with treason, which carried a maximum penalty of death. Private John Gordon Galaher was held in Reading Gaol, together with two other prisoners accused of similar charges, for several months after his arrest and the men were transported from there to Corunna Barracks, Farnborough daily throughout their trials, appearing in court handcuffed to the Canadian servicemen who were then staffing the establishment.

The trial, before a Canadian general Court-Martial sitting in camera, took place behind a thick veil of secrecy enforced by the military. Private Galaher had been taken prisoner-of-war by the Germans during the Dieppe raid on the French coast in 1942 and it was alleged that he had afterwards acted as an informer, passing on to his captors military secrets gleaned from other allied prisoners in the camp he was held in.

Throughout Galaher's high-profile, four-day hearing scores of newspapermen at Farnborough were barred from the trial room area, were refused details of the charge and could learn nothing from Canadian soldiers in the town, who were under strict orders to keep silent about the proceedings. 'From every military source in this headquarters town,' complained the press, 'there is a negative reply to questions about the trial.' Canadian Military Headquarters claimed that the reason for the security blackout was that the evidence would reveal 'highly secret methods used by military intelligence to pass information from prisoners of war to [the] authorities in England'. The authorities even went so far as to publicly deny the existence of three more Canadian soldiers in Reading Gaol awaiting trial.

The day after Galaher's trial concluded, Privates G. Hale and E. Martin were transported from Reading Gaol to Farnborough also to stand trial on treason charges. They were all found guilty and one month later were sentenced: Galaher to penal servitude for life, Hale to ten years in prison and Martin to 25 years' imprisonment.

The Headley rioters

In May 1945 the prison received 370 Canadian prisoners who were moved from Headley Detention Barracks in Hampshire after a riot there. During the VE celebrations on May 8-9 there had been large-scale rioting among Canadian servicemen at Headley. A substantial force of Canadian troops had to surround the barracks to prevent further trouble and many inmates were transferred to No. 4 Canadian Military Detention Barracks, Reading.

Subsequently 13 Canadian servicemen were charged at field-general Courts-Martial in connection with the riots. A press report of August 24 on the trial of Lieutenant G. E. Flaherty, charged with disorderly conduct, gives a flavour of the mayhem that had prevailed. It was alleged that Flaherty had:

> fired five rounds from his revolver into the officers' quarters, smashing windows and crockery. He also fired two rounds at electric lights in the provost orderly room, poured a pail of water and scattered books over the floor, and tossed a typewriter at a sergeant.

Flaherty, along with several others, was 'severely reprimanded' by the court.

The Aldershot 'glasshouse' rioters

On 4 and 5 July 1945 there were more riots amongst Canadian servicemen—this time in Aldershot. Hundreds of windows were broken in the shopping centre by men apparently impatient at delays in repatriating them. *The Maple Leaf* (the Canadian army newspaper) reported on August 23 that a Canadian Military Headquarters announcement had stated that sentences ranging from seven years' penal servitude to two years' imprisonment with hard labour had been imposed on three Canadian soldiers convicted by a general Court-Martial on charges arising out of these riots. With their usual secrecy, the Canadian authorities did not list the charges on which the soldiers had been convicted and a spokesman said there would be no further statement.

The last Canadian prisoner

The last and most infamous prisoner to be incarcerated in Reading by the Canadian military authorities arrived on 16 January 1946, to be held there for two weeks pending his transfer to Canada. Major-General Kurt Meyer SS had been sentenced to death by a military court for his part in the massacre of Canadian prisoners of war during the D-Day landings.

Meyer was a fanatical Nazi; he idolised Hitler and in 1933 he had joined Hitler's elite bodyguard (*Die Lebstandarte*). During the Normandy landings he had been in charge of the Hitler Youth Division (12th SS) which was responsible for murdering over 200 unarmed Canadian prisoners of war taken during the first couple of days of the landings. There was a public outcry, at the military trials that later followed, when French civilians related how these Hitler Youth soldiers would round up groups of POWs and murder them by firing squad, then mutilate the bodies and place dead soldiers propped up against signposts for all to see.

Meyer was captured by the American army in September 1944 and sent for trial charged with war crimes on 10 December 1945. He was found guilty and ordered to be executed by firing squad; this was later commuted to life imprisonment by General Chris Volkes of the Canadian Military in mid-January 1946—after which Meyer was sent to Reading Gaol. He was moved to Dorchester Prison in New Brunswick, Canada for five years before being transferred to a military prison in West Germany. He was finally released in 1954.

Overflow prison

On 19 August 1946, according to the prison records, Reading re-opened as an 'overflow prison', and W. G. Harding arrived to take up his post as governor. For the first couple of weeks, time was spent cleaning the prison and making all necessary arrangements for the arrival of the first group of 24 short term prisoners on September 24 from Birmingham Prison, to serve the remaining parts of their sentences. They worked in the grounds and gardens of the prison. In its new overflow role, Reading took people from all over the country, but this was not an ideal situation for the prisoners, their families or for the representatives of the various outside agencies who had to travel great distances to visit them. This situation could only be a stop gap and soon HM Prison Service was looking for ways to find a better role for Reading.

CHAPTER 9

A Pioneering Borstal Correctional Centre

> Each narrow cell in which we dwell
> Is a foul and dark latrine,
> And the fetid breath of living Death
> Chokes up each grated screen
> And all, but lust, is turned to dust
> In humanity's machine.
> (*The Ballad of Reading Gaol*, Oscar Wilde)

Towards the end of 1951, on December 10, Reading Gaol was reclassified yet again, and became a borstal correctional institution. Borstals had been in existence since their introduction in 1902, after the Gladstone Committee Report (1895) as championed by Sir Evelyn Ruggles-Brise, the sympathetic prison commissioner from Oscar Wilde's day. Named after the village of Borstal in Kent, England, where the first such establishment was conceived as an alternative to prison for young men and women aged 16 to 21, the whole ethos of the borstal system could in those days be summed up in three words: 'short, sharp, shock'. The idea was that a strict regime and a firm—even harsh—system of rules and discipline would shock young offenders (who became known as borstal boys and later borstal girls) and deter them from re-offending, while simultaneously training them for a productive working life upon release.

Reading's special role
Within the borstal system, Reading had a special role, as a correctional centre for young men. For a young offender to end up at Reading, he would first have been sent to a regular, training borstal where he would have received instruction in various types of work from gardening to manufacturing, depending on the particular institution. The period of training was indeterminate, anything from six months to two years in practice, and totally dependent upon how the individual behaved and conformed. Some borstal boys by their very nature rebelled against such strict, draconian regimes; others felt trapped and tried to abscond from work parties in the local community. When a boy had fallen into either of these categories he would be sent to Reading for a period of correctional training before being sent on to another borstal to complete his sentence.

Violence and abuse
Reading soon became synonymous with violence and brutality. Certain staff saw it as their duty to instil fear and intimidation into their young charges. From the

very moment a trainee entered Reading he would be subjected to verbal and physical abuse and intimidation by the staff. Almost every move he made was at the express orders of the prison staff; he had to march everywhere at the double, stand to attention, and so on. The place was run like an army camp and at 6 a.m. every morning the young men would be put through a rigorous physical routine in the gymnasium.

When I first joined HM Prison Service and came to Reading in 1988 I met a number of staff who had worked at the prison during those days. They could remember the severe regime and the many ways in which staff intimidated the trainees, particularly new ones. I was told, for example, about the 'procedures' for new trainees just arrived at the centre. Upon entering the reception area, a trainee would be instructed by a prison officer to stand, to attention, on a set of footprints painted on the floor. He would then be ignored for about an hour before another officer came along and shouted at him for standing in the wrong place. The trainee would be moved to another set of painted footprints, five feet away and told to await instructions. Then the first officer he had seen would come along and hit him from behind because he had moved from the spot where he had first been instructed to wait. The young lad would pick himself off the floor and again be subjected to abuse and intimidation.

The next 'game' that the reception staff would play involved the trainee being allocated to a cell and being told to go to Cell 12. The trainee would march at the double around reception looking for Cell 12. There was, in fact, no Cell 12. Just eleven single holding cells. Again the trainee would be subjected to abuse and intimidation for not being in the correct cell.

For these trainees daily life at Reading began with having to be ready beside their door at 'unlock' at exactly 6 a.m. They would already have folded their bedding into a bed pack (blankets and sheets folded into a perfect square block); with toiletries and utensils all displayed in neat order with specific distances between each item on the bed. The prison officer on the landing would survey each side of the landing to see if any trainee was standing too far outside his cell door and obscuring the officer's view. Anyone found breaking this rule would be singled out and abused; life was governed by physical exercise and abuse.

Borstal recall

In 1961 Reading gained a new distinction; as well as being a correctional centre it became one of the first borstal recall centres. Trainees who had failed their term of supervision under licence upon release (by re-offending) were recalled to borstal. This was the end of the road for these young offenders; they would spend the remainder of their sentence at Reading enduring the 'Short, Sharp, Shock' regime in place.

Bad press

On 17 September 1967 the *People,* the national Sunday newspaper, carried the banner headline 'Brutality at a Borstal'. The report contained allegations from six former borstal trainees at Reading that physical torture and brutality were endemic within the centre. The full page story sent shock waves through the Home Office and especially through Reading. The trainees made detailed and specific allegations of ritual torture and verbal abuse. The complaints were levelled not just at the prison officers but also at the Board of Visitors[1] which had apparently ignored complaints of brutality at the centre and thus been complicit in this.

The next morning *The Times* reported that a board of inquiry into the allegations was being set up by the Home Secretary (and future Prime Minister), James Callaghan (later Lord Callaghan). That board wasted no time and its members tried to interview all the people concerned. Such was the priority given to the inquiry—and it was conducted with such speed—that by 6 March 1968 the Home Secretary was able to declare its conclusions to Parliament:

> Two prison officers have been suspended ... in one case disciplinary action will be taken; the other case has been referred to the Director of Public Prosecutions for consideration of criminal proceedings ... the board of enquiry had unanimously concluded that there was substance in the allegations of irregular behaviour by certain officers.

James Callaghan decided to close Reading as a borstal correction and recall centre, giving a final operating date of 14 January 1969. From the very next day Reading would operate in a new role as a local prison.

The governor's journal, dated 18 October 1968, records what became of the two staff who were suspended. Officer A received a severe reprimand, was placed on probation (a period of close supervision) for a year and transferred to HMP Pentonville (an adult prison) with immediate effect. With regard to Officer B, the Director of Public Prosecutions decided not to initiate criminal proceedings, but the officer was transferred to HMP Oxford (another adult prison) with immediate effect.

The repercussions of the inquiry were felt all over the Reading centre. Gone were the 'short, sharp, shock tactics', to be replaced by a more humane and softer approach, and as an exercise in rebuilding public confidence it was decided to have an open day, with dignitaries invited from all over the country to look around the centre on October 26. The guest of honour was the Lord Mayor of Reading. According to a report in the local press, the governor, Mr Portch, informed his distinguished guests that while Reading had been a borstal, since 1951, it had received 9,191 boys. This figure included 2,000 who had been

---

[1] As it then was: now the Independent Monitoring Board or IMB.

recalled and to date 30 per cent had not re-offended. In his final speech he paid tribute to his staff:

> It would be unfair and uncharitable of me not to pay a tribute to my staff for their devotion to duty at all times, but particularly through the trying times of the last 12 months.

Those prison staff who worked at Reading during the borstal days to whom I have spoken tell me that they were ashamed of what went on, but one particular senior officer would revel in his description of the violence inflicted upon the trainees. He would look at the stairwell into E-wing (the old segregation unit) and laugh, remembering the times when he would harry someone down those stairs knowing that the person was going to get a beating when he reached the bottom. This officer gloried in his recollections of the reception process, described earlier. Thankfully he has since retired from HM Prison Service.

CHAPTER 10

Starting Again with a Clean Sheet

> Dear Christ! The very prison walls
> Suddenly seemed to reel,
> And the sky above my head became
> Like a casque of scorching steel;
> And, though I was a soul in pain,
> My pain I could not feel.
> (*The Ballad of Reading Gaol*, Oscar Wilde)

On 14 January 1969 HM Borstal Recall Centre (HMBRC) at Reading ceased to exist. All the borstal boys who were left, nine in number, were discharged on that day. The remaining prison staff commenced a three-day conversion course equipping them to adjust to dealing with adult prisoners. When working in a borstal environment staff would conduct themselves rather like taskmasters or sergeants on a parade ground, barking orders to everyone, making people jump when they spoke. Working with more mature prisoners, as the author has found, requires the ability to talk, listen and be less austere in manner, otherwise the adult prisoners will not conform and will rebel against the authority being exercised.[1]

With change pending there was great unease amongst the staff. People who were accustomed to working with youngsters would now have to work with a different type of prisoner: less volatile but certainly more cunning and devious.

Reading Gaol becomes an adult prison

The day after its closure as a recall centre, Reading reopened as a prison. From 15 January 1969 it became a gaol once again, holding sentenced adult prisoners who were all tradesmen who were to be utilised in the major rebuilding programme that was about to start. Much cleaning and basic house keeping was required before the new prisoners could arrive. New stationery had to be emblazoned with 'HMP Reading' instead of 'HMBRC Reading'. All prisoners' uniforms had to be changed, and other items even down to the security handcuffs: a borstal boy's wrist is usually much smaller than that of an adult.

Nearly two weeks later, on January 27, the first batch of 12 prisoners arrived from Oxford Prison to help clean up the inside of the prison ready for the

---

[1] It was once said to me by an old serving prison officer, 'Your job is getting the majority to do what the minority wants them to do'.

building work to commence. In total, over 50 prisoners were received with various trade skills to assist in the redevelopment programme. They were housed in the old female wing (E-wing) whilst the modernisation of B and C-wings was in progress. Upon completion of this the prisoners began renovating A-wing, then finally they moved into that wing and demolished E-wing, the female wing where they had been living to begin with.

MAJOR CHANGES

After being neglected for so long a massive upgrade was finally embarked upon: the exterior turrets, the old gatehouse, the governor's and the chaplain's residences were all demolished. The gatehouse was replaced by a new modern looking building rather out of character with the original rather handsome and ornate structure. E-wing, the old female wing—which had not housed women prisoners since 1915 and had been used during the First World War for the Irish Internees (*Chapter 7*)—was demolished, allowing the front wall to be extended forwards towards the road by some 50 feet. In its place was built a new administration block with a domestic visiting centre on the lower level, that was much more comfortable for visiting families than the old, austere room with a small window and large iron bars where Oscar Wilde last saw his wife, Constance.

Problems are always around the corner with Reading. Some people might say that nothing goes smoothly. Not for the first time in its history, the building contractors ran into financial problems, as the governor noted in his journal on 29 September 1972: 'All building work suspended, contractor in financial difficulties'. The governor wasted no time in securing all the building materials in the portakabins located in the car park outside the gaol, and he arranged for extra staff to patrol this area 24 hours a day until a security fence could be erected around the compound, which was done within a couple of days.

The prisoner labour supervised by uniformed work staff then began the major re-building programme. The establishment, which had formerly held up to 178 prisoners, was now being modernised and redesigned to cope with a population of over 350 men. All the cells had major upgrades, including the introduction of fluorescent lighting in place of gas lights. New flooring replaced the old cold slate tiles and a modern means of communication with landing staff replaced the system of brass levers which had served the prison since 1844. All the landing walkways had their slate tiles removed in favour of strong plywood boards; even the centre flooring was replaced and the once beautiful Victorian black and red tiles were lost for ever to be replaced with a more plain and basic variety.

The landings were all re-numbered: A1 landing became a purpose-built hospital wing with X-ray technology, a full dentistry centre and modern outpatient facilities. Oscar Wilde's cell on C3 landing ended up on what became C2 landing: because where the prison once had four landings (or levels), the underground landings (those under the centre, A1 and B1) now became a hospital wing and a close supervision wing and so that level no longer counted. The outcome, and something that has perhaps not been generally advertised, is that 'C.3.3' thus became 'C.2.3' in terms of its location. No doubt Wilde would have had some quip or witticism, perhaps about Reading Gaol having come down in the world. Even the trusty Haden boilers were replaced, which had served the prison for over 100 years. It is worth noting that in the 35 years since then the new boilers have been replaced three times!

Within the prison grounds new facilities were constructed: a large gymnasium on the ground floor and a substantial industrial complex to be used for all forms of repetitive, labour-intensive menial tasks, initially such as mail bag sewing.

RULE 43

The actual numbers of prisoners being sent to Reading was still low so that on 8 April 1970 a decision was taken that the prison required a new role. When B and C-wings had been modernised, a security fence had been erected across the entrance to A-wing totally closing this wing off from the main prison. A new idea was tried out at Reading, by making B-wing and C-wing open for a certain type of prisoner, known in prison terms as a 'Rule 43 prisoner', after the relevant prison rule under which someone could apply for protection from other prisoners.[2] This means that if a prisoner thinks that due either to the nature of his offence or personal status he is under threat from other prisoners, he can apply to be isolated from the general prison population. The rule is typically and predominantly relied upon by paedophiles, child molesters and other sex offenders, corrupt policemen, grasses, supergrasses and those who have turned Queen's evidence by giving testimony against a co-accused: all categories who within the prisoner culture and the informal hierarchy of prisoners are frowned upon.

Often, rule 43 prisoners are weak, insecure and vulnerable characters who require specialist psychological support through counselling, group work and workshops where prison officers and other specialists try to make them understand their actions and to address their offending behaviour. There are problems associated with housing this type of prisoner in a single establishment

---

[2] Now, in fact, re-enacted as rule 45 – but still referred to as rule 43 on an everyday basis.

and at the end of their sentence, where to resettle them following their release. Due to the very nature of their offence, they may have been ostracised by family members and their former local communities. When they eventually finish their sentence a return to their old home or local area may not be an option for some. It is said that within a short space of time a sudden increase in attacks within the Thames Valley area was attributed to some of these ex-prisoners.

READING ABBEY

Since Reading Gaol was built in 1786 upon the site of the ruins of Reading Abbey (*Chapter 1*), whenever any building work commenced, the ground would reveal a treasure trove of interesting finds and artefacts relating to the old abbey. With the building work at the turn of the twentieth century, in 1910 a large ornamental tiled pavement was uncovered, dating back to the thirteenth or fourteenth centuries, which had led from the cloisters of Reading Abbey to the Infirmary, which was located to the east of the present prison by the outer wall.

During the modernisation works on the prison between 1969 and 1978, Dr C. F. Slade from the Department of Archaeology at Reading University was able to conduct various archaeological investigations into the building work carried out over the years. Great concern at the prison was at first caused when human remains came to light. One such find was of a pit containing thousands of human bones, all dating from the thirteenth or fourteenth centuries (their origin is unknown, but speculation suggests that this may have been due to a plague or maybe it is a burial site for paupers).

Another more interesting discovery, according to staff serving here at the time, was of a number of headless bodies close to C-wing—the heads being found some distance away under the exercise yard on B-wing and C-wing (located to the south-west corner). It is known that in the thirteenth century there was a leper colony situated outside old Reading town—where A-yard is today—which is where the bodies probably came from. It was believed at that time that if the head of a leper were removed after death and buried separately from its owner's body, the evil inside them would go to Hell and their soul would go to Heaven.

Other items of historical interest

There was such a vast array of historical items and artefacts being uncovered that the governor at the time, Mr Richards, decided that some items were of such importance that they needed to be kept for posterity. The local museum was offered various items for public display on condition that these items were to be loans only and to remain the property of the Crown. Sadly this could not be agreed with the then curator of the museum so instead the items were placed in

storage within government storage facilities in November 1969. These items were:
- original centre box;
- Oscar Wilde's cell door;
- Oscar Wilde's shelf and writing table; and
- the governor's slate—a beautifully ornate writing tablet, with an oak carved frame enclosing a slate writing board.

Sadly the only item now remaining, according to correspondence dated 5 January 1972, is Oscar Wilde's cell door which went on show in the Prison Service Museum at Newbold Revel near Rugby until recently when it again went into storage with the closure of the museum display in 2005. Over the years some of the other artefacts seem to have disappeared and are lost for ever, possibly collecting dust in someone's attic rather than being on display in a museum for the benefit of all.

CHAPTER 11

Life as a Local Prison

> We sewed the sacks, we broke the stones,
> We turned the dusty drill:
> We banged the tins, and bawled the hymns,
> And sweated on the mill:
> But in the heart of every man
> Terror was lying still.
> (*The Ballad of Reading Gaol*, Oscar Wilde)

By 1980 there was an ever increasing prison population nationally and increasing demands on prison places. After a review of the situation by the Government it was determined that Reading should be re-classified once again, as a Category B local prison, returning it to much the same role that it had had when Oscar Wilde was incarcerated there. This remained its role throughout the 1980s. It involved taking prisoners, both adults and young offenders, remanded or convicted and serving a sentence, from a large catchment area spanning much of southern England. Principally this meant serving various courts in Berkshire, Hampshire, Oxfordshire, Wiltshire and Buckinghamshire and the associated transporting to and fro of prisoners. Following conviction, prisoners would be allocated to various training prisons suitable for their needs. Reading Gaol, with a design capacity of 184 places, was soon filling fast. By the end of the year its actual prisoner population had increased to over 350, making it one of the most overcrowded prisons in England and Wales. This often meant housing three prisoners in a cell designed for one.

Slopping out

With no form of in-cell sanitation since 1865 and only the use of a chamber pot for a toilet three people sharing a cell together meant for an unpleasant time for all. In-cell sanitation was eventually re-installed in 1990, which reduced the maximum number of prisoners sharing a cell to two. But this still meant that a prisoner had to eat, sleep and defecate in the same cell as someone else. It also involved the bizarre ritual of slopping out in the mornings, when a queue of prisoners lined up with their chamber pots on the prison landings on the way to flush them out in the recesses at the end of each wing. Today some of these recesses have been transformed into offices and classrooms.

The one thing that made Reading work was the large industrial workshops which had been built in 1969-1972. These were able to occupy a large number of prisoners so that they were involved in 'meaningful' or 'purposeful' activities rather than being incarcerated in their cells for 23 hours a day. In truth, this meant repetitive production line work, producing items for HM Prison Service as well as outside contractors. One such contractor used this vast untapped resource to produce up-market status carrier bags for leading department stores in London, including Harrods in Knightsbridge! The prison accounts show that this contractor paid eleven pence for every bag made, although the store sold them for £5.95 each. This lasted for a number of years until 1983 when a Sunday newspaper carried a report alleging 'Slave Labour at Reading Gaol'. By 31 August 1983 the local paper, the *Reading Evening Post* reported that this production line had ceased and the prisoners had been reallocated to the production of mail bags and newspaper delivery bags.

SOME INTERESTING READING PRISONERS

As in many other walks of life prisoners reflect a wide social spectrum and background, even if many are weak, vulnerable, mentally challenged, involved with drugs or ineffectual in dealing with their own lives. Many years service as prison officer tells me that when you work within a local prison you come across a huge array of individuals and types: from the first time offender to the hardened criminal; the petty car thief to the international drug smuggler; the person who has made a single, costly mistake but been caught out, to the recidivist who sees prison as an occupational hazard and the prison gate as a revolving door.

My very first day at Reading Gaol in 1988 brought me into contact with a family of recidivists: including two brothers who shall remain nameless purely in the hope that they might just have changed their ways and turned away from crime. They became notorious throughout the judicial system of Berkshire for their criminal exploits and particularly for the ways in which they were caught.

The Brothers: case one
The two brothers decided to break into a local factory complex and look around to see what they could steal; unfortunately the younger brother grew bored with looking into various drawers and cabinets, so he decided to play with the secretary's typewriter. There must have been only so much a young man could write before again becoming bored, and so he decided to type out his name and address! Within an hour of the robbery the police had apprehended the brothers and they were returned to Reading Gaol.

The Brothers: case two
Within two weeks of being released from prison the brothers decided to burgle a house within the area where they lived. This time they decided to take their pet

dog, which they tied up outside the house while they were inside burgling. When the owner came back to find his house had become another statistic in the local crime wave, the police were called and again the brothers were caught within an hour of the crime. They had left their dog still tied up outside with its name and address on its collar!

The Brothers: case three

One week after finishing a two-year sentence of imprisonment the brothers were at it again; this time they decided to be more meticulous with their preparation. No typewriters, animals or any other incriminating evidence was to be left behind. It was a cold January evening and the snow had begun to fall, when the brothers decided to burgle a local shop. Within five minutes they had accomplished it and were back at home, examining their hoard. Within ten minutes of the police arriving at the scene the brothers were caught. When arrested the brothers could not understand how they had been identified or why the police were laughing so much. It transpired that the police had simply followed two sets of footprints in the newly fallen snow—starting outside the shop and leading directly to their home.

Mr Big: the scam

I also came across a prisoner from the opposite end of the social spectrum, a Mr Big. This man was a very wealthy individual who owned a large car showroom dealing with top of the range cars. He was caught when a criminal associate informed on him to the police. The scam he used had been working for a number of years until the informant became incensed at being short-changed from a deal. by just £100.

The gang would receive an overseas order for a luxury motor car. They would then either search their register of recent sales or pay young lads to go around wealthy areas—such as Ascot and Windsor—looking for a particular make of car. Then using their motoring contacts they would contact the owner and pretend to be an insurance dealer offering them a quote for the car. Within the conversation they would find out the identity of the owner's current insurance company. The next stage was to steal the car (no alarm system was good enough to prevent them stealing it), strip it completely and dump the body shell on waste land.

The next stage was where all the planning came to fruition: knowing the name of the owner's insurance company, they would find out where the body shell was to be sold off at auction. They would then purchase it, put all the stolen bits back onto the car and ship it abroad in return for their fee.

The supergrass

At the same time that Reading was reclassified as a Category B local prison in 1980, a new Supergrass Unit was opened in E-Wing. It was situated within the old segregation unit and the bath-house where Oscar Wilde took his first bath at Reading. Prisoners from all over the country were located there for their own protection from reprisals by people on who they had informed to the police. Many of them had large contracts placed on them by the criminal underworld (a price that would be paid to anyone who killed them).

One such criminal I came into contact with was a former East End gangster whom I will call 'B'; he would show all the new officers who came into the unit at Reading his prized photographs of his time in the underworld. His pictures were always of himself and various notorious criminals, such as the Kray twins, who at the time of the picture controlled the northern part of London and the East End, whilst another picture showed the man with Charlie Richardson, the equally notorious gang leader of the 'Torture Gang' who ruled over London south of the River Thames. It was like a *Who's Who?* of London gangsters. The man had spent over 30 years as a guest of Her Majesty for one crime or another; his prison record even gave his occupation as 'armed robber'.

B had been caught by the television show *Crimewatch*, which had dedicated a whole programme to trying to catch him and his gang. The year was 1988 and B had already spent time in the Supergrass Unit for 'grassing' his previous gang and according to him he had survived numerous assassination attempts. He became the first person in British judicial history to become a supergrass twice. His reason for informing the second time was that his accomplice had failed to destroy the evidence from their last robbery. B was always meticulous in both his preparation and planning; he never used things more than once. He was caught when his accomplice put a device into his rubbish bin rather than destroying it as instructed. A local paperboy saw this device and took it home; some weeks later he was watching *Crimewatch* and informed the police of what he had in his bedroom. The accomplice was followed and both robbers were caught in the act of robbing a security van of hundreds of thousands of pounds.

The Hollywood prisoner

Like Oscar Wilde, from time to time other high profile individuals fall foul of the law and find themselves in prison. The well-known Hollywood actor Stacey Keach, prison number L55200, was sent to prison by Reading Crown Court in December 1984 for smuggling cocaine worth £4,500 into Heathrow Airport. He was sentenced to nine months' imprisonment and spent the six months he had to serve at Reading; the last three months being allowed for special remission on good behaviour.

The actor was appearing on television at the time playing the detective, Mike Hammer, in a long-running series of that name. Such was his notoriety that for his own safety (and because of a back problem) he was isolated from the main body of the prison and kept in the hospital wing for the first couple of weeks. Then as a final twist of irony he was located onto Oscar Wilde's landing, now C2[1] and given the same job as Wilde eventually was, that of prison librarian.

The suicide bomber

Before the prison escort service that transports prisoners to and from courts and other places was privatised by Margaret Thatcher's Government in the 1990s, prison staff had themselves to work as prisoner escorts in the cells of the local Crown Court centres. This involved a group of staff attending court before 10 a.m. and working all day, until the various courts had finished and those who had been sentenced to imprisonment were taken back to Reading Prison and processed through the standard reception procedures.

The biggest problem was that staff were dealing with an unknown quantity. Never was this more evident than in a case of a smartly dressed young man who had been sentenced to four years' imprisonment for attempting to blackmail the British Government. He had tried to extort money by claiming to be able to poison the water supply if he was not given a sum of money. This young man was the son of an army chaplain and presented himself as a smart, well mannered individual when he was taken down the stairs into the cells at Reading Crown Court. The dock officer (the name used for prison staff attending court) was a woman and therefore unable to search this individual thoroughly (as was usually done) before taking him down to the cells. He asked if he could go to the toilet and this request was granted.

He reappeared with a small package strapped to his neck and holding a switch in his left hand. The officer who was processessing all the new receptions at the court, was an experienced man and good friend of mine. Over all the years I had known him, nothing ever worried or fazed him; he would be calm no matter what the situation. This young man demanded to be released, claiming to have a bomb attached to his neck. Alan Stephens, the receptions officer concerned, looked at him totally unmoved and told him to sit down in his office and think about his actions. This gave time for Stephens to inform the senior officer, who gave instructions for the court house to be evacuated and the army bomb disposal team to be called in.

Alan Stephens showed immense courage in returning to his office and talking to the man for over two hours, eventually persuading him remove the device and place it in the rubbish bin. The bin was handed to a startled bomb disposal expert who undertook a controlled explosion; this home made device

---

[1] See the explanation as to how C3 became C2 in *Chapter 10*.

had been made of the highest quality explosive material and could have demolished a large proportion of the Crown Court buildings.

The prisoner concerned was charged with serious offences and placed on the Category A list (very dangerous criminals whose escape would be embarrassing to the Crown). Alan Stephens was awarded HM Prison Service Director General's Commendation for his bravery. To conclude on a somewhat sour note: the prisoner was never tried for these offences—and the staff concerned were never informed that the Crown Prosecution Service had decided that a conviction was not in the public interest and so to discontinue matters. It was left to a small paragraph in a Sunday newspaper to state that the reason was so as not to draw attention to the 'inadequacies of security at Crown Courts'.

The escapee
The last escape from Reading Prison was in September 1984 when a prisoner on a domestic visit was located in a room adjoining the visits hall, awaiting his return to the wing where he was being held during his sentence. The room was unsuitable for this purpose and letters had already been forwarded to HM Prison Service maintenance department requesting that extra security measures be put into place. The prisoner simply climbed through an open window and crawled in front of the visits building, then joined a group of visitors who had finished their trip and were being shown out of the front gate.

The prisoner simply strolled out with the others to his freedom; but he was recaptured within a day or so, because he went straight to his home address.

CHANGE

Spring 1992 saw the opening of a new prison in Oxfordshire called HMP Bullingdon, which was to take over the role of Reading and become the new local prison for the area. Being over twice the size of Reading, Bullingdon could accommodate all Reading's prisoners and the expected increases in prisoner numbers. It was decided that Reading would now be reclassified as a Remand Centre for Young Offenders. So totally unsuitable was the prison for holding young prisoners aged 17 to 21 years old that the staff feared the worst.

CHAPTER 12

HM Remand Centre and Young Offender Institution

> That night the empty corridors
> Were full of forms of Fear,
> And up and down the iron town
> Stole feet we could not hear,
> And through the bars that hide the stars
> White faces seemed to peer.
> (*The Ballad of Reading Gaol*, Oscar Wilde)

In the summer of 1992 Her Majesty's Remand Centre for Young Offenders, Reading began to take young offenders aged 17 to 21 from the Thames Valley area and beyond, increasing this prisoner population slowly until a maximum of 245 young men were housed there.

Young offenders are by far the most volatile and difficult individuals in the prison population; in addition, being on remand, they are, in the eyes of the law and as a matter of historic rights, innocent. There were no restrictions as to the type of offender: from car thief to serial killer—all were sent there. Reading was totally inappropriate for this task, lacking the space to expand to cater for these more active young men. A new, hard surface football pitch was built on B-yard and C-yard where Oscar Wilde once walked on exercise. Educational facilities were increased and the industrial workshops were removed to allow the large open space to be converted into an association area with pool tables, computer games machines, table tennis and televisions. Another innovation was a cardphone system that allowed prisoners to keep in contact with their families and friends. The system is identical to the payphones on street corners and so on except that prisoners need to purchase special phone cards from the prison shop with 'HMP' stamped on them.

PRISON REGIME

To accommodate the new type of prisoner a fresh regime was devised, which allowed two staff per landing. Each landing had a designated activity to do within its own, individual slot on the prison timetable, for example:

Landing	08:30-10:00	10:15-11:45	13:00-14:30	14:45-16:30
A1	Gymnasium	Association	Exercise	Domestics
A2	Domestics	Exercise	Association	Gymnasium
A3	Exercise	Domestics	Gymnasium	Association

The regime allowed prisoners to be out of their cells for up to nine hours a day, including evening association for either A-wing or B and C-wing on alternative nights. It soon became apparent that these prisoners were more lethargic and demotivated individuals than had ever been seen before by the Reading staff. Within a couple of weeks of opening the numbers at daytime education and gymnasium fell drastically. It was noted also that, whereas Reading had always prided itself on the clean and pristine condition of its cells and landings, standards had fallen dramatically.

Due to the majority of prisoners being on remand, they were not required by law to attend work, education or indeed to do anything. Whereas a convicted prisoner could be ordered to attend or be punished via the prison disciplinary system, these remand prisoners were untouchable and most of them would rather stay in their cells and do nothing. Much to the disgust of a number of older staff members, a new bonus scheme was introduced, allowing payment to every prisoner who attended education and the gym: 50 pence for every session attended, which may not appear a lot until it is considered that the basic wage for a prisoner is around £2.50 per week.

The new measure worked to an extent but did not address the declining standards of cleanliness within the cells. It was decided to introduce a grading system for the cleanliness of cells—grade A being the best and grade C the worst. If a prisoner had two consecutive grade Cs he would not be eligible for evening association. This had the effect of almost instantly transforming the cleanliness of the place and worked well until the practice was found to be unlawful so that it had to be terminated.

UNREST IN THE PRISON ESTATE

During the early 1990s there was much unrest within the whole prison estate; major acts of indiscipline and riots broke out at various prisons across the country of which the most notorious was the Strangeways riot at HM Prison Manchester that led to the Woolf Report by the future Lord Chief Justice Lord Woolf and the then Chief Inspector of Prisons, His Honour Sir Stephen Tumim.

To combat this, the government introduced a new charge of 'prison mutiny' for anyone found responsible for initiating a major act of indiscipline.

In 1990 HM Remand Centre, Pucklechurch near Bristol was set alight and extensively damaged, forcing it to close and most of the prisoners to be held in local police cells or adult prisons close by. This was an unsatisfactory situation and it was soon decided to move these young offenders. Thirty-two prisoners, including most of the riot ringleaders, were transferred from Pucklechurch to Reading, rather than being dispersed around other prisons. This had a major effect at Reading. The ringleaders soon became the focal point of all acts of indiscipline and the peace and relative calm were rudely interrupted. The new prisoners mostly came from the Bristol area and that part of south-west England, which was too far away from Reading for some families to visit. The young men seemed determined to cause trouble so as to be sent to a prison closer to their home city.

At Christmas 1992 a riot took place that changed the face of Reading. The following account is compiled from prison and court records and the first-hand recollections of prison officers.

Trouble brewing

In the period before the riot staff had been informing the prison's security department that informers were warning them that trouble was being planned. Security Information Reports (SIRs) were being submitted by staff detailing such information weeks beforehand. The number of prisoners at Reading at that time was 131, very low, and it was felt that with those numbers any act of indiscipline could be contained.

Christmas Day 1992

Most of the SIRs indicated Christmas evening association (B-wing and C-wing) as being when and where trouble might start so extra staff were deployed into the association area. The evening went without incident except that it was noticeable that a number of prisoners had decided not to attend association that evening. When association had terminated and the prisoners were returning to their cells, most of the men in A-wing began to bang their cell doors and create a disturbance.

Boxing Day

The day passed relatively calmly with no acts of violence or indiscipline, and it was decided to again put an extra member of staff into the association room, complementing the senior officer and four other officers present at that time who were watching 49 inmates. It was later detailed in evidence from staff that inside the association room there was a group of seven or eight individuals going around the various groups within the room fomenting trouble (these were the ringleaders). The time was 6.45 p.m.-7 p.m.

A riot breaks out
Officer Phil Maher was playing pool with a prisoner; Phil has a great rapport with young offenders and is a credit to HM Prison Service. At 7.15 p.m. a prisoner behind Phil grabbed hold of his key chain, trying to take his keys. Phil was very strong in the arms (being a former carpenter) and was able to take hold of this prisoner and lift him onto the pool table. Phil was then hit on the side of his face by a pool ball, fracturing his cheekbone and disorientating him. Then began an orgy of violence directed towards the six members of staff who, for protection, lifted a table-tennis table onto its side to use as a shield and moved towards the double-door entrance to the association area. The prisoners used everything they could get their hands on to throw at the staff.

By 7.16 p.m. the staff had managed to get out of the area and were going down the corridor adjourning the association area to the main prison. The other staff on duty were at this time coming to their assistance, as the senior officer had pressed the alarm bell at the start.

At 7.17 p.m. the orderly officer (who is in charge of the prison on an evening) accompanied by some of the staff from the association room, proceeded to secure the prison. This was done by double-locking all the metal gates to the living area of the prison. This meant that only one key could now open these gates and the key the rioters had was rendered useless. This one action was later praised by the Director General of HM Prison Service as the act that saved the prison.

Inside the association room some prisoners were sitting in a corner, not wishing to participate in the destruction taking place around them, whilst the majority began demolishing anything and everything. The prison shop which was in this area was ransacked and most of the produce was later passed to prisoners locked up in their cells through the cell windows on the ground floor.

Fire
A group of prisoners made their way into the gymnasium and started a fire in the staff office, whilst another group went into the education block and totally demolished all the classrooms and offices there.

Escape attempt
The main ringleaders had decided to use this night to try and escape. They 'hot-wired' the prison van and drove it against the outer east-facing wall adjacent to the abbey ruins. They had also removed a set of goal posts from the football pitch, placed these on top of the van and climbed onto the prison wall. Thankfully, staff within the control room had seen them and informed the local police who encircled the entire prison with uniformed staff and dog handlers

within ten minutes of being informed of the situation, thus preventing a mass breakout.

Staff reinforcements

Within ten minutes of the incident, staff from all over the local area and beyond began arriving at the prison wearing riot gear and taking up positions ready to retake the prison. Unknown to staff coming in, the prisoners had control of the van which became evident when a group of staff going into the main prison were chased by it being driven towards them. The prisoners had failed in their attempt to escape, so they drove the van around the prison grounds a couple of times in a highly erratic and dangerous manner. They then tried to ram the doors to the hospital wing; presumably to get into the drug store which was located there. Unable to succeed in this, their attention turned to the maintenance department's welding storeroom. This was rammed a couple of times but as it was on a slight slope, the van ended up becoming jammed onto the curb and unable to move.

Recapture

As soon as staff reached the prison, they were dispatched in three-officer teams into the grounds to catch the prisoners, who by this time had become bored with their destruction and were walking around aimlessly. Full control of the prison was regained and a prisoner head count was taken at 11 p.m. Some trouble was still being caused by prisoners located on the ground floor of the prison; they had been given weapons and various items from the prison shop through their cell windows by the rioters. It took some time to demolish the barricades erected inside these cells.

An inquiry

In the official inquiry held into the incident it was noted that:

> It speaks well for the staff professionalism that there were no reported injuries to inmates throughout the incident and no inmates subsequently complained of ill treatment ... staff used their initiative and were a major factor in bringing the incident to a satisfactory end.

The total cost of damage caused by the rioters was £153,000.

Criminal proceedings

These commenced on 17 May 1993: 23 former prisoners were charged with various offences and eight ringleaders with the more serious offence of prison mutiny. They received sentences consecutive to the ones they were already serving of up to five years' imprisonment. The sentences sent a clear message to other would-be rioters that this type of action would not be tolerated. The trial judge, Judge Leonard Gerber, said on sentencing the rioters:

There was no overcrowding, there were excellent facilities and I am satisfied all the staff were highly professional ... there seems to have been an influx of an unruly element who where intent on having a violent confrontation with prison staff on Boxing Day ... there was a wicked attack on prison officers, an elderly officer had his keys snatched and there were attacks on other officers who fled for their lives.

The end result

Since the riot major changes that were long overdue have taken place. The education block which was totally destroyed has been relocated in a much larger area inside the old association area. All the wings have been fenced off and gated, the grounds have been sectioned with high security fencing and the exercise area is now totally enclosed with high security fencing and gates. Around the entire perimeter of the prison there is a network of CCTV cameras, in addition to that of internal cameras on constant watch, 24 hours a day. All these measures are designed to control and isolate any acts of indiscipline and prevent them from spreading to other parts of the prison.

CHAPTER 13

'Reading Gaol' Today and in the Future

> And all men kill the thing they love,
> By all let this be heard,
> Some do it with a bitter look,
> Some with a flattering word,
> The coward does it with a kiss,
> The brave man with a sword!
> (*The Ballad of Reading Gaol*, Oscar Wilde)

After the riot of 1992 outlined in *Chapter 12* there was a drive by the Home Office to try and change for the better various areas within Reading Gaol. Money was allocated with a view to developing those areas that had been damaged and improving the facilities overall. The large open area known as the association room, where the riot had started, was sectioned into two parts. One side was used again as an association area and the other side was developed into a new education facility. This consisted of six purpose built classrooms, where a number of courses were on offer ranging from computing to cookery, with the staff trying to address the young prisoners' educational needs.

KENNET UNIT

One area that benefited greatly from the extra development was the old education block. This had been totally destroyed by the rioters on Boxing Day night 1992 and with the educational facility now moved upstairs into one half of the old association area, there was the chance to create a unique development at Reading on this site. Accordingly, a new facility was built, called the Kennet Unit.[1] This unit was to serve as a pre-release facility, allowing young long-term prisoners who were coming towards the end of substantial sentences the opportunity to work in the community and begin to integrate themselves back into society in preparation for their release.

This new unit comprises 20 beds in 16 rooms, with each occupant having his own room key and unrestricted access within the unit 24 hours a day, allowing a sense of freedom and degree of personal responsibility never before seen at Reading Gaol.

---

[1] After the Kennet Canal that flows behind the rear of the prison.

From the outset, the young men were encouraged to work with various employers within the community on job placements and in local charity shops. One national company gave the prison a grant of £50,000 to train 50 young men in forklift truck operation: a course designed to fill a local skills gap within the market place. Over 70 per cent of the young offenders who attended that course found employment upon their release and to date just six per cent are known to have re-offended, compared with a national average of around 72 per cent of young offenders offending within two years of release (Social Exclusion Unit, 2003).

With this new unit, which opened in 1996, Reading was reclassified from a Remand Centre to Her Majesty's Prison and Young Offender Institution, making this the thirteenth different role for the prison.

A whole new ethos started to develop at the prison, with a dedicated group of staff working closely with local and national companies looking for work placements and different avenues of helping to rehabilitate the young offenders. This was a massive step forward in the way prisoners were treated and it reflected nationwide changes in the culture of HM Prison Service, which were being rolled out across the country under various initiatives. Gone now, at Reading and some other prisons, are the days of simply locking a prisoner up for 23 hours a day. They have been replaced by a more humane and relaxed atmosphere in which the young men are encouraged to take responsibility for their own actions and lifestyles, in an attempt to re-focus their lives away from the cycle of custody-release-reoffending-return to custody.[2] For the first time these prisoners are enabled to address their re-offending, empowering them with a much needed sense of belief in themselves and an understanding that they can change.

Sadly the ethos and initiatives pioneered within the Kennet Unit and to some degree on the main resettlement wing (C3 and B3) were marred by a negative culture within the rest of the prison and poor industrial relations with the local branch of the Prison Officers Association (the prison officer's union).

PERFORMANCE TEST

In 2001, criticism of Reading led to the establishment being one of the first prisons in the country to be selected to meet the challenge of Performance Testing as part of the Bench Marking programme (a programme set up by the Prison Board to ensure that all prisons meet a minimum standard in terms of decency, performance and regime). The reason for Reading being selected was that performance was at that time deemed unacceptably poor in relation to

---

[2] Sometimes called 'revolving door syndrome'.

regime, industrial relations, compliance with HM Prison Service standards and the treatment of young prisoners within the prison.

For the staff a sense of uncertainty and apprehension prevailed over life at Reading, morale was at an all time low. Under performance testing, the managers and staff were required to demonstrate improvements or face the prospect of being run by a private sector company. This meant that a private contractor could be brought in to operate the gaol, and staff would then become private sector employees, losing their status as civil servants with major implications for their working conditions and pensions.

Reading needed a new focus and new drive. A new governor was brought in, tasked with turning around a perceivedly failing prison. Nick Leader proved to be one of a new breed of proactive and dynamic governor, such had never been seen before at Reading. From the very start he showed huge willingness and a belief that Reading could win the forthcoming performance test; he was going to be taking Reading from the nineteenth century into the twenty-first century. Nick was a workaholic. He would start at four in the morning and not finish until nine in the evening, working for weeks at a time without a break. His dynamic approach was infectious with the staff; leading from the front he tried imaginative and refreshingly different approaches to prison life.

The result was that Reading won its performance test in April 2003 and according to the report of HM Inspectorate of Prisons in 2004:

> Reading won its performance test with some very imaginative and proactive initiatives.

VOCATIONAL TRAINING CENTRE

One of the initiatives praised in the report was the new Vocational Training Centre (VTC). This was funded by the Offender Learning Skills Unit, which awarded a grant of half-a-million pounds to develop the old association area into a purpose built educational unit housing seven classrooms, two large workshops, showering facilities, stand down area (a place for prisoners to relax and make tea) and access to the modern-day prisoner PIN phone system that replaced the card phone system mentioned in earlier chapters.[3] The centre was designed by myself and a colleague, Marcus Gale. Together we tried to make the whole environment conducive to learning and remove it from the austere and claustrophobic atmosphere of a prison. The main focus of the centre is on nine

---

[3] The PIN phone system is incorporated into all prisons today. It allows the operator to call only telephone numbers preselected by the owner. This goes some way to preventing the bullying and intimidation from other prisoners that used to be endemic in all prisons using a card phone system.

key areas identified by the Government's Social Exclusion Unit in 2003 as the main factors in re-offending:

- education;
- employment;
- drug and alcohol misuse;
- mental and physical health;
- housing;
- financial support and debt;
- family networks;
- attitudes and self-control; and
- institutionalisation and life skills.

Classrooms One and Two: Induction

These classrooms are designed for educational inductions. It is a requirement that all new prisoners receive an induction. On the first day, they undergo a basic skills assessment in literacy and numeracy. The same test is given to them again at the end of the week and the results are analysed. The reason for repeating the tests is that when someone first comes into prison they arrive with a whole host of problems and issues. From drug dependency to social and family problems, these are all addressed in the first week's induction, with representatives of various agencies and support networks attending lessons and placing students on relevant courses that will help them.

Classroom Three: Fitness

This classroom is used by the gymnasium department, running an accredited fitness courses with excellent outside links placing some of the students into employment upon their release within local fitness centres and sporting facilities.

Classroom Four: Drugs rehabilitation

Those students who have had or are still faced with drug related issues can attend drug rehabilitation courses here, addressing their dependency with the support of a dedicated group of medical nurses and drug counsellors. Voluntary drug testing is also undertaken to prove to both families and the courts that the reason for the person's incarceration, if it involved drugs, is being addressed.

Classroom Five: Job placement

This classroom, the smallest in the unit, is used for one-to-one interviews with representatives from Job Centre Plus, Connections and other government-funded agencies to assist the young adults with finding employment upon their release.

Classrooms Six and Seven: Pre-release courses

Attendance on these courses is a pre-requisite before a prisoner can be considered for any possible early release on licence before the end of his sentence. The courses address offending behaviour, making the student look at the implications of crime and how it affects individuals and places the emphasis on each person to identify his own particular causes of crime. The aim and hope is to stop them from re-offending; as well as teaching them various coping strategies to reinforce this.

Workshops One and Two: Plan-a-Kitchen

The Plan-a-Kitchen course is unique, developed by myself and a colleague. As the name suggests, it is based around designing a kitchen. The course runs for four weeks and is open to all students with an educational ability of entry Level 3 (basic literacy and numeracy) and above. Students attend this course on a full time basis; with theoretical sessions in the morning and practical ones in the afternoon. The practical sessions are very 'hands on' and teach the students skills in building kitchen units, plumbing, painting and decorating. Gaining these skills also develops in the students a much needed self-belief and self-esteem. The course is fully accredited with nationally recognised qualifications and there have been some excellent examples of students progressing into outside employment upon release.

Case study 1
James entered Reading prison in 2003, sentenced to 18 months' imprisonment for driving offences. Prior to this he had been without any qualifications and was unemployed. When he attended the Plan-a-Kitchen course, he passed with flying colours and was top of the class. James indicated that plumbing was his preferred vocation. With our links with various colleges and employers we were able to start him off on day release from prison to work with a plumbing firm and attend Reading College. James has now finished his prison sentence and is a fully qualified heating and plumbing engineer.

Case study 2
Daniel was a recidivist: in the previous five years he had spent just three months in total at home, having been sentenced to prison seven times. He is one of seven children from a run down area of Reading, two of his brothers are also incarcerated. His mother has never visited him whilst in prison and he looked upon prison as an occupational hazard. Educationally he has no qualifications and cannot remember ever going to school. Daniel attended the Plan-a-Kitchen course and found that he had a hidden talent with carpentry. He showed exceptional promise and during the course photographs of his work were taken to send to his mother. She visited him at the end of the course, for the first time in five years. At the time of writing, Daniel is in the last two months of a five year sentence before he is eligible for parole. He is

working for a small construction firm in Reading and at present is in his final year of an NVQ Level 2 course in site carpentry.

In 2005 the Adult Learning Inspectorate examined the educational facilities at Reading and commented that the Plan-a-Kitchen course showed one of the best examples of embedded Key Skills in both literacy and numeracy Level 1 that they have seen in both prison and outside educational facilities.

Family contacts
To promote family contacts it was decided by myself and Marcus Gale that at the end of every course the students' families could come into the prison and attend a passing out ceremony. This has proved to be a considerable incentive for the students. They are able, some for the first time, to prove to their families that although they were a failure once, they are now trying to address their own problems and to demonstrate that they can achieve something.

LIFE IN READING GAOL TODAY

Today the emphasis within the prison can be summed up by saying that it is totally focused upon addressing re-offending and as the new motto suggests, *Turning Lives Around*.

Education
As noted earlier, every new prisoner undergoes a week-long induction to establish his educational levels in literacy and numeracy. At the same time the prisoner is encouraged to take responsibility for his actions. A great many offenders have had a poor experience of schooling in their formative years and it appears, from government reports into re-offending and research such as that shown in the table below, that low educational attainment is one of the main factors in re-offending.

Education inside prison has to be focused on the individual's needs and not purely on pressure to fill spaces. To work, prison education has to allow the individual to take control of his or her own learning, so that he or she finds the whole learning environment enjoyable and rewarding. Today more than 71 per cent of all the women and 51 per cent of the men inside prisons throughout England and Wales have no academic qualifications (Social Exclusion Unit, 2003).

Educational comparison between the general population and prisoners

Characteristic	General population	Prisoners
Regularly truanted from school	3%	30%
Excluded from school	2%	49% of male, 33% female
Left school at 16 or younger	32%	89% of male, 84% female
Attended a special school	1%	23% male, 11% female
Have no qualifications	15%	52% male, 71% female
Numeracy at or below level 1	23%	65%
Reading ability at or below level 1	21-23%	48%
Writing ability at or below level 1	No comparison	82%

Source: Social Exclusion Unit (2003)

I have found through my teaching role at Reading that education allows a prisoner to regain a sense of self-belief and personal pride, something that is often lost when someone enters prison. It means a lot to see the smiles on their family's faces when they see the young lad receive his qualification at a presentation in the prison and watch him grow both in self-belief and in terms of a stronger personality, away from his problems, sometimes a drug dependency, into the young man once thought lost by his family.

Drugs and security

Drugs inside prisons today are a massive issue; many prisoners will use any means to get them. Two of the most common techniques are:

- receiving drugs during a visit from a loved one or acquaintance. They can be secreted, e.g. inside a baby's nappy or hidden upon the person;
- before going into court the drugs are either swallowed or hidden.

The human body has an immense capacity for hiding things; from drugs to weapons and prisoners have become adept in the art of concealment. Over my years as a prison officer I have seen an array of items—from mobile phones to seven-inch lock knives—hidden inside the bodies of new prisoners on their arrival. To combat this, in 1994 HM Prison Service introduced drug dog teams into most establishments. 'Buzz' the Border Collie entered Reading with his handler and almost immediately made an impact upon drugs detection. Today there are two types of drug dogs in Reading:

- passive dogs: these are used when the searching of individuals is required. Their acute sense of smell will pick up any traces of drugs on the individual, even if the drugs were used the previous day; and
- active dogs: these dogs are used for searching cells and other open areas away from the public and prisoners.

In addition, both mandatory drug testing (MDT) and voluntary drug testing (VDT) schemes have been introduced: VDT is coupled with an extensive drug rehabilitation program to facilitate a prisoner's wish to change his lifestyle and end his dependency on drugs. With advances in modern technology metal detectors, both small, hand-held ones and the large, walk-through 'airport' variety, are now used all over the prison, coupled with CCTV cameras that closely monitor all prisoner movement.

Mental health

With the gradual closure of the old Victorian psychiatric hospitals and a greater emphasis on care in the community, mental health has become a major issue in prisons across Britain. At Reading, across the years I have witnessed an enormous increase in the number of prisoners with severe mental health issues. Sometimes a young man will spend months in custody at Reading waiting for a space at a secure mental health facility, or to be assessed medically by defence and prosecution teams prior to his trial. I have known of many cases where a prisoner has been sent to a high security hospital (such as Broadmoor, Ashfield or Rampton) only to be deemed untreatable and sent back to prison. According to the Prison Reform Trust (2005) 72 per cent of male prisoners suffer from two or more mental health disorders.

Addressing re-offending

One of the main functions of Reading prison today is to protect society and address re-offending; according to HM Prison Service's statement of purpose:

> Her Majesty's Prison Service serves the public by keeping in custody those committed by the courts. Our duty is to look after them with humanity and help them lead law-abiding and useful lives in custody and after release.

Fundamental to this statement is addressing re-offending; at Reading there are dedicated teams of staff psychologists, probation teams, healthcare and drug workers, chaplaincy staff and prison officers who all have a major part to play in this regard. When a new prisoner comes in through reception, he is seen on the morning after he arrives by representatives of all the above teams. A sentence plan is initiated which is structured to address the cause of that individual's offending behaviour. To achieve the best results, the sentence needs to be sufficiently long to allow time for these issues to be addressed, but in many instances the courts give offenders short sentences (less than six months) that allow insufficient time to do this. This has the inevitable consequence of the prisoner re-offending, spending further time in prison, and costs to the taxpayer.

CLOSING THOUGHTS

Reading Gaol has now existed in one form or another for over 500 years, protecting the public of Berkshire and beyond across the centuries. It stands as a monument to British penal history, from the early, dark days of sometimes cruel punishments to the more humane and rehabilitating regime of today. The whole ethos is now geared towards crime prevention and rehabilitation rather than punishment. In terms of relationships, staff address prisoners on first name terms and the silence of the Victorian separate system has been replaced at times by laughter and friendly banter between staff and prisoners.

Today's Prison Service as a whole is more focused than ever before on addressing the causes of re-offending and trying to change the lives of its charges for the better. When I first trained to become a prison officer in 1988 there appeared to be a negative culture. All through that training instructors kept repeating a tired old phrase, 'Happiness is door shaped'; meaning that when prisoners are locked in their cells most day to day problems go away. But for officers like me, problems did not go away. The public would be faced again by the prisoner, his troubles and offending, on his release; making it worse if he is more bitter, resentful, disturbed and institutionalised than before.

At first I was simply annoyed by the idea that problems go away just because a cell door is locked behind a prisoner; then, like other colleagues, I realised that such attitudes had to change. Thankfully my faith in the majority of prison staff has proved me correct. I know that at Reading there is a nucleus of exceptional staff who sometimes work in difficult conditions with some volatile and unpredictable individuals. Officer Phil Maher, who was attacked by the rioters on the night of Boxing Day 1992, still plays pool with his charges, friendly and professional, always trying to do his best for the prisoners. The one thing all the staff at Reading Gaol have in common is their dedication and seeking to make a difference to their charges' lives. We all hope beyond hope that this will be the last time a prisoner spends time inside the walls of a prison and that he will go on to become an integral part of his community, not a drain on society, a life lost to crime and incarceration. This is what keeps us going.

Appendix 1: Arrested Development

Arrested Development by Theodore Dalrymple

First published in *The New Criterion*, June 2002

The last time I attended a hanging in the prison it was a murder, not a suicide. I arrived too late to bring the hanged man back to life: for, if there are degrees of deadness, he was by then already very dead.

The cellmate of the hanged man did not so much confess as boast that he had intimidated the dead man into hanging himself. He had threatened to cut his throat in his sleep if he did not hang himself first, and the man, who was two weeks from his release, chose the rope—or rather, the bedsheet torn into strips, dampened and braided into a noose. The cellmate helped him up on to the chair and obligingly kicked it away from under him.

The hanging before last that I attended was complicated by the fact that the dead man had on his chest a small puncture wound that penetrated to his heart, inflicted by the thrust of a ball-point pen, which I had not until then considered a potentially lethal weapon. No explanation of how the man came by this wound was ever forthcoming: but it seems that, even where there is a high illiteracy rate, as in prison, the pen is as mighty as the sword.

There have been many more hangings in my prison since the abolition of the death penalty than there ever were before. It is as if the gods demand human sacrifices, and if the state does not carry them out, the prisoners themselves have to step into the breach in their own amateur fashion. It seems from the statistics that an official execution, with all its attendant solemnity and ceremony, is more pleasing to the gods than three or four suicides and murders. The gods like a little formality.

I suppose it will be granted that sentimentality is unlikely to remain for long the vice of the prison doctor, though cynicism might easily replace it. Sometimes I wonder whether, through constant contact with the sordid, I have or might one day become the 'coarse-mouthed Doctor' of *The Ballad of Reading Gaol* who

> ... gloats and notes
> Each new and nerve-twitched pose,
> Fingering a watch whose little ticks
> Are like horrible hammer-blows

and who later comforts the condemned prisoner thus:

> The Doctor said that Death was but
> A scientific fact.

Irrespective of the ethics of capital punishment, I am glad that among my duties has never been that of pronouncing a man fit for execution: for by what criterion is the doctor supposed to judge? Is the fitness to be thus pronounced physical or mental, a lack of incapacitating anxiety, perhaps? (Albert Pierrepoint, one of the last hangmen of England—a position for which, in the days of judicial hanging, the Home Office used to receive five applications a week, year in, year out—wrote in his autobiography that all the condemned men he knew behaved correctly at their execution, save one: 'and he,' wrote Mr Pierrepoint by way of explanation, 'was a foreigner.') The last doctor I met who had examined men for fitness for execution—in a former British colony—was an alcoholic, though I cannot positively say that he was driven to the bottle by a disturbed conscience.

Whenever I enter my prison, I am always accompanied by *The Ballad of Reading Gaol*— not literally, for my own copy, written by Oscar Wilde and published by Leonard Smithers in 1898, is too valuable for me to risk in a congregation of thieves—but mentally. This invariable accompaniment is strange, because Oscar Wilde is not a literary figure I much admire: though brilliantly gifted, he was one of the first authors to prefer the route of publicity and self-promotion to that of achievement, and his actual work paid the price. Not only was he himself ultimately the victim of his own choice, but he was a harbinger of genuine decline to come.

I first heard *The Ballad* read over the radio when I was a child, and its pathos moved me, though I knew nothing of prisons and could not have guessed that I would ever enter one. Wilde was still considered a slightly risqué figure at the time, over whose personal proclivities it was best to draw a veil of silence, and though his works were published and performed, he was not yet the hero and martyr he was soon to become. I remember my father spluttering with outrage at the film made with Peter Finch in the title role of *The Trials of Oscar Wilde*: not at the injustice or cruelty of the eventual sentence, but at the idea that anyone should have thought Wilde innocent or undeserving of his punishment.

My prison belongs, architecturally, to the same era as Reading Gaol. It is of the panopticon type, so that, theoretically speaking, the whole prison could be surveyed from an observation point at its centre. The Victorian ironwork is magnificent, and in a happier context would invite admiration; and though the outer aspect of the prison is forbidding, there are features of the gothic revival within. The prisoners still trudge round the exercise yards as depicted in Victorian paintings.

Prison is another country: they do things differently there. I go abroad every time I enter it, and even the sky changes for me. Like a cheap tune whose chorus infects the brain as an insect bores into wood, I recall the lines

> ... that little tent of blue
> Which prisoners call the sky.

Later in *The Ballad*, the famous line becomes more personal

> ... that little tent of blue
> We prisoners call the sky.

and the change from the third to the first person reminds me of my own recurring nightmare, in which I am received into the prison not as a doctor, but as a prisoner. I wake up in a sweat: How will I bear the humiliation of it and the need constantly to ask permission of the warders to do even the simplest things? Or will I, like Dr. Ragin of Ward No. 6, who is admitted as a lunatic to his own ward in Chekhov's story of that name, sink into despairing apathy and die for lack of will to live? In fact, educated and intelligent people survive surprisingly well as prisoners, perhaps by detaching themselves from their predicament and observing everything around them in a deliberately unemotional way: but their surprising resilience does not prevent my nightmare from recurring.

Some things have not changed very much since Wilde's days in Her Majesty's penitentiaries. Men who live in the most squalid and litter-strewn parts of our cities are transformed temporarily into fanatics of cleanliness: brass railings are polished over and over until they gleam and glitter.

> We rubbed the doors, and scrubbed the floors,
> And cleaned the shining rails;
> And, rank by rank, we soaped the plank,
> And clattered with the pails.

It is still as if, in the official mind, a spotless floor and an immaculate railing signified a reformed character: a sound mind in a clean prison, as it were.

Because there are no executions any longer, there is no prisoner who

> ... does not bend his head to hear
> The Burial Office read,
> Nor, while the terror of his soul
> Tells him he is not dead,
> Cross his own coffin, as he moves
> Into the hideous shed.

But the execution chamber of my prison is still colloquially known as the Topping Shed, and the (no doubt apocryphal) story is told in the prison of how one of the last prisoners to be executed there was taken from the condemned cell to the gallows, passing a little space of open air *en route*, and, looking up at the little tent of grey we English call the sky, said to the warders accompanying him, with the banality of finality, 'Looks like rain.' 'It's all right for you,' one of them replied, 'you're not coming back.'

When a prisoner is suicidal, warders may still, as in Wilde's day, be set

> Who watch him night and day;
> Who watch him when he tries to weep,
> And when he tries to pray;
> Who watch him lest himself should rob
> The prison of its prey.

But it is here that, realistic and truthful as Wilde's lines undoubtedly are, other reflections rise to my mind based upon my own experience: for though Wilde is speaking the truth, it is not the whole truth by any means. His poem is programatic or propagandistic in intent, a clarion call to prison reform in times of indisputable harshness, and nonetheless worthy for that: but reformers are apt to lose sight of Man's fallen nature in their zeal for betterment, and this leads to wilful simplification.

When a man is known in prison to be suicidal, he does not necessarily arouse the compassion of his fellow-prisoners, contrary to Wilde's letter to *The Daily Chronicle* soon after his release, extolling prisoners' 'sympathy for each other, their humility, their gentleness, their pleasant smiles of greeting when they meet each other.' On the contrary, they will do everything possible to aid a man in his efforts to kill himself, from providing the pills to passing the razor blade. They do this not because they believe in an abstract, Humean right to suicide, or because they have a personal grudge against the person who is suicidal, but because they know that a suicide embarrasses the authorities, and a man's life is a small price to pay for doing this. I recall, for example, a man who had repeatedly cut his wrists and his throat, who was under the direct observation of two warders night and day. It is surprisingly difficult to observe a man constantly without lapses of concentration: and when the man saw that the two warders were temporarily abstracted, he slipped out a razor blade that he had inserted between his gum and his cheek and gashed his throat with it (not fatally, in the event). The razor blade had been passed to him in his food by a well-wishing fellow-prisoner, and he had secreted it in his mouth, to await his opportunity to use it. And prisoners, who usually hang on to their medication as something very precious, are quite prepared to donate it to others in a good cause such as a suicide attempt.

On the night before an execution in Reading Gaol

> ... there is no sleep when men must weep
> Who never yet have wept:
> So we — the fool, the fraud, the knave —
> That endless vigil kept,
> And through each brain on hands of pain
> Another's terror crept.

Then came the morn of the execution itself:

> With sudden shock the prison-clock
> Smote on the shivering air,
> And from all the gaol rose up a wail
> Of impotent despair,
> Like the sound that frightened marshes hear
> From some leper in his lair.

But it is different when a man hangs himself in prison: if he is a run-of-the-mill prisoner, the life of the prison continues as if nothing has happened. He disappears like a pebble in a pond, but without the ripples, and he is not spoken of again. If, on the other hand, he is a notorious sex-murderer, as one who hanged himself in my prison not long ago was, news of his death is greeted with triumphant cheers, the entire prison erupts with glee, the building echoes with a joyous percussive chorus of struck metal pipes and railings. If the very same man had been officially executed, his death would have been the object of the despair Wilde describes, because it was the authorities that hanged him: and the despair he describes is therefore that of antinomian solidarity defeated, not a manifestation of humanitarianism. And in *De Profundis*, Wilde's long letter to Bosie from Reading Gaol, he states quite openly that he is 'a born antinomian,' as if it were something rare and precious, as if he were one of the elect: 'I am,' he wrote, 'one of those who were made for exceptions, not for laws.'

The Ballad of Reading Gaol is dedicated to 'C. T. W. Sometime Trooper of the Royal Horse Guards. Obit H.M. Prison, Reading, Berkshire, July 7th, 1896.' C. T. W. was Charles Thomas Wooldridge, a soldier who killed his estranged wife in a fit of jealous fury 'and so he had to die.'

> He did not wear his scarlet coat,
> For blood and wine are red,
> And blood and wine were on his hands
> When they found him with the dead,
> The poor dead woman whom he loved,
> And murdered in her bed.

Wilde heightens the pathos by famously suggesting that we are all, at heart, or potentially, C. T. W.:

> Yet each man kills the thing he loves,
> By each let this be heard,
> Some do it with a bitter look,
> Some with a flattering word.
> The coward does it with a kiss,
> The brave man with a sword!

There is an undoubted humanity in these verses. The murderer is my brother, he is a member of the human race, his passions are human, all too human. Recently in the prison, for example, I spoke for several hours to a murderer who had killed from motives of jealousy. I could not but recall C. T. W. as we spoke, and the man's story aroused my pity. Murder may be the worst of crimes in the eyes of the law, but murderers are often not the worst of criminals.

The man was in his middle age, of previous good and upright character, and had been married for 30 years to the wife he eventually killed. She was a terrible drunkard, whom I had seen, as it happens, several times in my hospital. When drunk, as she was most days, she was unbearable in her shrewishness. She denied that she had ever touched a drop even with a glass of whisky in her hand. She drank so much that she became doubly incontinent. When still capable of some degree of coordination, she was violent, and had stabbed her husband, bitten and scratched him, thrown saucepans at his head. She turned their house into a cesspit, secreted bottles everywhere, and destroyed everything of value by smashing it. Into the bargain, she was intensely jealous, phoning him ten times a day at work, and creating a violent scene at home if he were a minute late from work or shopping.

'For 30 years,' he said, 'I looked after that woman. I provided for her, I cleaned up after her, I washed away the vomit, I cleaned her, I put her to bed. She couldn't have survived without me.'

'Why did you do it?' I asked.

'I loved that woman, I worshipped the ground she stood on.'

At such moments, one has difficulty in understanding what understanding would be: at what point can one say, like Archimedes, 'Aha, now I understand!'? My murderer-patient mused on.

'Then she announced one day that she was returning to her first lover. He had become a very rich man. I said, "You can't do this to me, not after 30 years. I've looked after you for 30 years, and now you're just going to leave me all alone. You've taken 30 years of my life." She said, "Well, I'm going anyway." '

'And so you killed her?'

'I don't remember. I don't remember. But I loved her, and my life is over without her.'

Several times before and since, he has tried to end his life. I caught him once with a noose around his neck—he was going blue—and had to wrestle it from him. His self-pity was far greater than his guilt, of course, but his story was nonetheless tragic and pitiable. I congratulated myself for being so sympathetic a listener, and felt the warm glow of rectitude suffuse my being as he thanked me for my kindness to him.

This warm glow is precisely the sensation that Wilde's poem imparts to us, as we compassionate with the wretched and the despised: how broad are our sympathies, how generous our sentiments!

Perhaps not quite broad or generous enough, however: or perhaps they need to be a little more firmly under intellectual control. I have omitted certain details from my account of my murderer: he gouged his wife's eyes out and decapitated her. Likewise, and for precisely the same emotional effect, Wilde, to heighten our sympathy for C. T. W., says he murdered her in her bed. This suggests to us that he suddenly lost control, that he was momentarily overcome by passion, as any of us might be in the right circumstances. But Wooldridge's plea for clemency was turned down because, in actual fact, he did not kill the thing he loved in her bed: he lay in wait for her with a razor at the ready and cut her throat three times. This indicated an unforgivable degree of premeditation, and he was hanged.

One imagines from reading *The Ballad* that Reading Gaol was an insatiable Moloch, waiting to be fed victims, indifferent to the justice of the proceedings. But in the half century of Reading Gaol's existence before Wilde's arrival, there were actually only five executions there: that of Thomas Jennings in 1844, for having poisoned his four-year-old son with arsenic, which he deliberately misled him into thinking was salt; that of John Gould in 1862, for having cut his seven-year-old daughter's throat; that of Henry and Francis Tidbury in 1877 for the joint murder of two policemen; and that of John Carter in 1893, for the murder of his third wife, he being strongly suspected of having murdered his second wife as well. Wilde was 'lucky,' therefore, at least in the literary sense, to be incarcerated when there was an execution to give power to his poem, for the statistical chances were against it. And in the remaining 71 years in which the death penalty was still in force, there were only four further executions at Reading Gaol.

The tragedy of C. T. W. is not that of harsh and rough justice meted out to him: it is that of a man who acted from motives understandable and perhaps even shared by everyone, and yet whose crime had to be expiated for the good of society. Even without the execution, or with a last-minute reprieve, there was no possible happy ending to the all-too-human story: and that, not ill-treatment, is its tragedy.

The power of *The Ballad* is not in its propagandistic or prison-reformist message, therefore, but in its implicit recognition of the frailty and imperfectibility of man. No number of prison reforms would reduce it to a document of merely historical interest. We know that there will still be C. T. W.s in the best-ordered societies, because man is a fallen creature, and the passion to which C. T. W. succumbed springs eternal, just as the need to punish springs eternal. The law ('I know not whether Laws be right,/ Or whether Laws be wrong') can perhaps control or tame such passion a little, but never eliminate it finally: and we would not wish it to if it could, for all the misery it causes. Life can never be unblemished joy, though that is what we should like it to be.

The Ballad occupies a special place in Wilde's *oeuvre*, of course. It was the last thing he wrote for publication, and the only one after his release from prison. He was a broken man, but was he broken only by the harsh treatment he had received? For a brilliantly gifted man who had moved only in the *beau monde* of late Victorian England, prison gruel, oakum picking, floor scrubbing, and buckets for excrement must, of course, have been a severe shock. He was used to ceaseless conversation and gaiety, and in prison there was enforced silence; a great reader, he was reduced to one book a week, and that a mere crude religious tract.

But the shock, I suspect, was far deeper than any supplied by physical hardship, serious as this was for him. Only a few months before he went to jail, when he was no mere youth any longer but a man of 40 years of age, he had written *Phrases and Philosophies for the Use of the Young*, for an Oxford undergraduate magazine called *Chameleon*. These few maxims were a quintessence of what he claimed to believe, and of the attitudes upon which he had built his glittering career. Here is a sample:

The first duty in life is to be as artificial as possible.

Wickedness is a myth invented by good people to account for the curious attractiveness of others.

If the poor only had profiles there would be no difficulty in solving the problem of poverty.

Nothing that actually occurs is of the smallest importance.

In all unimportant matters, style, not sincerity is the essential. In all important matters, style, not sincerity, is the essential.

No crime is vulgar, but all vulgarity is crime.

Any preoccupation with ideas of what is right or wrong in conduct shows an arrested intellectual development.

The sheer callow, shallow, spoilt-child silliness of all this—upon the propagation of which the brilliantly gifted Wilde wasted so much of his life and energy and which ruins so much of his work—must have been obvious the very moment he passed through the prison door. Wilde was never a wicked man. It was nevertheless only in prison that he learned the value of truth, sincerity, and goodness, and by then it was too late.

Prison has taught me much also.

© 2002 Theodore Dalrymple

Appendix 2: Rules for Prisoners (c.1850)

COUNTY GAOL
RULES FOR PRISONERS

1. The bell shall ring at the opening and locking up of the rooms and cells, which shall be, from Lady Day to Michaelmas Day, at six o'clock in the morning and eight o'clock in the evening; and in the winter months at day-light in the morning and eight in the evening; and at all times the prisoners shall be locked up in their day rooms before dusk in the evening.

2. No person shall be allowed admission into the prison during the hours of prayer, the time for public worship, or before unlocking or after locking up hours; and no person (except a barrister or solicitor), unless in the presence of the Keeper [Prison Governor] or some person appointed by him, shall remain within the prison after hours of locking up, except in case of sickness of a prisoner, or some other cause assigned to the satisfaction of the Keeper.

3. Every prisoner shall attend prayer and public worship, except in case of illness, or other reasonable cause, to be allowed by the governor or a visiting justice.

4. Every prisoner guilty of drunkenness, blasphemy, swearing, or any improper expression, or any abuse or disorderly conduct, shall be punished at the discretion of the governor.

5. Every prisoner shall make his or her own bed, and be washed before nine o'clock every morning, on pain of forfeiting one day's allowance of provisions.

6. No tobacco to be used in the prison.

7. All prisoners who shall not be at work shall be required to walk round the yards, or be locked up in solitary cells.

8. The chambers and cells shall be swept out and thoroughly cleansed by the prisoners every morning before they are left.

9. No wine, ale, beer, porter, or spirituous liquors of any kind, shall be admitted for any convicted prisoner under any pretence whatever, unless ordered by the surgeon in his journal.

10. Every prisoner shall, at locking up time, present himself in the yard, and also at the door of the cell, to the turnkey.

11. Silence must be observed on all occasions by day and night.

12. Every prisoner guilty of any of the following offences will subject himself to punishment:-

- Talking, shouting, cursing, swearing, singing, whistling, attempting to communicate by signs, by writing or in any other way.
- Unnecessarily looking around or about at any time.
- Having in possession or attempting to receive money, tobacco, knives.
- Looking out, or attempting to look out, at window or door of a cell.
- Not folding a bed in the proper manner … in bed after 6 a.m. or before 8 in the evening.
- Stealing any property of the prison or of a prisoner … trying to take anything left from another prisoner's meal.
- Spitting on, or disfiguring the prison walls and floors.
- Irreverent behaviour in chapel either before, during, or after service.
- Striking, or in any way assaulting or threatening, another prisoner or officer.
- Attempting to escape, or assist other to do so.
- Not folding up clothing in a proper manner.
- Not washing feet twice a week, prior to using the water to clean the cell.
- Not ready to leave cell when unlocked by officer for exercise, chapel.

Prisoners wishing to see the Governor, Chaplain, or Surgeon must apply to the officer when paraded for exercise in the morning, who is bound to attend to such applications.

PRINTED AT THE OFFICE OF J. MADOCKS.

Appendix 3: Prison Dietary Scales (c.1850)

COUNTY GAOL.

....

DIETARIES.

....

The following are the prescribed rates of **DIET**

Class 1.
Prisoners confined for any term not exceeding seven days.

Breakfast	1 pint of Oatmeal Gruel	1 Pint of Oatmeal Gruel
Dinner	1lb. of Bread	1lb. of Bread
Supper	1 pint of Oatmeal Gruel	1 pint of Oatmeal Gruel

Class 2.
Prisoners for any term not exceeding a month.

Breakfast	1 pint of Oatmeal Gruel	1 Pint of Oatmeal Gruel
Dinner	1lb. of Bread, 1lb. of Potatoes	1lb. of Bread, 1lb. of Potatoes
Supper	1 pint of Oatmeal Gruel	1 pint of Oatmeal Gruel

Class 3.
Prisoners exceeding a month.

Breakfast	1 pint of Oatmeal Gruel	1 Pint of Oatmeal Gruel
Dinner	1 ½lb. of Bread, 1lb. of Potatoes	1lb. of Bread, 1lb. of Potatoes
Supper	1 pint of Oatmeal Gruel	1 pint of Oatmeal Gruel

(Male and Female prisoners of this class to have 1½ lb. of Scouce (Stew) on every Monday, Wednesday and Friday, instead of potatoes).

Class 4.
Prisoners sentenced by the Court to solitary confinement.

The ordinary diet of their class.	The Ordinary diet of their class.

Class 5.
Destitute Debtors.

Class 3. diet.	Class 3. diet.

Class 6.
Prisoners under punishment for prison offences, for terms not exceeding three days:-

1lb. of Bread *per diem*.

Note.- The Gruel, when made in quantities exceeding 50 pints, to contain 1½ oz. of Oatmeal per pint; and 2oz. per pint when made in less quantities. The Scouce to be made of Beef, cut in small pieces, and Potatoes,-- the proportions to be 9lb. weight of Beef to 90lbs. weight of Potatoes.

....

PRINTED AT THE OFFICE OF J. MADOCKS

Appendix 4: List of Executions

Based on the prison *Execution Log* and other primary sources

I. Executions at the 'first gaol' at Reading 1800-1843

Date	Condemned man	Offence
6th March 1800	John Hutt	Murder of Ann Pearman
16th July 1801	James Dormer	Murder of Mr Robinson
29th March 1802	John Ryan	Murder of Henry Frewin
29th March 1802	Edward Painter	Theft of two Heifers.
19th March 1803	Dennis Daly	Forging cheque for £10
23rd March 1811	Thomas Cox (20)	Bestiality
26th March 1814	Charles White	Horse stealing
25th March 1815	John Newcombe	Uttering forged notes
15th July 1817	Thomas Ayres	Housebreaking with Violence
2nd August 1817	James Castle	Sheep stealing
7th August 1819	Edward Tooley David Patience	Housebreaking
18th March 1820	George Wiggins	Robbery at Thatcham
4th March 1824	Daniel Grimshire	Murder of his infant son
28th May 1824	William Giles	Uttering forged £5 note
22nd March 1828	Henry Burnett Thomas Field Samuel White	Shot a Gamekeeper while poaching
January 1831	William Winterbourne	Robbery, during the 11th Agricultural riots.

25th February 1833	John Carter	Arson
4th August 1833	Edward Green Thomas Lincoln James Morris	Burglary
3rd March 1834	George King *(19)*	Murder of Mrs Ann Pullin Landlady of the 'The White Hart', Wantage

II. Executions at Reading Gaol since 1844

Date	Condemned man	Offence
22nd March 1845	Thomas Jennings	Murder of his four year old Son. The first public hanging at the new Gaol.
20th March 1846	William Spicer	Basket maker of Howard Street, Reading, who Murdered his wife by beating Her with a metal poker.
14th March 1862	John Gould	Last public hanging at the New Gaol He murdered his 7 year old Daughter by cutting her throat With a razor.
12th March 1877	Henry Tidbury Francis Tidbury	First non – public hanging at the Gaol. For the Murder of P.C. Drewit And Inspector Shorter.
5th December 1893	John Carter	Murder of his third wife, also believed to have murdered his two previous wives (but not proved).
7th July 1896	Charles Thomas Wooldridge	Murder of his wife at Clewer. The subject of Oscar Wilde's *The Ballad of Reading Gaol*.
28th November 1899	Charles Scott	Murder of Eliza O'Shea at Windsor.
5th November 1907	William George Austin	Murder Unity Alice Butler (13) At Clewer.
24th November 1910	William Broome	Murder of an elderly Shopkeeper in Slough.
4th February 1913	Eric James Sedgwick	Murder of a young woman at Eton College. The last hanging at Reading.

Primary Sources, Internet Sites and Select Bibliography

Primary sources These include:
Archives, various, including of HM Prison Service, Reading Public Library, Governors' Journals, Visiting Committee Book (1878-1920 (Two volumes), Reading Museum, Public Record Offices, Chaplains Journal, 1878-1884, Commissioner's Minute Book, 1946-2000, Governors' Journals, (1940-1959) (1968-1976), Home Office Letter Book, 1917-1918, Home Office Standing Orders and Prison Rules, 1938, Inspector's Minutes, 1887-1919, Nominal Register, 1916-1918

Official Report of an Enquiry into a Major Incident at HMRC Reading, an Executive Summary May 1993

Plan of Burial Ground, 1923

Photograph Albums, 1883-1915 (Four volumes)

Register of Executions, 1893-1913

Register of Graves, 1845-1913

Report by Councillor Smart, 1938

Various Historical papers, Home Office Instructions, Newspaper cuttings, Official Letters, Plans, Prisoner Correspondence

Visiting Committee Book.

Internet Sites Available by searching: British History Online, Huntley & Palmers Collection, National Archives, Oscar Wilde, Reading Library Services, Reading Museum, Thames Valley Police, University of Reading, Wikipedia Encyclopaedia.

Select bibliography
Betjeman, John, 'The Arrest of Oscar Wilde at the Cadagon At Hotel', *Selected Poems*, John Murray, 1976.

Ellis, J., *Diary of a Hangman*, Forum Press /True Crime Library, 1996.

Ellmann, R., *Oscar Wilde*, Random House Inc, 1988.

Field, Rev. J, *Prison Discipline*, Vols 1 and 2, Longman, Brown, Green and Longmans Reading, 1848.

Figgis , D., *A Chronicle of Jails*, Talbot Press, Dublin, 1917.

Hyde, H. Montgomery, *Oscar Wilde*, Farrar, Straus and Giroux, 1975.

Long, R., *Murder in Old Berkshir:, A Collection Of Sudden Deaths in and around the Old County*, Barracuda Books, 1990.

Long, R., *I'll Be Hanged: A Saga of Sudden Death in and around Old Berkshire*, Quotes Ltd., 1991.

Mayhew, Henry and Binny, John, *The Criminal Prisons of London and Scenes of London Life*, Griffin, Bohn and Co, London, 1862.

McLaughlin, S., *Execution Suite: The History of the Gallows at Wandsworth Prison, 1879-1993*, HMP Wandsworth, 2004.

McLoughlin, I., *Berkshire Murders*, Countryside Books, 1992.

Morris, Rothman, *The Oxford History of the Prison: The Practice of Punishment in Western Society*, New York, 1995.

Prison Reform Trust, *Bromley Briefings*, Prison Reform Trust, London, 2005.

Ruggles-Brise, E., *The English Prison System*, MacMillan and Co., London, 1921.

Sawers, Geoff, Hay,Peter, *A Ladder for Mr. Oscar Wilde*, Puddle Books, Reading, 2002.

Sherard, R. H., *The Life of Oscar Wilde*, T. Werner Laurie, London, 1906.

Southerton, P., *The Story of a Prison*, Osprey, Reading, 1975.

Social Exclusion Unit, *Reducing Re-offending by Ex-offenders*, Office of the Deputy Prime Minister, London, 2003.

Stanford, P, *The Outcasts' Outcast: A Biography of Lord Longford*, Sutton Publishing, 2004.

Stern, V. (1987), *Bricks of Shame*, London: Penguin.

Stacey, C. P. and Wilson, Barbara M., *The Canadians in Britain 1939-1946*, (Historical Section of the General Staff, Canadian Military Headquarters in Great Britain), King's Printer, Ottawa/University of Toronto Press, 1987.

Thomas, J. E., *The English Prison Officer Since 1885: A Study in Conflict*, Routledge & Kegan Paul, London, 1972.

Wilde, O., *The Portable Oscar Wilde*, Edited by R. Aldington and S. Weintraub, Penguin Books, 1981.

Woodley, L., *The Last Patrol: Policemen Killed on Duty While Serving in the Thames Valley*, The Book Castle, 2001.

Index

Illustrations are listed at p. viii

abuse 45 144-7
air raid wardens 139
alcohol 19-20 89 109
Aldershot glasshouse rioters 142
Anatomy Act 1832 53
Army Recruiting Office 139
army surplus clothing store 139
'Arrested Development' 174
artefacts 151-2
association 127-8 160

badge 38
Ballad of Reading Gaol 30 44 46 55 74-5 77 83 88-9 93 103-18 127 139 144 153 159 165
beggars 45
Betjeman, John 78-9
Billington, James 54-5 75 107-8 110
birch rod 50
birth 18
Black Act 1723 52
Bloody Code 18
Board of Visitors (BOV) 49 146
books 79 81 85 91-2
borstal boys 140
Borstal Correctional Centre 144-7
borstall recall centre 145 148
bricks of shame 115
bridewell 17-20
buildings 18 20 132
  alterations 23 30 127-8 148-50 164-5
  cells 34 112 149-50
  condemned cell 65 70 139
  execution centre 56-9 76 122 139
  gatehouse 33 66-7 72 149
  layout 32-7
  photographic house 73-4 76 107
  turrets 32-3 149
building work 22-3 28 31 148-50
burials 67 108 113-4 151

C.3.3 77 103 126 150
Callaghan, James 146
Calcraft, William 53-4 59 67 72
Canadians 15 97 130 *et seq.*
Capital Punishment Act 1868 56-7 71 74
Castle Street gaol 17-20
cat-o-nine tails 44 50
Cavanagh, Bernard 25
Centre (The Centre)
chapel 37 101
chaplain 18 20 22 25 30 32 34 36 39 49 66-7 70-4 80 84 91 119
Chamberlain, Ada 43 48
children 50 116
Clarke, William 98
Collins, Denis 26
Colville, Reverend J B 70
conditions 18-9 23 38-9 103-18
Corresponding Societies Act 1799 27
Cosgrave, W T 134
costs 19-22 27 31 163
county secure food store 138-9
County Gaol Rules 46
cleanliness 160
Cress, Louis 137-8
Criminal Law Ammendment Act 1885 78
Criminal Justice Act 1967 51
Cubitt, Sir William 22
culture 127 150 166

Dalrymple, Theodore vi xi 174
dark cells 38 44 47
death 39
debtors 17 19-20 23 109
Defence of the Realm Act 1914 130 132 138
de la Escosuras, Carlos Kuhne 136-8
De Profundis 80-1 85-6 88 93
design 24
deterrent 44 127 144
diet 23 38-9 42 44 130 183
discipline 39 44-51

Dobson, Reverend 31
Douglas, Lord Alfred 77-8 85 106
driving test centre 139
drugs 171-2
Du Cane, Edmond 42 45 103
Dyer, Amelia 33-4 55

Earles, Arabella 96
Easter Rising 127 131-4
education 127-8 167-71
eighteenth century 18
Ellis, John 55-6
enquiry 84-5 89-90 92 146 163
escape attempts 22-3 28-9 39 41 43 136-8 158 162-3
ethos 127 144 166
execution
  execution centre 122
  executioners 52-7 60 67 71 74 110
  Execution Log 53 114-5 102
  executions 17-8 33 52-76 103 108 110 112-5 128 185
  execution process 56-9 106 115
  execution party 106
  private execution 72-6
  public execution 18 56
exercise area 36-7 105 122

felons 17-20
Field, Reverend John 18-9 22 66-7
Figgis, Daniel 136
flogging 44 88 116
Folkestone, Lord 27-8
fools parade 103 105
Forbury House of Correction 20
Franks, Winifred Amy 129
Friend, Reverend MT 84

gag 44
Galaher, John Gordon 141-2
Gale, Marcus 167 170
Galloway, Alexander 27
gallows 52 54 56 57 108 112
gallows tree 108
gardens 36-7 50

Gate/Gatehouse 97 123
George V 129
general amnesty 129
Ginnell, Laurence 134 136
gin trap 107
ghosts 59
Gladstone Committee 90 127 144
Gould, John 68
government convicts 40
governor 24 47 82-4 91 136-8 140 143 146-7 149 151-2 167
Graham, Sir James 24
Grey, Sir George 71
Griffith, Arthur 134

Habeas Corpus Act 1679 26
hair 82 86 92
Haldane, R B 79-82 90-2 127
hand crank 45
Harding, W G 143
hard labour 41-2 44-5 83 90 110 127
Headley rioters 142
Henry VIII 17
Hirons, Thomas 40
HMP Reading 148-52
HMP & YOI Reading 166-74
Hodgson, Richard 27
homosexuality 77-8
House of Correction 48
Howard, John 19-21
hunger strike 134 137
Huntley & Palmers 82 86 92 119

inquiry, see *enquiry*
inquest 113
inspections 24
Inspector of Prisons 41
internees 130-8
internment 127
invisible prisoners 139 *et seq*
Irish republicans 131-6
iron gin, iron town, etc. 108 110 112 113 116
Isaacson, Colonel 50 82-5 92

Jennings, Thomas 59-68
juries 53

Keach, Stacey 156-7
Kennet Unit 165-6

Leader, Nick 167
Le Maitre, Paul Thomas 27
lepers 151
library 85
lighting 34 59 149
light labour 44-5
local prison 153-8
luxury motor car scam 155

MacSwiney, Terence 134
magistrates 24 32
Maher, Phil 162 173
marriage 18
Martin, Thomas (Warder Martin) 85-90 92-3
Marwood, William 54 74
Meyer (internee) 136-7
Meyer, Major-General Kurt 142-3
military detention centre 141
mill house 41
Morgan, Captain 130
Morrison, Reverend WD 80
murder 33-4 59-76 143 185

nationalisation 42 46
Nelson, Major 85 92
newspapers 19 22-5 29 31-2 34 38-9 47 50 70-2 83 86 88-9 93 103-4 128 137-8 146 154
Nichols, William 26
nineteenth century 18

overcrowding 19 21-2 153
overflow prison 143

Palmer, George W 82 85-6 91-2 100
Penal Servitude Act 1853 41
Pentonville Prison 30 79-80 91
performance testing 166-7

petitions 65 72
Photographic House 56 73 74 76 96 107
physical restraints 47-8
Pierrepoint, Albert 52
Pierrepoint, Henry Albert 55
pit of shame xii 117
Pitt, William 26
Place of Internment 129-38 140-3
plan-a-kitchen 169-70
plants 93 131
poetic licence 104 107 110
population 20-1 40 153 159 161
Prison Act 1781 20
Prison Act 1865 42 45 83 104
Prison Act 1877 42-3 46 81
Prison Act 1898 49 90 127 129
Prison Commissioners 42 49 79 84-5 87 89-91 93 127-33 136-8
prison mutiny 160-4
Prison Rules 44-7 79 85-7 91-2 109 128 181
prisoners 18-9 25-9 38-9 111 148-51 153-8 159-64
  numbers 38 83
privilege 26 128
professionalism 42 163-4
public sentiment 68 118
Pucklehurst rioters 161
punishment 38 41-2 44-52 83-4 88 127-8

Queensbury, Marquis of 77-8

Reading Abbey 20-1 23 151
reception 19 36 38 79 145 147 157-8 173
recidivism 87 146-7 154-5 166 168-70 172-3
reform 24 115 118
reformation 44-5 128
reformatory school 50
regime 37 116 128 145 159-60
remand 17 90 105 153 158-64

Remand Centre for Young
   Offenders 158-64
resettlement 128
Rich, Sir Almerich 140
Royal Canadian Air Force 140-3
Ruggles-Brise, Sir Evelyn 49 80 90
   127 144
'Rule 43' 150-1

sanitation 83
Schoolmasters Orderly 85
Scott, Charles 76
Scottish cap 30 37-40 46-7 105 128
Sedgwick, Eric James 76
separate system 30-43 46 79-80 90
   101 120 128
seventeenth century 17
Sidmouth, Lord 27
silent system 30
Sinn Féin 134-6
sixteenth century 17
Sixth Protocol to the European
   Convention On Human Rights xv
   52 118
Skeffington's gyves 111
soldiers 132
solitary confinement 47
special treatment 84 86 88-93
staff 17 20-1 110 128 130-3 136 144-8
   157-67 172-4
   see also turnkey
star class 87
Stephens, Alan 157-8
straight jacket 48
Straw, Jack MP 52
suicide bomber 157
supergrass 156

Table of Drops 53 58
Thirteenth Protocol to the European
   Convention On Human Rights xv
   52 118
Tidbury, Henry and Francis 72-4
trafficking 86 90 93 133

training 144
treadmill 22 24 41
treason 26-8 141-2
Truelove, Mabel 128-9
turnkey 19 22 29-30 35 42 48
typhus 19

Vagrancy Act 1824 25
visiting 36 44 71 84 149
Visiting Committee 42-3 45 47 82 84-
   5 89 91-2 100 109 132
Vocational Training Centre 167-70

Wallis, William and Edith 25
Wandsworth Prison 80-1 91
Warder Martin See *Martin, Thomas*
Wilde, Constance 77 82 84 86
Wilde, Oscar 36 38 45-6 49-50 55 74-
   5 77-94 103-18 150
witchcraft 25
women 33 129
Wooldridge, Charles Thomas 46 55
   74-5 88-9 103-18
work in the community 165-6 168
workshops 150 153 159
World War I 129-34
World War II 139-43

young offenders 153 165-74
   see also borstal

Pit of Shame is published by

Waterside Press

For further books on crime, punishment and penal affairs, please visit Waterside Press Online at

www.watersidepress.co.uk

Whores and Highwaymen: Crime and Justice in the Eighteenth-Century Metropolis
by Gregory J. Durston

The 'whores' and 'highwaymen' of Gregory Durston's title are just some of the dubious characters met with in this absorbing work, including thief-takers, trading justices, an upstart legal profession whose lower orders developed various ways to line their own pockets and magistrates and clerks who often preferred dealing with those cases which attracted fees. The book shows how little was planned by government or the authorities, and how much sprang up due to the efforts of individuals—so that the origins of social control, particularly at a local level, had much to do with personal ideas of morality, class boundaries and perceived threats, serious and otherwise. Based on news reports, Old Bailey and local archives, and other solid records the book weaves a compelling picture of a critical time in English history, through the voices of contemporary observers as well as the best of writings by experts ever since. At its broadest point, the book spans the period from the Glorious Revolution to the early 1820s.

'A very-well-researched and readable book… a bit of a romp': *The Law Society Gazette*

Hardback & ebook | ISBN 9781904380757
2012 | 672 pages

A History of Criminal Justice in England and Wales
by John Hostettler

John Hostettler's work is an ideal introduction. It charts all the main developments of criminal justice, from Anglo-Saxon dooms to the Common Law, struggles for political, legislative and judicial ascendency and the formation of the modern-day Criminal Justice System. Among a wealth of topics the book looks at the Rule of Law, the development of the criminal courts, police forces, jury, justices of the peace and individual crimes and punishments. It locates all the iconic events of criminal justice history and law reform within a wider background and context—demonstrating a wealth and depth of knowledge. John Hostettler is well-known to readers of Waterside Press books. He is just as at home discussing the Star Chamber or Seven Bishops as he is the impact of the executions of King Charles I, Derek Bentley or Ruth Ellis. From Victorian policing to madness and mayhem, hate crime and miscarriages of justice to radicals, terrorists, human rights or restorative justice, *A History of Criminal Justice in England and Wales* contains an enormous supply of facts, information, and ideas.

'Every student entering law school should have a copy and read it: *Criminal Law and Justice Weekly*

Paperback & ebook | ISBN 978-1-904380-51-1
2009 | 352 pages